American Ideal

American Ideal

Theodore Roosevelt's Search for American Individualism

Paul M. Rego

LEXINGTON BOOKS

A division of
ROWMAN & LITTLEFIELD PUBLISHERS, INC.
Lanham • Boulder • New York • Toronto • Plymouth, UK

LEXINGTON BOOKS

A division of Rowman & Littlefield Publishers, Inc.
A wholly owned subsidiary of The Rowman & Littlefield Publishing Group, Inc.
4501 Forbes Boulevard, Suite 200
Lanham, MD 20706

Estover Road
Plymouth PL6 7PY
United Kingdom

British Library Cataloguing in Publication Information Available

Library of Congress Cataloging-in-Publication Data

Rego, Paul M., 1979-
  American ideal : Theodore Roosevelt's search for American individualism
        / Paul M. Rego.
     p. cm.
  Includes bibliographical references and index.
  ISBN-13: 978-0-7391-2607-3 (cloth : alk. paper)
  ISBN-10: 0-7391-2607-5 (pbk. : alk. paper)
  1. Roosevelt, Theodore, 1858–1919—Political and social views. 2.
  Roosevelt, Theodore, 1858–1919—Language. 3. Roosevelt, Theodore,
  1858–1919—Influence. 4. Political leadership—United States—History. 5.
  Individualism—United States—History. 6. Rhetoric—Political aspects—
  United States—History. 7. Public interest—United States—History. 8.
  Progressivism (United States politics)—History. 9. United States—Politics
  and government—1901–1909. I. Title.
  E757.R34 2008
  973.91'1092—dc22   2008001517

Printed in the United States of America

⊗™ The paper used in this publication meets the minimum requirements of American
National Standard for Information Sciences—Permanence of Paper for Printed Library
Materials, ANSI/NISO Z39.48–1992.

To my mentor and friend, Jerry Mileur, who suggested this project, read the manuscript several times, and offered continuous advice, encouragement, and laughter.

To my parents, Mike and Linda, who nurtured my love of politics and history. In fact, my first lesson in American political history—the difference between Washington and Lincoln—was given by my mother on President's Day 1984.

To my wife, Trisha, who is my best friend, the love of my life, and the greatest of the many gifts with which I have been blessed.

Contents

Introduction

Early in George W. Bush's presidency, Karl Rove, the president's top political adviser, recommended that his boss read *Theodore Rex*, Edmund Morris' account of Theodore Roosevelt's presidential years. Shortly after Christmas 2001, Bush told reporters that he had just finished the book and recommended it highly. In the wake of September 11, it is easy to imagine Bush reading excitedly about the parallels between Roosevelt's circumstances and his own. TR believed that "anarchism, that plague of European government," also threatened both order and freedom in the United States. After all, an anarchist had been responsible for the assassination of his predecessor. As President, Roosevelt intended to "war with ruthless efficiency" against this terrorism of his time, and he addressed the threat with the same language of moral outrage that Bush adopted in the War on Terror.[1] More recently, Rove furthered the comparison between Roosevelt and Bush, suggesting that, given "a choice between Wall Street and Main Street," the 43rd President, like the 26th, would "choose Main Street every time." He argued as well that Roosevelt would stand up and applaud Bush's initiative on healthy forests, noting that there are currently more trees in the United States than when TR was President.[2]

Bush, however, is not the only recent President who has sought to establish a connection with Roosevelt. Bush's father, George H. W. Bush, repeatedly praised Roosevelt's positive moral example, and even invited TR biographer David McCullough to the White House to lecture on Roosevelt's valor. Bill Clinton often referred to Roosevelt as one of his favorite Presidents. He hung a portrait of TR by the entrance to his private study, off the Oval Office, and posthumously awarded him the Congressional Medal of Honor. As President, Clinton expressed admiration for Roosevelt's trust busting, advocacy of child-labor laws, and efforts to protect the public from unsafe food. Again and again, he spoke about the parallels between TR's time, when an agrarian economy was becoming industrial, and his own, when an industrial economy was becoming information-based.[3] As a former President, Clinton has continued to invoke the memory of Roosevelt. In an August 2004 op-ed piece for the *Los Angeles Times*, he reminds readers that, despite Roosevelt's warning against the waste and destruction of natural resources, the Bush administration has proposed ending limitations on the development of approximately 60 million acres of national forests where no roads have been built. Pointing to examples such as these, Clinton maintains that, if the Rough Rider were alive today, he "would have been a Democrat."[4]

Similarly, various pundits have used Roosevelt to serve their respective political agendas. When Senator John McCain challenged Bush for the Republican Party's presidential nomination in 2000, Richard Lowry of *National Review* noted McCain's frequent mentions of Roosevelt and described the senator's calls for a renewed spirit of American citizenship as "Rooseveltian." Alleging that both Roosevelt and McCain associated wealth with selfishness and were unwilling to acknowledge that such virtues as "thrift, foresight, and service to others" underlay democratic capitalism, the Lowry article concludes that a number of McCain's proposals, such as the Patient's Bill of Rights and campaign-finance reform, fit TR's brand of progressivism, which "wasn't just about energy, but also about fear and control, and grabbing power back from grubby businessmen and putting it in the hands of middle-class, college-educated experts."[5] At the same time, David Brooks of *The Weekly Standard* has expressed admiration for Roosevelt's foreign policy, which he believes placed moral concern over the maintenance of international political stability. In a review of *Theodore Rex*, Brooks wonders if Morris overlooks how willing Roosevelt was to "upset equilibriums and [transform] the status quo" for the sake of a cause he thought just.[6]

In sum, politicians and political activists of diverse beliefs and ideologies all lay claim to the mantle of Theodore Roosevelt, borrowing particular pieces of his legacy. Conservatives embrace Roosevelt's strong belief in the power of self-improvement, his commitment to individualism, and his willingness to preach about the loss of virtue; but they completely ignore his support for the regulation of business. On the other hand, liberals tend to ignore most of the above and celebrate only Roosevelt's conservationism and his willingness to regulate the economy to counter many of the negative consequences of large-scale industrialization.

Far too often, then, Roosevelt is cast as either "conservative" or "liberal," but his political thought defies so simple an interpretation; it was more nuanced and had a larger purpose than mere ideology. This study demonstrates that Roosevelt spent most of his life trying to reconcile two often-competing values: the collectivist spirit of Progressivism and the individualism of the American founders. As President, TR used the power of the national government to break down obstacles that prevented many Americans from competing on a reasonably level economic playing field, thereby providing them with opportunity to realize their individual potential. At the same time, he believed that much depended on the *character* of the individual. He therefore relied on personal example, the bully pulpit, and an extraordinary number of public writings to preach the values of fair-play, decency, hard-work, self-control, and duty to family, community, and nation. Economic regulations, coupled with the power of rhetoric and the inspiration of his example, were the means by which Roosevelt attempted to reconcile the tension between individualism and collectivism. In office, as in life, he was the embodiment of boldness, energy, and resoluteness. He had an aggressive fighting style, but he also had a capacity to empathize with the plight of others. In essence, Roosevelt played the role of the kindhearted tough guy—*his American ideal*—and he hoped that his words and deeds would inspire his fellow citizens to appreciate the importance of both individualistic and collectivistic qualities.

Roosevelt accepted largeness in American life, including the new corporate scale of the economy. He rejected both the Wilsonian desire to break up corporations and the Socialist wish to nationalize them. He preferred instead to strengthen the regulatory powers of the federal government, while remaining devoted to the principle of individual responsibility. He was simply unwilling to regard structural solutions like statutes, constitutional amendments, and regulatory bodies as an appropriate response to all of society's problems. With regard to both economic and social/moral issues, Roosevelt also regarded rhetoric and personal example as an effective means of encouraging Americans to embrace both individualistic and collectivistic values. Thus, as Michael McGerr observes, TR was not in the mainstream of Progressive reformers in that he set out to reform, not forsake, the individualist values that prevailed during the 18th and 19th centuries.[7] The sum of Roosevelt's efforts (both institutional and personal) offers a third way that transcends the liberal-conservative dichotomy of modern American politics.

This book examines TR's third way. It is an *intellectual* biography about a man not usually thought of as an intellectual, but who was perhaps our most scholarly President. It takes Theodore Roosevelt seriously as a man of ideas, a thinker who was deeply committed to addressing the problems of his generation.

This is also a study of TR as a leader, one who used rhetoric to shape the American mind in ways that he thought proper. Central to this rhetoric was his effort to reconcile the American tradition of individualism with a new concern for the social good (that is, an individual's responsibility for and obligation to his community). The focus, therefore, is on the *public* Roosevelt—his speeches, books, articles, and essays that, unlike his personal correspondences, were addressed to and readily accessible to the general public. To be sure, one might wonder whether, in analyzing Roosevelt's public writings, it may be safely assumed that his words are not merely what he thought his audiences wanted to hear rather than what he actually believed. This can be a problem with any intellectual biography, especially one that focuses on so-called "political men." I can only respond to this concern by noting how surprised I was to discover the remarkable similarity between Roosevelt's privately expressed thoughts and his public words.

It is not just political actors who have claimed Roosevelt's legacy for their own conservative or liberal purposes. Many scholars also interpret his thought and actions as representative of one or the other of these two dimensions. Conservative interpretations[8] tend to see Roosevelt as interested in enacting economic reform for the rather *conservative* end of preserving stability and order. With a few exceptions,[9] they conclude that Roosevelt was skeptical of individualism, viewing it as a source of social conflict. In doing so, they overlook the fact that, throughout his public life, Roosevelt stressed his firm belief in the value of fair economic competition as well as the need for certain individualistic qualities like self-reliance. On the other hand, liberal treatments[10] tend to emphasize TR's inherent sympathy for the underprivileged. Simply stated, these works see a basic *liberal* strain in most of what Roosevelt said and did as a regulator of big business, even as he was pulled more and more to the left over the course of his political career. Admittedly, most representatives of this group mention Roosevelt's attraction to individualism, but they tend to focus more on his devotion to the collective good. Moreover, they offer no discussion of how TR used his public writings and his personal example in an effort to reconcile independence and interdependence.

The fact is that most studies of TR do not really seek to resolve the central tension in his thought; however, a recent study by Michael McGerr moves in this direction. McGerr sees the response to the beginning of modern America, with the dominance of large-scale businesses, the explosion of wealth, rapid industrialization, and mass urbanization, as one in which a group of middle class Americans set out to remake American society. According to McGerr, their crusade was not an ambiguous or nebulous one against some imagined or hypothetical enemy. The enemies were real, and they included not just large business conglomerates and corrupt wealth but also alcohol, prostitution, divorce, and indecent entertainment. McGerr insists that Progressive reformers seldom suggested that the middle class was a problem in the new, modern America. Rather, they argued that the major problems rested with other classes and were eager to use the government to police a variety of social and economic activities.[11]

McGerr notes that a few reformers did worry that certain regulatory laws and institutions would diminish emphasis on individual self-control and personal responsibility, and one of these was Roosevelt. To McGerr, Roosevelt acknowledged the limits of the individualist creed, arguing that "[n]o small part of the trouble that we have comes from carrying to an extreme the national virtue of self-reliance, of independence in initiative and action," yet he could not abandon his belief that the individual was preeminent. "Much can be done by wise legislation and by resolute enforcement of the law," TR observed in 1906. "But still more must be done by steady training of the individual citizen, in conscience and character, until he grows to abhor corruption and greed and tyranny and brutality and to prize justice and fair dealing." Nonetheless, McGerr finds that Roosevelt was "the one endorsing large scale business organizations and building an intrusive government." In short, the defender of individualism was one of the principal architects of modern governmental regulation. McGerr concludes that Roosevelt appeared to understand this, for he "openly tied himself in knots" in a vain attempt to reconcile these opposing forces.[12]

McGerr avoids simply categorizing TR as either a conservative or a liberal. Indeed, Roosevelt defies mere ideological interpretation, for his thought had a larger purpose: striking a balance between the interests of the individual and the needs of the community. Thus, McGerr is correct in arguing that Roosevelt's willingness to strengthen the regulatory powers of the federal government did not imply a rejection of America's long-standing devotion to individualism.

At this point, it is important to note that my book has profited greatly from (and, no doubt, builds upon) McGerr's insightful scholarship. Specifically, McGerr introduced me to the following ideas: first, that Progressivism was, above all, a rejection of individualism; second, that Roosevelt never stopped emphasizing the importance of the individual and, unlike other Progressives, worked hard to reform the individualistic values of the nineteenth century; and third, that Roosevelt's dedication to the individual was most evident in his approach to social reform, where he "mostly confined his involvement . . . to sermonizing."

But McGerr stresses the contradiction between Roosevelt's embrace of individualism and his willingness to strengthen the regulatory power of the federal government, concluding that, while Roosevelt spoke openly and vigorously about the issues of individual effort and governmental control, he could *not* reconcile these "opposing forces." My analysis yields a different conclusion. For Roosevelt, the concepts of personal autonomy and civic concern were not mutually exclusive. This belief was the crux of his thought. Roosevelt argued that it was because the principles of self-reliance and personal freedom were important that it was sometimes necessary for the entire community to use its collective power—and, if necessary, the institutions of the government—to enable individuals to do what they could not do alone.

Moreover, while it is certainly true that Roosevelt's devotion to American individualism prevented him from relying exclusively on governmental coercion to effect needed change, McGerr gives the reader the impression that Roosevelt reserved most of his "sermonizing" to social problems. TR understood, in contrast to many other Progressive reformers, that inspirational rhetoric and positive personal example could be as good as institutional reform and the force of law in achieving *both* economic and social reform. Finally, I am stressing that there is evidence of Roosevelt's political preaching in the most unlikely of places, including his writings on hunting, ranching, western settlement, and the great figures of history. Nearly all of Roosevelt's myriad public writings, even those which do not focus exclusively on politics per se, reflect his belief in the value of individualism, his respect for the concept of the social citizen, and, in most cases, a determined effort to show compatibility between the two.

Before we delve into Roosevelt's thought, however, it is necessary first to step back and set this study in the proper intellectual context, which involves exploring not only Social Darwinism, the Social Gospel movement, Pragmatism, and Populism but also explaining their connection to Progressive thought in general.

NOTES

1. Burt Solomon, "The Cult of TR," *National Journal*, February 15, 2002, <http://wwwkencollier.org/classes/PSC448/reading448/CultofTeddyRoosevelt.html> (August 9, 2004).

2. Quoted in Solomon, "The Cult of TR." See also Richard W. Stevenson, "Top Strategist Terms Bush a Populist About Taxes," *New York Times*, January 23, 2003, <http://www.politicalposts.com/news/index.asp?id=166002> (August 9, 2004).

3. Solomon, "The Cult of TR."

4. Quoted in Solomon, "The Cult of TR." See also Bill Clinton, "Our Forests May Be on a Road to Ruin," *Los Angeles Times*, August 4. 2004, <http://politicalposts.com/news/index.asp?month=8&year=2004> (9 August 2004).

5. Richard Lowry, "TR and His Fan: Roosevelt and McCain, for good and ill—John McCain models himself on Pres. Theodore Roosevelt," *National Review*, February 7, 2000, <http://findarticles.com/p/articles/mi_m1282/is_2_52/ai_58836292/print> (August 9, 2004).

6. David Brooks, "TR's Greatness: Edmund Morris' return to Teddy Roosevelt," *The Weekly Standard*, November 19, 2001, <http://www.weeklystandard.com/Utilities/printer_preview.asp?idArticle=519&R=9F6925A2F> (August 9, 2004).

7. Michael McGerr, "Theodore Roosevelt," in *The American Presidency*, eds. Alan Brinkley and Davis Dyer (Boston: Houghton Mifflin Company, 2004), 279.

8. See John Morton Blum, *The Republican Roosevelt* (Cambridge: Harvard University Press, 1981) and John Milton Cooper, *The Warrior and the Priest: Woodrow Wilson and Theodore Roosevelt* (Cambridge: Belknap Press, 1997).

9. See Richard Hofstadter, *The American Political Tradition and the Men Who Made It* (New York: Vintage Books, 1989). Hofstadter argues that Roosevelt spoke for an American middle class that had become uneasy with the growing power of the trusts on one side and the labor and Populist movements on the other. In a reinterpretation of the American political tradition, in which he alleges that most of the major figures who have influenced the course of American history were flexible, crafty, and opportunistic men who shared a common devotion to the values of capitalism (i.e., private property rights, economic individualism, and competition) and never strayed far from the views of their constituents—the American people, Hofstadter charges that Roosevelt's willingness to fight both the rich and the organized power of the masses was a purposeful attempt to entertain, distract, and please the great number of middle class Americans who were vainly seeking money and social standing during the Gilded Age.

10. See George E. Mowry, *Theodore Roosevelt and the Progressive Movement* (New York: Hill and Wang, 1960); G. Wallace Chessman, *Theodore Roosevelt and the Politics of Power* (Prospect Heights: Waveland Press, 1994); and James MacGregor Burns and Susan Dunn, *The Three Roosevelts* (New York: Grove Press, 2001).

11. Michael McGerr, *A Fierce Discontent: The Rise and Fall of the Progressive Movement in America (1870–1920)* (New York: Free Press, 2003), 94.

12. McGerr, *Fierce Discontent*, 177–78.

Chapter One

Individualism and Its Discontents

Alexis de Tocqueville, traveling through America in the 1830s, observed that democracy worked here because most people were able to balance competitive individualism with their concern for their local communities. But, between 1865 and 1900, a new industrial economy replaced an older agricultural order, and the United States underwent what Eric Foner calls "one of the most profound economic revolutions any country has ever experienced."[1] By the first decade of the twentieth century, American manufacturing production had surpassed the combined total of Great Britain, Germany, and France; railroad mileage had tripled; millions of Americans had moved from the farm to the city; and giant corporations had come to dominate such industries as steel, oil, sugar refining, and meatpacking. In cities like New York and Philadelphia, individuals continued to work as independent artisans or domestic laborers, but the factory system increasingly came to dominate manufacturing and to employ the bulk of laborers. This was the world into which Theodore Roosevelt was born; it was the world he knew as he grew to adulthood.

A massive industrial work force was emerging, but this hardly meant prosperity and greater freedom for more people. Although real wages rose throughout these years, the result of monetary deflation and falling prices, the depressions of the 1870s and 1890s kept most of the working class close to poverty. Skilled craftsmen in certain industries were able to exercise control over such matters of production as work rules, output quotas, and the training of apprentices, but economic freedom of this sort applied only to a small portion of the industrial workforce. Most workers were unskilled, more expendable, and therefore less autonomous. But, at the other end of the economic spectrum, Foner notes, there was "an unprecedented accumulation of wealth."[2] By 1890, the

wealthiest one percent of Americans not only received the same total income as
the bottom half of the population but also owned more property than the remaining ninety-nine percent.

In the eyes of many, the concentration of wealth and capital was a natural
by-product of an ever-expanding mass market in which "the modern corporation has replaced the independent producer as the driving force of economic
change." Attempting to justify the new order, economists maintained that
wages were determined by the iron law of supply and demand, and that
wealth rightly belonged to those with the vision and the ability to satisfy the
needs and demands of consumers. "The close link between freedom and
equality," Foner concludes, "forged in the Revolution and reinforced during
the Civil War, appeared increasingly out of date," adding that the purpose of
the new social sciences was now to devise ways of making "men who are
equal in liberty" content with "inequality in . . . distribution [of wealth]."[3] Just
as many whites had asserted their "natural superiority" over blacks to justify
slavery, social theorists in the "Gilded Age"[4] invoked science and drew analogies to the natural world in order to defend unfettered capitalism and explain
the success and failure of individuals in the marketplace. Language such as
"natural selection," "the struggle for existence," and "the survival of the
fittest" comprised the laissez-faire (or "let it be") outlook of the time. Social
Darwinism, as it was to be called, was used to criticize nearly all forms of
state interference with the "natural" laws of the economy.[5] Tocqueville's
America was disappearing, as the balance between competition and social responsibility was threatened by the new urbanization and industrialization.

THE FOUNDATIONS OF AMERICAN INDIVIDUALISM

Theodore Roosevelt came to manhood in the 1880s, in an era dominated intellectually by the new evolutionary science of Charles Darwin. Through the
efforts of Herbert Spencer and William Graham Sumner, the ideas of Darwin
were adapted to a new theory of society. "Social Darwinism," as it came to
be called, was radically individualistic and hostile to any governmental actions that might interfere with the natural evolution of society—the process
of natural selection and the survival of the fittest. But the questions it posed
about an overly expansive and overly activist government were not new in the
American experience.

Indeed, as H.W. Brands explains, "From before they had become a nation,
and continuing until almost the middle of the twentieth century, Americans
registered chronic skepticism regarding a more active role for the federal government in their lives."[6] It was, after all, a desire to escape England's perse-

cution of their religious beliefs that led the Puritans to settle New England, and during colonial times, the acceptance of British regulations on manufacturing and trade did not prevent the American colonists from smuggling and "doing a hundred other things" forbidden to them. Brands adds that protests against taxation without representation had less to do with the demand for representation than with the colonists' rejection of taxation by a centralized and tyrannical authority.

Indeed, the Revolutionary era revealed the colonists' deep-seated distrust of centralized authority, even centralized American authority, and their greater confidence in themselves as individuals. George Washington, for example, was constantly frustrated not only by the refusal of a jealous Continental Congress to grant him the necessary power to prosecute the war for independence effectively but also by the refusal of jealous states to supply the Congress with the means to fund the war. In most states, many Americans insisted on attaching bills of rights to their state constitutions, and when the Articles of Confederation later proved ineffective, many accepted a stronger national government on the condition that specific restrictions be placed on its powers. James Madison reluctantly agreed to draft a bill of rights as the price of ratification, but within a decade, he joined Thomas Jefferson in using the first of these amendments to oppose the Sedition Act and the consolidated government power it represented.[7] In fact, in the first decade of the Republic, Madison and Jefferson, along with many former Anti-Federalist opponents to the Constitution, organized the Democratic-Republican Party to resist the efforts of Federalists like Alexander Hamilton to centralize administrative power in the hands of the national government.

When the Democratic-Republican Party won control of the national government in 1800, President Jefferson was able to implement his vision of "a wise and frugal government which shall restrain men from injuring one another, shall leave them otherwise free to regulate their own pursuits of industry and improvement, and shall not take from the mouth of labor the bread it has earned."[8] In practice, however, Jefferson was somewhat less devoted to small, restricted government than in theory. As Brands explains, "Jefferson was hardly the last president to discover that power wasn't half as bad when wielded by oneself as it had been in the hands of those rascals who went before." The purchase of the Louisiana Territory and the embargo against both British and French goods required Jefferson to abandon his principle that the Constitution should be interpreted literally as permitting the national government to exercise only those powers that specifically had been delegated to it. Even his supporters had difficulty accepting Jefferson's sweeping assertions of federal power, and "Jefferson left office to the jeers of his enemies and the embarrassed silence of many of his friends."[9]

After the "Era of Good Feelings" (1816–1824), some members of the new National Republican Party like Henry Clay of Kentucky urged that the national government support such "internal improvements" as road and canal construction, renewing the charter of the national bank, and a tariff on any foreign imports that competed with American-made goods. Congress voted to fund a national road. But this activist program split the National Republican Party, and a faction led by Martin Van Buren and President Andrew Jackson, which subsequently took the name "Democrats," arose in opposition. Jackson fulfilled his promise to "kill" the bank by vetoing its recharter and transferring federal funds to the state banks. Of this great battle Tocqueville observed, "the prominent feature of the administration in the United States is its excessive decentralization." Tocqueville added that the American preference for local control had "been carried further than any European nation could endure without great inconvenience." Americans clearly preferred local government, in which they could play an immediate role, to state and especially national levels of government.[10]

The Civil War was the great exception to this pattern, as it led to unprecedented expansions of national power. War and preservation of the Union led Americans to accept the necessity of a more energetic role for the national government. In the 1860s, the national government established the first federally-controlled paper currency ("Greenbacks") and required most creditors to accept it for the payment of debts. Congress passed a National Banking Act that authorized the federal chartering of banks that could issue bank notes (which, in turn, were backed by federal bonds). Congress also levied new taxes on alcohol, tobacco, playing cards, billiard tables, jewelry, yachts, medicines, newspaper ads, professional licenses, business receipts, dividends, inheritances, and stamps; passed a stopgap measure to tax income; and created a Bureau of Internal Revenue to collect the taxes. It also funded the construction of a transcontinental railroad and instituted a military draft.[11] Other expansions of federal power, such as the suspension of *habeas corpus* and the emancipation of slaves in rebel territory, came not from Congress, but from actions taken by President Abraham Lincoln.[12]

But many of these increases in the power and authority of the national government did not survive for long after the end of the war. Conscription, detention without trial, and the suppression of political dissent ended almost immediately with the conclusion of hostilities. The federal income tax ended in 1872, and the federal government's military presence in the South was removed officially in 1877.[13] In short, the actions of the federal government during the Civil War were part of a pattern in American history that began in 1781. Americans were willing to accept an expansion of federal authority during wartime, but they expected this expansion to last only as long as the war itself. During the Civil War, Americans permitted the national government to do whatever was necessary to provide for the common defense, but with the war's end, their preference for relying on the private sector to provide for their prosperity and happiness returned.[14]

In the private sector, according to Sidney Fine, eighteenth and nineteenth century American hostility to governmental intervention into the economic marketplace was rooted in the doctrine of natural rights, American faith in the self-sufficiency of the individual, and the teachings of classical political economy.[15] In the first half of the nineteenth century, appeals for the protection of private property rights against both the acts of legislatures and the decisions of state and federal courts were often made to the "principles of natural justice." Many Jacksonian-era courts permitted *state* legislatures more discretion in regulating certain economic matters, but by the 1850s, there was a renewed effort to protect private property rights from the actions of both Congress and state legislatures. Adding further support to the "hands off" doctrine of laissez-faire was American faith in the self-sufficiency of the individual. Steeped in a Protestant tradition that emphasizes the spiritual rebirth of individuals, and further strengthened by Transcendentalism, which identified the consciousness of the individual with God, Americans have tended to trust the individual more than the government and to view most exercises of governmental control as a threat to self-reliance and personal moral accountability. Finally, laissez-faire was at the center of the economic doctrines that America imported from England and France.[16] In the eighteenth century, for example, Adam Smith advocated replacing the excessive mercantilist regulations of his day with a new system based on natural liberty, or the belief that "every man, as long as he does not violate the laws of justice, is left perfectly free to pursue his own interest, his own way, and to bring both his industry and capital into competition with those of any other man, or order of men."[17]

Like Brands, Fine notes that American hostility to governmental action, especially in economic matters, was given full expression by the followers of both Jefferson and Jackson. He explains, "That government should minister directly to the needs of the people by positive action, that it should regulate to any extent the economic life of the nation, were ideas foreign to the liberals of Jefferson's and Jackson's time." When and where government oversight and control were needed, these liberals would entrust such activities to the state governments, which were closer to the people and, arguably, more accountable and amenable to popular control. All the while, they restricted the national government to those powers that were specifically enumerated in the Constitution and sought to promote an agrarian society that allowed the people to retain maximum power at the expense of the regulatory state. Jefferson declared that "agriculture, manufacturers, commerce, and navigation, the four pillars of our prosperity, are the most thriving when left most free to individual enterprise." Government existed merely to prevent men from infringing upon the lives, liberties, and property of others.[18]

At the same time, the liberal tradition of Jefferson and Jackson, with its hostility to the idea of positive state power, was not accepted by all Americans. Alexander Hamilton, for one, sought to use the national government to promote industry and commerce. Rejecting the Jeffersonian idea that industry prospers "in direct proportion to the degree in which it is left alone," he pinned his hopes for national prosperity on both the national government's aid to business and its simultaneous unwillingness to regulate the economic marketplace. "In matters of industry," he argued, "human enterprise ought, doubtless, to be left free in the main; not fettered by too much regulation; but practical politicians know that it may be beneficially stimulated by prudent aids and encouragements on the part of the government." On these grounds, Hamilton advocated the establishment of a national bank, the national government's assumption of the existing national and state debts, and a protective tariff to assist domestic manufacturers.[19]

Later, Henry Clay championed national power, supporting the protective tariff as an aid to American industry and advocating for internal improvements on the grounds that sufficient private capital was not available to construct needed roads and canals. Thus, Hamilton and Clay rejected strict laissez-faire, especially when it suited their interests. Both would use the powers of the national government to grant favors to the business classes, while Clay also advocated governmental assistance to western farmers. Yet they shared with Jeffersonians and Jacksonians a belief that the government should not act as a regulator of business.[20]

Throughout the nineteenth century, the federal government, for the most part, refrained from regulation of the private economy. There were exceptions. It forbade the use of liquor in the fur trade. It also required the licensing and bonding of private fur traders and established its own fur factories to serve as a "yardstick" for the private sector. Relying on compulsory monthly deductions from the wages of seamen, the federal government constructed marine hospitals to care for sick and disabled sailors. Finally, it regulated both the codfish industry and interstate steamboat operations. Nonetheless, as Fine observes, the federal government intervened "less rather than more in the economic sphere."[21] Indeed, despite enormous growth in the scale and scope of American enterprise and finance in post-Civil War America, the period between 1865 and 1901 saw the greatest promotion of laissez-faire principles. The Progressive Movement in general — and Theodore Roosevelt in particular — grew to maturity in these new conditions of American life, and in reaction to the doctrines of Social Darwinism with which they were regularly defended.

SOCIAL DARWINISM IN AMERICA

It was the Englishman Herbert Spencer who inscribed Social Darwinism upon America. His progeny of scholars, housed in the nation's leading universities, brought the teachings of Spencer to a generation of college students in the final decades of the nineteenth century. So sweeping were the doctrines of Spencer that, as Richard Hofstadter notes, "It was impossible to be active in any field of intellectual work without mastering Spencer. Almost every American philosophical thinker of first or second rank . . . had to reckon with Spencer at some time." He influenced a whole generation of intellectuals. Whether they agreed or disagreed with his writings, the post-Civil War generation could not ignore them.[22] Even criticism "was another measure of the man's towering influence," and the brutally honest manner in which Spencer articulated his views certainly invited criticism.[23] After all, this was a man who unabashedly proclaimed, "The whole effort of nature is to get rid of [the unfit], to clear the world of them, and make room for better. . . . If they are sufficiently complete to live, they do live, and it is well they should live. If they are not sufficiently complete to live, they die, and it is best they should die."[24]

According to Spencer, individuals were free to do whatever they pleased, so long as they did not infringe upon the freedoms of others. In his view, the only role for the state was to ensure that this individual freedom was not violated.[25] Moreover, if the human species was to be preserved, it had to permit the distribution of economic rewards in proportion to merit. Spencer reasoned that, if individuals received either rewards or punishments based on their actions, then those best adapted to their environment would prosper most, while the least well adapted would prosper least. He believed that progress was guaranteed, if the fittest survived. But, if the superior were forced by the government to care for the inferior, then the progress of the whole society was stifled.[26]

Viewing society as an organism that was subject to the laws of nature, Spencer criticized reformers whose actions presumed the existence of human will and choice. The evolution of society, like the evolution of all natural species, he argued, could not be altered according to the planning and effort of mere humans. It was, indeed, an "impious presumption" for "political schemers, with their clumsy mechanisms," to attempt superceding "the great laws of existence." To Spencer, any government official who assumed that legislation and bureaucratic regulation could effectively "patch" nature or alter its great plan was naive beyond belief.[27] Furthermore, he argued that, because of the complexity and interdependency of society's institutions, all of the consequences of specific political acts could not be foreseen. Legislators, he said, had to realize that their laws rarely produced the results intended. They were most likely to obstruct the operation of nature's laws; they certainly could not improve upon them.[28]

Spencer believed in progress, which was measured in large part by the movement of society from more to less government over time. In *The Principles of Sociology*, he writes that there are two types of society: military and industrial. In military societies, the interests of the individual are subordinated to the state's need to preserve itself, because the government must produce weapons and military machinery. It also trains its citizens for warfare and compels a great deal of cooperation on the part of its people. In essence, military states are despotic, and those who are best adapted to a militant lifestyle will dominate these societies. But Spencer argues that such states are destined to evolve: as the strongest and most adapted militant societies conquer the weaker ones, there is less conflict and more internal peace.

In this new environment, Spencer suggests, the industrial arts prosper and a new type of society emerges: an industrial society.[29] According to Spencer, industrial societies, unlike militant ones, are marked by contract. No longer subordinated to the state, the individual is defended by it. Simply put, life, liberty, and property are protected by the government, and because economic reward is based entirely upon merit, the survival of the fittest is assured.[30] Spencer believes that, as long as the government restricts its activities to protecting the rights of citizens, it will enjoy universal support. Moreover, the individual whose abilities are fully developed requires no assistance from the government, and any attempt by the state to assist such an individual will only prevent him from exercising his freedoms and realizing his full potential. On the other hand, state aid is harmful to the individual whose abilities are deficient, for it prevents him from making the necessary adaptation to his environment, thereby hindering his growth and potential.[31]

After the Civil War, the American reading public became enamored with Darwinian theory and was eager to explore any political, economic, or sociological idea that was rooted in Darwinism.[32] This was not surprising in a society that had just experienced the horrible bloodshed of the Civil War, where whole communities had lost an entire generation of able-bodied men. The war had taken a grisly toll on the nation, with over 600,000 men dying in action or of disease—almost as many as would die in all of America's subsequent wars combined. Much of the carnage was due to the fact that the weapons were modern, while the tactics were pre-modern. Developed during the era of the musket, a gun with a range of about 80 yards, the close-order infantry charge was no match for the new rifles, which had a range of 400 yards. The lesson for many was that an inability to adapt to changing circumstances would lead to death. Moreover, Darwinism seemed to confirm the American experience as a story of change and evolution (i.e., territorial expansion and increasing industrialization), and for the victors of the Civil War, Darwinism could even appear to support the outcome of the war: the fittest—morally, politically, and economically—had survived.

Darwin's ideas, as Hofstadter stresses, held a special appeal to American conservatives, who called upon Darwinian principles to justify the economic inequality and hardships associated with the marketplace.[33] Social Darwinism differed from traditional conservatism in that it was devoid of any reverence for state authority, completely unsentimental, and more secular in its outlook. Hofstadter qualifies this claim by conceding that Social Darwinism was "a kind of naturalistic Calvinism in which man's relation to nature is as hard and demanding as man's relation to God under the Calvinistic system." In other words, the ethic of Social Darwinism, like the Puritan ethic, valued hard work, self-restraint, and self-reliance. Leisure and waste would result in failure.

Differences between Social Darwinism and traditional conservatism notwithstanding, the fact remains that the former became a tool of the latter. American conservatives were attracted to Social Darwinism because it defended the status quo and justified attacks on reformers.[34] Businessmen, of course, approved of such government programs as the protective tariff and internal improvements; they only railed against the regulation of their business practices. Many economists, sociologists, and political scientists were less zealous than Spencer in their advocacy of laissez-faire, for unlike him, they were willing to permit the state to run schools, post offices, and even hospitals for the "unfit." Unlike the business community, many in the academy opposed such state interference in the economy as the protective tariff and felt the regulation of "free" labor to be an oxymoron.[35]

According to Fine, not only did Spencer's application of Darwin's theory to society appeal to American businessmen and intellectuals, but his "optimistic presentation of the beneficent operation of nature's laws was thoroughly consonant with the American faith in progress." Moreover, Spencer's individualism, "although it went too far for most Americans, was nevertheless in the best American tradition."[36] Spencer did not have to introduce the American people to individualism or to the concept of the negative state, for these had been woven into the fabric of the American political tradition a century before. Instead, Spencer's significance lies in how he reinforced these ideas and grounded them in science. "The American advocates of laissez-faire," Fine writes, "were ever ready to use Spencer's arguments and Spencer's language to support their views, even if they were reluctant to go quite so far as he did. In Herbert Spencer, the cause of laissez-faire in America had gained a major ally."[37] Hofstadter also concludes that Spencer became the spokesman for the American tradition of individual freedom, and while he did not change the course of mainstream American political thought, his contributions certainly "swelled the stream of individualism."[38]

William Graham Sumner was both a leading proponent of Spencer's views and typical of the adaptation that many American intellectuals made to his thought. But Sumner was no blind follower.[39] He rejected Spencer's belief in natural rights, declaring that "a man has no more right to life than a rattlesnake; he has no more right to liberty than any wild beast." The only true liberty, he maintained, was civil liberty, or liberty under the law.[40] In addition, Sumner did not accept the inevitability of progress. "Under our so-called progress," he writes in "The Challenge of Facts," "evil only alters its forms, and we must esteem it a grand advance if . . . on the whole, and over a wide view of human affairs, good has gained a hair's breadth over evil in a century."[41] Nonetheless, Sumner did accept Social Darwinism. His support of laissez-faire was based, in part, on his association of man's struggle with the larger struggle for existence in nature. In his view, this struggle for existence was basically a contest between man and nature, with man constantly striving to enhance his power over nature. In this struggle, nature could be made to submit, but only to the fittest men. Sumner reasoned that, if the state did not interfere in the social and economic order, men would be rewarded in proportion to their efforts, but if the state attempted to lessen inequality by taking from the successful and giving to the failures, the result would be the end of civilization.[42] Sumner argued that everyone was entitled to a chance at success, but no one was entitled to success itself. In his view, those who were "sober, industrious, prudent, and wise" would succeed, while those who did not possess these qualities would fail and had no reason to expect help.[43]

Like Spencer, Sumner also accepted social determinism, arguing that social institutions were complex and beyond man's control. The industrial organization, he maintained, rested on constant forces like competition and self-interest. Sumner believed these economic forces acted in accordance with natural laws, and nothing could be done to change this fact. Reformers, he declared, who believed that problems like poverty existed because society had been organized badly, did not understand that it made as little sense to alter the social world as to alter the physical world. According to Sumner, the most that a man could do was to ruin, by ignorance and lack of foresight, the natural laws that governed society. In fact, Sumner argued that the ills of his time were, in no small part, the consequences of past reforms. He often said that it would take years and years of effort just to eliminate these past mistakes of reformers and philosophers, and even still the hardships of life would continue. In short, Sumner believed that human planning was inadequate to deal positively with social problems. He advised man to sit back and allow the forces of nature to unfold freely.[44]

Despite his many similarities to Spencer, Sumner did not believe that the state would disappear once man's moral sense had been developed sufficiently. For him, history demonstrated that ambitious people and classes had always attempted to gain control of the state in order to live off the earnings of other people and classes. Democracies were no exception to this rule. In fact, Sumner found that democracies were more likely to become paternal and interfere with private property rights, because popular majorities seemed to believe that only kings and aristocrats were wrong to exercise arbitrary and irresponsible power.[45] Yet, he concluded, if the state were to confine itself merely to the task of maintaining order, there would be no need for the ambitious to control it. From Sumner's standpoint, legislators were not to study the problems of society in the hope of devising plans to regulate social and economic activity, for this power would only be exploited by the ambitious. His brand of reform meant greater security for property rights; it did not mean positive state action to help the underdogs weather the struggle for existence. Sumner maintained that, if the state assumed new functions, it only lost its ability to perform the one function for which it was established: maintaining peace and order.[46] Fine concludes that Sumner "did not push his hostility to state action quite so far as Spencer," although he did oppose most of the new functions assumed by the governments of his day. While Sumner supported efforts to protect women and children workers, believing that they could not look out for themselves, he was opposed to any and all state action to protect male laborers, and he especially despised the protective tariff.[47]

THE CHALLENGE TO SOCIAL DARWINISM

In college, TR heard Sumner teach that the plight of the poor was the result of their inability to adapt to a changing economic and social environment. Even then, however, Roosevelt had doubts about the application of Darwinian theory to human society, a view that was likely reinforced by Nathaniel Shaler, Roosevelt's natural history professor. Shaler was a Christian evolutionist, who believed in the interdependence of species. Specifically, he taught about the dangers of deforestation and the need for land reclamation. Such teaching illustrates that, while the views of Spencer and Sumner were widely embraced in business and academia, not all of their contemporaries opposed an activist state.

Initially, objections to the purely negative state found expression in the Social Gospel movement. Originating in the 1870s, the Social Gospel movement was a reaction against the excessive individualism of traditional Protestantism that showed little concern for the new problems associated with mass industrialization and urbanization. Rejecting the view that the church should focus exclusively on individual conversion to Christ, Social Gospel advocates emphasized the need to save society as a whole. They concerned themselves with the family and the nation, with both social and commercial life. They stressed the importance of environment as a cause of sin and sought to apply the principles of Christianity to the many problems of the age.[48] As Fine explains, "Society itself was to be redeemed and Christianized, and although individuals were still to be converted, they were to be provided with a Christian society in which to live. Only if a regenerated individual were able to live in a regenerated society could he be expected to lead a Christian life."[49] Social Christians denounced the philosophy of laissez-faire as "selfish," "inhumane," "unethical," "immoral," and "barbaric." Many of them regarded competition as antisocial and un-Christian; a kind of warfare in which the strong won and the weak were crushed. A Christian society, they argued, demanded organization on the basis of cooperation, not competition.[50]

In the beginning, Social Gospel advocates did not place much emphasis on solving social problems through state action. Rather, they stressed the need for social regeneration through individual self-sacrifice and the voluntary adoption of Christian ethics. In addressing various urban problems, they relied on the institutional capacities of the church as well as social settlements. Over time, however, they came to realize that it was not enough to hope that individuals would voluntarily embrace the Golden Rule. To achieve the desired reform, state action might be needed as "an important ancillary to Christian ethics."[51] Fine concludes that the most important contribution of the Social Gospel movement was its attack on the philosophy of laissez-faire.

By contending that laissez-faire was an unethical and un-Christian view of the social order, the Social Gospel movement helped to discredit Social Darwinism and thus "clear away a formidable obstacle in the path of the general welfare state." The movement did not convert many conservatives, but it did influence the emerging Progressive thought and individuals like Theodore Roosevelt, for it enabled reformers to "justify social change in terms of Christian doctrine," link their cause with tradition, and thereby give it greater authority.[52]

But Social Gospelers were not the only critics of Social Darwinism. Sociologists like Lester Ward also challenged the application of Darwinian theory to society, and they were joined by Pragmatists like William James in their assault on social determinism. Ward believed that the purpose of sociology was to better society, and he recognized two types of social progress: genetic (or passive dynamic) and telic (or active dynamic). In his *Dynamic Sociology*, he writes that genetic progress is the kind that has occurred in the animal and vegetable worlds. It is completely passive evolution in that it is acted upon by the forces of nature and cannot be influenced by the actions of its subjects.[53] But human evolution, Ward continues, involves something more than the unconscious working of social forces. Man has intellectual ability, and this, Ward contends, has resulted in a different type of social progress, namely "telic" progress.

Telic progress is the result of man's intellect applied to nature, where man has the ability to guide the forces of nature to his advantage.[54] Ward does not accept that the ways of nature are necessarily superior to the ways of man. In truth, he observes, nature is extremely wasteful, noting that an octopus must lay 50,000 eggs to maintain itself and a codfish must hatch one million young fish in order for two to survive. In the vegetable kingdom, he continues, a single plant has been found to contain more than three million spores. Indeed, Ward concludes, terms like "natural selection" and "survival of the fittest" refer to the fact that much is not selected and only a few survive. In addition, he finds that nature is not as peaceful as many would like to believe and that the constant strife in nature, in fact, leads to a lower level of development in surviving life-forms than would occur through cooperation.[55]

In contrast to the wasteful ways of nature, the telic method of man, characterized by will and purpose, achieves truly economic results. Ward notes that man's interference with the competition in nature has produced horticulture and breeding (i.e., cereals, fruit trees, and domesticated animals). Thus, he concludes, through invention, foresight, and design, man has managed to control natural forces to serve his needs. In short, whenever man has directed nature, he has improved upon it. Human progress, Ward argues, has been more the result of artificial selection than of natural selection.[56]

Still, Ward is quick to add, artificial selection (or the telic method) has been employed, for the most part, by individuals, not by society as a whole. Moreover, it has been applied primarily to physical and mechanical problems, not to social problems. For the time being, he asserts, society operates in a rather random manner. As a result, the soil is exhausted, forests are destroyed, cities are unplanned, labor and capital refuse to cooperate, millions are unemployed, and unrestrained competition resulting from the natural laws of trade only invites combination, which leads to monopoly and higher prices.[57]

If government has failed in past efforts to promote the general welfare, Ward argues, it is only because of inexperience. If government is to solve social problems, legislators must become sociologists, and the operations of government must be treated as an applied social science. Society, Ward concludes, must direct social forces in order to shape its own destiny. If social laws really are analogous to physical laws, and if man is able to control natural forces for the benefit of all, then in Ward's mind, there is no reason why humanity cannot utilize social forces for the common good.[58]

Pragmatists also challenged the determinism of Social Darwinism as reducing man "to a mere automaton in a world where the laws of nature ruled supreme."[59] Pragmatists like William James were interested in the uses of knowledge and ideas. For the Pragmatists, Louis Menand explains, "there is no noncircular set of criteria for knowing whether a particular belief is true, no appeal to some standard outside the process of coming to the belief itself."[60] In *Pragmatism*, William James writes that truth "*happens* to an idea." In other words, an idea "becomes true, or is made true, by events. Its verity is in fact an event."[61] Pragmatists like James argued that thoughts were not divine revelations of some external truth, but rather were tools for adapting to reality. An individual chose to believe in something because events and experience showed that it paid to believe in it.[62] Thus, James refused to believe that human behavior was merely a reaction to purely physical events over which the mind had no control; he made the creative and active individual the centerpiece of his thought.

In *The Principles of Psychology*, James argues that human consciousness transforms the concept of survival from mere hypothesis into an "imperative decree." The mind is "fundamentally active and creative" and not simply a passive adjuster to the world around it. In "Remarks on Spencer's Definition of Mind as Correspondence," he argues, "mental interests, so long as they are bases for human action—action which to a great extent transforms the world—help to make the truth which they declare." In short, the mind has "a vote" and can be spontaneous; the struggle for survival is more than the adjustment of the body and the mind to their external environment.[63] James therefore rejects Spencer's "block universe" philosophy, which ruled out chance and spoke only of natural laws and "predetermined tendencies." The world, he writes in "The Dilemma of Determinism," is a "pluralistic and restless universe, in which no single point of view can ever take in the whole scene," and the active mind has a role to play in shaping this uncertainty and incompleteness.[64]

Most Americans, Ralph Gabriel contends, readily accepted James' version of Pragmatism. James was, after all, "the enemy of authority and dogma, of fatalism, of despair, and escapism, of stagnation, of inhumanity, and of the oppressive weight of established things." Moreover, he wished to see ideas applied to the real world, and when he made the creative and active individual the centerpiece of this thought, he placed his philosophy in the mainstream of American political thought and tradition.[65] Americans, Gabriel concludes, accepted James' brand of Pragmatism, because it "urged activism in a society whose culture was charged with activism." Because James believed that ideas must be applied to real problems and judged by their results, his philosophy was in accord with an American tradition of empiricism. Indeed, the founding fathers themselves had looked upon the Constitution of 1787 as an experiment. Moreover, James' belief in the power of the autonomous and creative individual was reminiscent of the Declaration of Independence, the frontier, and the yeomen farmer in whom Jefferson placed his trust, as well as with "the central doctrine of the American democratic faith, that of the free and responsible man and citizen."[66] Pragmatism therefore fit with American values every bit as much as did Social Darwinism.

FROM PROTEST TO PROGRESSIVISM

James was one of Roosevelt's favorite professors at Harvard and, while the headstrong Theodore did not accept all of his teachings, much of his later thought, like Progressivism in general, shows the influence of James' Pragmatism. Even though James was not really interested in social reform, Progressives like Roosevelt borrowed from his Pragmatic tradition in their approach to national economic planning. Gabriel notes that a careful examination of the books and speeches of the Progressive era shows the significant influence that Pragmatism had on Progressive thinkers.[67] "This is a world of experiment and change," Charles E. Merriam declared, "a world in which constant readjustments are being made in the future even more rapidly than in the past, as man's control over the forces of nature, including human nature, expands and develops and reaches points hitherto unattained." Similarly, Herbert Croly wrote, "The planning department of the democratic state is creation for action. . . . It plans as far ahead as conditions permit or dictate. It changes its plans as often as conditions demand. It seeks above all to test its own plans, so as to discover whether they will accomplish the desired result." No doubt, such sentiments drew upon Pragmatism to determine how planning should be conducted in the era of the positive state. The answer lay in empiricism. Gabriel explains, "Progressivism was an aspect of the rising cult of science." At the same time, Progressives did not want to become slaves of science. "Democracy," Croly declared, "can never permit science to determine its fundamental purpose, because the integrity of that purpose depends finally upon a consecration of the will . . . " Progressives, Gabriel suggests, were attempting to "smuggle ethical absolutism in through the back hall of his philosophical edifice to give support to a brave facade of Pragmatism." Thus, while they borrowed heavily from the Pragmatic tradition in their approach to national economic planning, the Progressives also injected it with moral certitude, as modified by the Social Gospel. They were optimistic that science and experimentation (social planning) could be guided and controlled by moral certainty, or truth.[68]

In its opposition to laissez-faire as well as its advocacy of social reform, Progressivism would borrow heavily from both Pragmatism and the Social Gospel movement, but it was not just religious leaders and academics who issued the call for reform that was Progressivism. Reform was born in protest as well. Farmers and laborers were also unhappy with growing inequalities in wealth, the control of political and economic power by wealth, unprecedented unemployment, and the poor living conditions of the have-nots. They would be the foot soldiers of Progressivism. Indeed, farmers, who believed they were not sharing fairly in the rewards of the emerging national economy, were among the first groups to voice their discontent with the new economic order. The drop in the price of farm commodities in 1868 only fueled the fires of their discontent. By the mid-1870s, more and more farmers, mostly in the Midwest and the South, joined the Granger movement to promote their economic interests, which railroad magnates and eastern financiers sought to ignore. "Granges" were formed originally to compensate for the isolation and loneliness of farm life. Through lectures, discussions, picnics, and other family entertainment, they provided farmers with social and intellectual opportunities, but they also built a sense of social solidarity. The meetings increasingly focused on the economic issues of importance to farmers, such as the declining price of wheat and the increasing costs of railroad transportation. While the constitution of the Granges precluded participation in politics, members skirted this prohibition by formally adjourning their meetings after the customary literary or musical program. They were then just regular farmers gathered together, who could discuss political issues and how to promote their cause, which came to embody a whole host of concerns.[69]

Farmers in Iowa, Nebraska, and Kansas, in particular, complained about the high costs of shipping corn to the markets in the East. Farmers in Minnesota and the Dakotas said the same of wheat. All of them criticized the policy of the grain elevators, which stored their wheat and corn until it could be transported by rail. Often, elevator operators offered farmers low prices for high-quality produce, and the farmers were usually forced to accept these unfair deals, because there was nowhere else to store their grain. Southern and western farmers were also frustrated with the limited credit that banks were willing to extend to their regions. National banks, which had been established during the Civil War, did not exist anywhere in the South; and few existed in the West because Congress required a minimum capital of $50,000, which few western towns could raise. As a result, the availability of loans was limited in these parts of the country.

For their part, midwestern businessmen also objected to the absence of sufficient credit, and, like the farmers, they complained of high railroad rates and the preferences that railroads gave to long-distance shippers, who, with lower shipping costs, could undersell them. This general discontent led states to enact Granger laws, which set maximum charges for grain operators and railroads. Not surprisingly, the railroads and grain elevator companies challenged the constitutionality of these acts, but the United States Supreme Court upheld the right of the states to regulate rates in *Munn v. Illinois* (1877). Ultimately, these regulations proved to be ineffective, as many were either repealed or greatly modified to the point of impotence.[70]

At the same time, labor protested many of the inequalities associated with the new industrial system. As business activity declined by about one-third in the 1870s, many workers were laid off and others suffered pay cuts. Most economists and wealthy businessmen regarded this "panic of 1873" as a normal part of the natural workings of the economic order. But the search for relief from the depression led some workers, especially in the coalmines, to take matters into their own hands. A group called the "Molly Maguires" gained power in the anthracite coal region of Pennsylvania and soon mine owners began to report that the "Mollies" were intimidating and even murdering mine bosses and superintendents. Eventually, a number of alleged ringleaders were arrested, based on the dubious testimony of a paid informant. Twenty-four of them were convicted in late 1876, and disturbances ended for a time.

But, in 1877, when eastern railroad managers cut wages by ten percent, workers on the Baltimore and Ohio Railroad went on strike and took possession of various rail yards. Employees of the other eastern railroads also went on strike, and when local and state government proved unable to deal with the crisis, President Rutherford B. Hayes used the army to break the strike. Subsequently, states began to pass laws against labor organizations, and the courts began to invoke "the doctrine of malicious conspiracy" to break strikes.[71] Rejecting direct action as counterproductive, however, some laborers sought economic relief by turning to the political system, particularly independent political parties like the Greenbacks that advocated issuing more paper money to provide relief from the depression. The Greenbacks also favored regulating working hours and restricting Chinese immigration.[72]

The Greenbacks were just one party that organized to protest the unwillingness of both Democrats and Republicans to address the mass inequality of the Gilded Age. Also contesting national, state, and local elections in the decades following the Civil War were political parties like Prohibition, Anti-Monopoly, Labor Reform, Union Labor, United Labor, Workingmen, and hundreds of local and state independent parties. By 1892, however, a potentially broader union of these alienated grassroots champions of small farmers and wage earners had organized. Most of the base of the new People's Party consisted of debt-ridden cotton farmers from the South and wheat farmers from the Midwest, but the party reached out, with some success, to the anti-saloon crusaders of the Women's Christian Temperance Society and the Prohibition Party, to Christian Socialists, to advocates of a single tax on land, and even to a few workers of the Knights of Labor and the American Federation of Labor.[73]

The People's, or "Populist," Party was indeed "an unstable amalgam of social groups and political organizations of clashing priorities." Debt-ridden small farmers wanted to inflate the money supply, while urban workers feared a hike in prices for food and rent. Prohibitionists opposed the sale of liquor, while currency reformers opposed big money and the constriction of credit. The hope was that all of these various reformers would unite behind one simple message: the need to save the people from concentrated wealth and corrupt state power.

Populism was to be a crusade against plutocracy. Central banks, creditors, railroad barons, and industrial monopolies were the principal villains. It was they who held great influence over state governments, and their grasp needed to be broken for the sake of "the people"—the "producing class." The producing class included just about everyone except bankers, land speculators, liquor dealers, and monopolists. Certain immigrant groups like the Chinese were also excluded, for it was believed that they were too easily manipulated by the economic elite. Even those who reached out to immigrant laborers never abandoned the belief that Anglo-American culture was superior to all others. African-Americans who rejected Black Nationalism and accepted white dominance of the movement were welcome in the People's Party, however.[74]

The Populist attack on wealth, Michael Kazin explains, was often rooted in the language of Christianity. Reformers opposed monopolies that seemed to mock the teachings of Jesus about sacrifice, charity, and brotherhood. Kazin stresses that these Christian appeals were not intended to convert more souls for Jesus; rather, Populist reformers used "a Christian vocabulary" because it allowed them to speak about social problems with great emotion, thereby positioning themselves in stark contrast to the scientific and rational appeals of the Social Darwinists.[75] The specific platform of the party promised farmers an increase in the money supply, a ban on alien land ownership, and state-run railroads. For wage earners, it endorsed a shorter working day and abolition of the strikebreaking Pinkerton Agency. Both currency reformers and the residents of western mining states were promised an unlimited coinage of silver and gold, and Union veterans were assured the continuation of generous pensions. What was not mentioned in their official platform, but was "woven throughout the language of most committed Populists," was an emphasis on promoting public virtue and ridding society of all forms of corruption. Kazin notes that, with the exception of the pension issue ("a Republican standby"), the Populist agenda was one that neither the Democrats nor the Republicans would support.[76]

In all, the Populists argued for a stronger state that could counter both the exploitations of big business and the corruption of party machines, but not all agreed as to the wisdom of calling for an expansion of governmental power. Some of their heroes like Jefferson and Jackson had advocated small, limited government as well as a strictly literal interpretation of the Constitution. Ultimately, however, the Populists concluded that state power in and of itself was not the problem. The problem was with the character of the men who served in the state legislatures, governor's mansions, Congress, and the White House. The politicians, in other words, were to be faulted for "using the people's money against the people's interests."

This was the message that the Populists preached, and the results of the elections of 1892 and 1894 seemed encouraging.[77] In 1892, the Populist presidential nominee, James Weaver received over one million votes and won a majority of the popular vote in Colorado, Idaho, and Nevada. Two Populist governors were also elected that year. In 1894, the party enjoyed greater success, when its candidates won over 1.5 million votes. Seven of its nominees for the U.S. House of Representatives and six of its candidates for the U.S. Senate won their elections, as did hundreds of state legislative candidates. At the same time, the party's success was limited regionally, for the Populists made all of their gains in the Deep South and Rocky Mountain states. They failed to attract the support of most craft and industrial workers in urban areas, many of whom were neither native-born nor Protestant.[78] In 1896, the Democratic Party, hurt by a severe depression that began in 1893, endorsed the coinage of silver and gave its presidential nomination to the Populist William Jennings Bryan. Most Populists thereupon decided to support Bryan and the Democrats, but a majority of voters outside the South and West either did not agree that America faced a great crisis or feared that the Populist alternative would be worse than the current state of affairs. Bryan's pious criticisms of urban life also offended the traditionally Democratic voters who lived in various eastern and midwestern cities, and he was defeated. But, while the Populist Party disappeared from American politics, its influence lived on in the Progressive crusade of the early twentieth century.[79]

Progressivism, Frank Freidel writes, was "a continuation and coalescing of the many reform movements that had been active in the last decades of the nineteenth century." The movement included political reformers, as well as followers of the single tax, social justice, women's rights, temperance, and Social Gospel movements. Many former Populists joined the Progressive ranks and brought their direct democracy enthusiasm to the Progressive program.

The similarities between the Progressive and Populist agendas were such that William Allen White, a Progressive Kansas newspaper editor, once quipped that the Progressive leaders had "caught the Populists in swimming and stole all of their clothing except the frayed underdrawers of free silver."[80]

At the same time, there were important differences between the Progressives and the Populists. The Populist Party had consisted primarily of debt-ridden southern and midwestern farmers as well as advocates of both Prohibition and currency reform. It had reached out with little success to northern and eastern laborers. Progressivism, on the other hand, consisted of men and women from all over the United States, although it was especially prevalent in the Northeast and Midwest. Moreover, Progressives tended to be not only white, native-born, and Protestant but also urban, middle class, college-educated, and either small businessmen or self-employed professional men. In addition, most Progressives were Republican, although some Democrats were active in the movement.[81] But, regardless of party affiliation, Progressives were united by a common determination to transform America. Theodore Roosevelt entered public life imbued with the Progressive spirit, informed by the political and intellectual ferment of his times, determined to make his mark on the public life of the nation.

INDIVIDUALISM AND ITS TORMENTS

Individualism was the credo of the American upper classes in the late nineteenth century. A half century earlier, Tocqueville had coined the term *individualism* to describe the American spirit, and it was now the heart and soul of late nineteenth century Victorian culture, which celebrated self-discipline and self-reliance as vital to success and attributed the plight of the poor to individual shortcomings rather than to the economic system.[82] But the culture of the upper classes was almost impossible for the wageworkers and farmers to understand. Wageworkers, in particular, barely made enough to support themselves, let alone their families. They lived with the constant threat of unemployment that came with the periodic depressions and, even when employed, had to fear injury on the job or early death due to hard labor, poor working conditions, and/or poor diet. Most working class women, unlike ladies of the upper classes, had to work to help support a family. Children worked as well. There was little time for leisure.[83]

Farmers too had little in common with the upper classes, for they too lived with insecurity. Whole families—women and children, as well as men— toiled together in the work of farming. But, unlike wageworkers, farmers never completely lost their economic independence. As Michael McGerr notes, "They ruled over their own domain, however small."[84] Isolated by poor roads and poor mail service, farm families had reason to feel independent, and they taught their children to be tough and self-reliant. This set farmers apart from industrial workers, as well as from the rich. Farm life allowed little time for leisure, and most agrarians used what free time they had to hunt, fish, and attend revivals.[85]

The different experiences of the upper classes, the wage workers, and the farmers begged a fundamental question: What role should Victorian values continue to play in the new industrial society? At a time when farmers, workers, and the wealthy were too divided to provide an answer to this question, a new college-educated and more professional middle class seized the initiative. This was the soil from which the Progressive movement in America grew. Increasingly dissatisfied with the economic conditions around them, these middle class men and women, raised to revere individualism, self-discipline, and self-denial, sought a new way of living, a new ideology that, would put an end to "the friction and conflicts of the industrializing nation."[86]

Without a doubt, class conflict was the major problem that the Victorian middle class saw in the world around them. "We do not like to acknowledge that Americans are divided into two nations," Jane Addams declared. Middle class reformers like Addams saw what the rich refused to see, specifically that men exist in two classes: the working class and the upper class. McGerr notes that, after the turn of the century, middle class reformers would pay more attention to the plight of the nation's farmers, but in the last two decades of the nineteenth century, "it was the wage earners and the rich who preoccupied the Victorian imagination." They found fault with both the wealthy and the working class whose values they regarded as foreign and degenerate. Moreover, both classes seemed to be selfishly unconcerned with how their demands and actions would impact the rest of society. The middle class, McGerr concludes, was "trapped in a no-man's land." Comfortable with neither the upper class nor the working class, it found itself "caught in a crossfire," and its individualistic values were of no help whatsoever. More and more, the middle class saw individualism as the reason for the crisis in the first place. Victorian men and women were now willing to question their longstanding devotion to individualism.[87]

The new middle class also came to reassess its dedication to hard work, thrift, and self-denial. As the American economy grew, the middle class became more and more seduced by leisure, abundance, and consumerism, and increasingly, the view was held that, while work was important, one could work too hard or too much. Leisure time took on a new importance, as the new middle class found new interests like church services, museums, concerts, tennis, baseball, self-improvement lectures, classes, and vacations to either the shore or the woods.[88] They began to spend more freely on gifts, dinners, entertainment, clothing, cosmetics, and home improvements, but they were careful to balance the pursuit of pleasure with self-restraint. This self-discipline was, perhaps, nowhere more apparent than in the efforts of many in the new middle class, men and women alike, to make themselves more physically fit and sexually chaste.[89] "By the turn of the century and the approach of Queen Victoria's passing," McGerr observes, "the American Victorians were no longer Victorians. . . . [R]ejecting individualism, reconsidering work and pleasure, and redesigning the body, middle class men and women had cast off much of their old identity. Strengthening themselves, they were becoming new people."[90]

Focused on the *interdependence* of the men and women of all classes, middle class reformers came to believe that the well-being of society rested on a form of association that rejected not only individualism but also the working class and agrarian brands of mutualism that were based merely on common class identity. The concept of association "grew out of a sense of difference . . . it meant crossing class lines to bring together people of diverse identities and conditions." Yet, even as the middle class began to consider the need for association among varying economic interests, it looked also for "a more coercive replacement for individualism" and found it in state power.[91] By the end of the nineteenth century, middle-class reformers had rejected their "longstanding individualism" and adopted in its place the concept of collectivism. They came to rely more and more on the power of the state to end class conflict and to solve the myriad other problems associated with industrial capitalism. By the turn of the century, the Victorians had become Progressives.[92] They were determined to promote the ideal of collectivism and develop the regulatory powers of the state, and because there were many ways to accomplish these goals, Progressives could pursue various reforms without stepping on one another's toes.

"Rather than turn into a nineteenth century symphony orchestra," McGerr writes, "they became like a musical innovation of their own time, the jazz band, in which each instrumentalist improvised a unique melody on top of a shared set of chords."[93] Wealth, it was argued, made the upper class behave in a selfish and indulgent manner, so some Progressives advocated taxes on inheritance and income.[94] The problems of the poor and working classes were the product of preventable conditions that other Progressives sought to correct: poor sanitation and safety at home and work; no access to recreational facilities; lack of education; limited competition in the marketplace; or no public regulation of working hours, wages, and standards in business.[95] Finally, fearing the extent to which Social Darwinism had perverted the principle of individualism, and believing that the public's appetite for pleasure encouraged individualism, some Progressives even attempted to regulate private adult behavior (alcohol, gambling, prostitution, divorce, and indecent entertainment).[96] Regardless of their specific agenda, these new middle-class reformers advanced the Progressive agenda of antiindividualism, collectivism, and enhanced state power, all grounded in the conviction that people changed when the character of both their private and public environments changed. Individualism aside, they held that society was interdependent.

This, then, was the world in which Theodore Roosevelt grew to maturity, carrying a strong belief in the virtue of both individual and social growth. He embraced the Progressive belief in the interdependence of society, which led to his advocacy of legal and institutional restraints on industrial capitalism. But he also celebrated the idea of individual freedom and personal responsibility that many Progressive reformers rejected as products of Social Darwinism. The intellectual challenge for Roosevelt was to integrate collectivism and individualism into a coherent body of thought and action. He accepted that the government should not allow powerful businessmen to do whatever they wanted in the name of individual freedom. At the same time, he never lost sight of his belief that the individual was preeminent, and that there must be a way to reconcile Progressive collectivism with the individualistic tradition of the United States.

NOTES

1. Eric Foner, *The Story of American Freedom* (New York: W. W. Norton and Company, 1999), 116–17.
2. Foner, *Story of American Freedom*, 117–18.
3. Foner, *Story of American Freedom*, 118–19.
4. The term was coined by Mark Twain to depict both the boom-and-bust speculative mentality of post–Civil War era businessmen and the unquestioning willingness of politicians to serve the interests of big business.
5. Foner, *Story of American Freedom*, 120–21. See also Richard Hofstadter, *Social Darwinism in American Thought* (Boston: Beacon Press, 1992).
6. H. W. Brands, *The Strange Death of American Liberalism* (New Haven: Yale University Press, 2001), 1–2.
7. Brands, *Strange Death*, 3–4.
8. Quoted in Brands, *Strange Death*, 4–5.
9. Brands, *Strange Death*, 5–6.
10. Brands, *Strange Death*, 6–7.
11. Brands, *Strange Death*, 30–31.
12. Brands, *Strange Death*, 32–33.
13. Brands, *Strange Death*, 50.

14. Brands, *Strange Death*, 47. See also Jerome M. Mileur and Ronald Story, "America's Wartime Presidents: Politics, National Security, and Civil Liberties," in *The Politics of Terror and the U.S. Response to 9/11*, ed. William Crotty (Boston: Northeastern University, 2004), 95–133.

15. Sidney Fine, *Laissez Faire and the General-Welfare State* (Ann Arbor: The University of Michigan Press, 1964), 8. Please note that most of my summary and discussion of Social Darwinism and its critics is reliant on Fine.

16. Fine, *Laissez Faire*, 5.

17. Fine, *Laissez Faire*, 7.

18. Fine, *Laissez Faire*, 12–13.

19. Fine, *Laissez Faire*, 15.

20. Fine, *Laissez Faire*, 16.

21. Fine, *Laissez Faire*, 19.

22. Hofstadter, *Social Darwinism*, 33.

23. Hofstadter, *Social Darwinism*, 35.

24. Herbert Spencer, *Social Statics* (New York: D. Appleton and Company, 1864), 414–15.

25. Fine, *Laissez Faire*, 33. See also Spencer, *Social Statics*, 79–80.

26. Fine, *Laissez Faire*, 34. See also Herbert Spencer, *Principles of Ethics*, vol. 2 (New York: D. Appleton and Company, 1895–1898), 6–7, 17; Herbert Spencer, "Sins of Legislators," in *The Man versus the State* (New York: D. Appleton and Company, 1885), 64–66; Herbert Spencer, *The Study of Sociology* (New York: D. Appleton and Company, 1896), 315.

27. Fine, *Laissez Faire*, 35. See also Spencer, *Social Statics*, 293–94.

28. Fine, *Laissez Faire*, 35. See also Spencer, *Study of Sociology*, 1–21, 245, 365–67; Spencer, "Sins of Legislators," 74–77; Spencer, *Principles of Ethics*, vol. 2, 428.

29. Fine, *Laissez Faire*, 36. See also Herbert Spencer, *The Principles of Sociology*, vol. 2 (New York: D. Appleton and Company, 1876–97), 620–28.

30. Fine, *Laissez Faire*, 36. See also Spencer, *Principles of Sociology*, vol. 2, chap. 18.

31. Fine, *Laissez Faire*, 37–38. See also Spencer, *Social Statics*, 280–82.

32. Hofstadter, *Social Darwinism*, 5.

33. Hofstadter, *Social Darwinism*, 6.

34. Hofstadter, *Social Darwinism*, 7–10.

35. Fine, *Laissez Faire*, 29–30.

36. Fine, *Laissez Faire*, 43.

37. Fine, *Laissez Faire*, 46.

38. Hofstadter, *Social Darwinism*, 50.

39. Fine, *Laissez Faire*, 81.

40. Fine, *Laissez Faire*, 81. See also William Graham Sumner, "The Boon of Nature," in *Essays of William Graham Sumner*, vol. 1, ed. Albert G. Keller and Maurice R. Davie (New Haven: Yale University Press, 1934), 385.

41. Fine, *Laissez Faire*, 81–82. See also William Graham Sumner, "The Challenge of Facts," in *Essays*, vol. 2, ed. Albert G. Keller and Maurice R. Davie (New Haven: Yale University Press, 1934), 119.

42. Fine, *Laissez Faire*, 82. See also Sumner, "Challenge of Facts," 87–93, 95–97; William Graham Sumner, "The Influence of Commercial Crises on Opinions about Economic Doctrines," in *Essays*, vol. 2, ed. Albert G. Keller and Maurice R. Davie (New Haven: Yale University Press, 1934), 56.

43. Fine, *Laissez Faire*, 82–83. See also William Graham Sumner, "Protectionism: The –Ism Which Teaches That Waste Makes Wealth," in *Essays*, vol. 2, ed. Albert G. Keller and Maurice R. Davie (New Haven: Yale University Press, 1934), 435; William Graham Sumner, "The Abolition of Poverty," in *Essays*, vol. 1, ed. Albert G. Keller and Maurice R. Davie (New Haven: Yale University Press, 1934),109.

44. Fine, *Laissez Faire*, 84. See also Sumner, "Influence of Commercial Crises," 46–47; Sumner, "Challenge of Facts," 99–100; William Graham Sumner, "The Absurd Effort to Make the World Over," in *Essays*, vol. 1, ed. Albert G. Keller and Maurice R. Davie (New Haven: Yale University Press, 1934), 94.

45. Fine, *Laissez Faire*, 86. See also William Graham Sumner, *What Social Classes Owe to Each Other* (New York: Harper and Brothers, 1883), 30–33; Sumner, "Challenge of Facts," 119–22; William Graham Sumner, "State Interference," in *Essays*, vol. 2, ed. Albert G. Keller and Maurice R. Davie (New Haven: Yale University Press, 1934), 142–45.

46. Fine, *Laissez Faire*, 88. See also William Graham Sumner, "Democracy and Plutocracy," in *Essays*, vol. 2, ed. Albert G. Keller and Maurice R. Davie (New Haven: Yale University Press, 1934), 217–19; William Graham Sumner, "Separation of State and Market," in *Essays*, vol. 2, ed. Albert G. Keller and Maurice R. Davie (New Haven: Yale University Press, 1934), 240–41.

47. Fine, *Laissez Faire*, 89.

48. Fine, *Laissez Faire*, 170.

49. Fine, *Laissez Faire*, 171.

50. Fine, *Laissez Faire*, 172–74.

51. Fine, *Laissez Faire*, 179–80.

52. Fine, *Laissez Faire*, 196–97.

53. Fine, *Laissez Faire*, 254–55. See also Lester Ward, *Dynamic Sociology*, vol. 1 (New York: D. Appleton and Company, 1883), 56–57.

54. Fine, *Laissez Faire*, 255. See also Ward, *Dynamic Sociology*, vol. 1, 28–30; Lester Ward, *Outlines of Sociology* (New York: The Macmillan Company, 1898), 179–82, 235; Lester Ward, *The Psychic Factors of Civilization* (Boston: Ginn and Company, 1893), 242–44; Lester Ward, "Mind as a Social Factor," in *Glimpses of the Cosmos*, vol. 3 (New York: G. P. Putnam's Sons, 1913–18), 367–69.

55. Fine, *Laissez Faire*, 255. See also Ward, *Dynamic Sociology*, vol. 1, 72–73; Ward, *Dynamic Sociology*, vol. 2, 86–88; Lester Ward, "Scientific Basis of a Political Economy," in *Glimpses of the Cosmos*, vol. 3, (New York: G. P. Putnam's Sons, 1913–18), 33–34; Ward, *Psychic Factors*, 251–52, 260–61.

56. Fine, *Laissez Faire*, 256. See also Ward, "Scientific Basis," 36–37, 47–48; Ward, "Mind as a Social Factor," 369–74, 375–77; Ward, *Dynamic Sociology*, vol. 1, 33–35; Ward, *Dynamic Sociology*, vol. 2, 205–06; Ward, *Psychic Factors*, 256–57, 260–62.

57. Fine, *Laissez Faire*, 257. See also Ward, "Scientific Basis," 34–36; Lester Ward "The Sociological Basis of Protection and Free Trade," in *Glimpses of the Cosmos*, vol.

4 (New York: G. P. Putnam's Sons, 1913–18), 186–89; Ward, *Dynamic Sociology*, vol. 1, 29–30; Ward, *Psychic Factors*, 263–76.

58. Fine, *Laissez Faire*, 258. See also Ward, *Dynamic Sociology*, vol. 1, 37; Ward, *Dynamic Sociology*, vol. 2, 249–52.

59. Fine, *Laissez Faire*, 280.

60. Louis Menand, *The Metaphysical Club: A Story of Ideas in America* (New York: Farrar, Straus, and Giroux, 2002), 353.

61. William James, "Pragmatism," in *The Works of William James*, ed. Frederick H. Burkhardt (Cambridge: Harvard University Press, 1975–1988), 97.

62. Menand, *Metaphysical Club*, 358.

63. Fine, *Laissez Faire*, 282. See also William James, *The Principles of Psychology*, vol. 1 (New York: Henry Holt and Company, 1890), 138–41; William James, "Remarks on Spencer's Definition of Mind as Correspondence," in *Collected Essays and Reviews* (New York: Longmans, Greens and Company, 1920), 67.

64. Fine, *Laissez Faire*, 282. See also William James, "The Dilemma of Determinism," in *The Will to Believe* (New York: Longmans, Greens and Company, 1897), 151–53, 176–79, 183.

65. Ralph Gabriel, *The Course of American Democratic Thought* (New York: The Ronald Press Company, 1956), 344–45.

66. Gabriel, *Course of American Thought*, 346–47.

67. Gabriel, *Course of American Thought*, 364.

68. Gabriel, *Course of American Thought*, 365.

69. David Herbert Donald, *Liberty and Union: The Crisis of Popular Government, 1830–1890* (Boston: Little, Brown and Company, 1978), 238–40. See also Elizabeth Sanders, *Roots of Reform: Farmers, Workers, and the American State, 1877–1917* (Chicago: The University of Chicago Press, 1999).

70. Donald, *Liberty and Union*, 240–41.

71. Donald, *Liberty and Union*, 241, 243–44.

72. Donald, *Liberty and Union*, 242–43.

73. Michael Kazin, *The Populist Persuasion: An American History* (Ithaca: Cornell University Press, 1998), 28.

74. Kazin, *Populist Persuasion*, 30–31, 34–35.

75. Kazin, *Populist Persuasion*, 33.

76. Kazin, *Populist Persuasion*, 38–39.

77. Kazin, *Populist Persuasion*, 41–42.

78. Kazin, *Populist Persuasion*, 42–43.

79. Kazin, *Populist Persuasion*, 43–46.

80. Frank Freidel, *America in the Twentieth Century*, 4th ed. (New York: Alfred Knopf, 1976), 18.

81. Freidel, *America in the Twentieth Century*, 19–20.

82. Michael McGerr, *A Fierce Discontent: The Rise and Fall of the Progressive Movement in America (1870–1920)* (New York: Free Press, 2003), 9.

83. McGerr, *Fierce Discontent*, 16–17, 19–21.

84. McGerr, *Fierce Discontent*, 24–26.

85. McGerr, *Fierce Discontent*, 27.

86. McGerr, *Fierce Discontent*, 42.
87. McGerr, *Fierce Discontent*, 54–56.
88. McGerr, *Fierce Discontent*, 60–61.
89. McGerr, *Fierce Discontent*, 62–63.
90. McGerr, *Fierce Discontent*, 64.
91. McGerr, *Fierce Discontent*, 66–67.
92. McGerr, *Fierce Discontent*, 68.
93. McGerr, *Fierce Discontent*, 73.
94. McGerr, *Fierce Discontent*, 98.
95. McGerr, *Fierce Discontent*, 99.
96. McGerr, *Fierce Discontent*, 84.

Chapter Two

Years of Preparation

Darwinism had a profound influence on TR's generation. Many economists, sociologists, political scientists, and historians, from 1865 to 1901, had applied Darwin's theories of adaptability and change to their own disciplines and, following the intellectual lead of Herbert Spencer, made "survival of the fittest" not just the law of nature but also the law of society. Many social theorists invoked science and drew analogies to the natural world to defend unfettered capitalism and explain the success and failure of individuals in the marketplace. Language such as "natural selection," "the struggle for existence," and "the survival of the fittest" epitomized the predominant social outlook of the time, especially in economic matters. Many argued that, because evolution, both natural and social, lent itself to the progress of a species, it should not be altered. If economic reward and punishment were based upon individual actions and behavior, then those best adapted to their environment would prosper most, and those least adapted would prosper least. If the fittest survived, progress was assured; however, if the superior were forced by the government to care for the inferior, then the progress of the whole society would be stifled.[1]

TR AND SOCIAL DARWINISM

Like so many of his generation, Roosevelt accepted the scientific theories of Darwin. Interested in nature and biology since he was a boy, Roosevelt delighted in reading about evolution and the natural world. Along with his brother and sisters, his earliest playmates were mice, guinea pigs, chipmunks, and squirrels. He was also interested in birds, carefully inspecting their coloring and

observing their habits, and in addition spent summers in the countryside study-
ing flora and fauna. Roosevelt kept notebooks full of detailed natural observations, including a seven-page study on the natural history of ants, which he
wrote at the age of nine. At college and in the Dakota Territory, he continued to
examine and record the natural habitats of various creatures. Professional scientists were subsequently to draw upon his studies of the wapiti, cougar, and
other animals of the western plains and the Long Island swamps.[2] In his autobiography, Roosevelt traces his interest in observing, capturing, and even preserving natural specimens to a boyhood encounter with a dead seal that had
been laid out on a New York City street. Young TR measured the mammal with
a pocket ruler that he always carried and recorded detailed field notes. Before
long, he started gathering all sorts of small rodents and other creatures. With
self-taught taxidermy methods, he preserved and stored them in his bedroom,
which he dubbed the Roosevelt Museum of Natural History. By the time he was
eleven, Roosevelt had over 1,000 specimens in his collection. After the maid
complained, the most offensive specimens were removed, but this did not stop
Theodore from storing dead rodents in the icebox.[3]

As a naturalist, Roosevelt accepted that life was a struggle and that both individuals and societies progressed if they possessed the ability to endure
hardship and adjust to change, yet he also believed that there were limits to
how Darwin's theories, in particular, could be applied to society-at-large.
"The progress of mankind in past ages," Roosevelt writes in an 1895 review
of Benjamin Kidd's *Social Evolution*, "can only have been made under, and
in accordance with, certain biological laws, and . . . these laws continue to
work in human society at the present day. . . . [They] govern the reproduction
of mankind from generation to generation, precisely as they govern the reproduction of the lower animals, and . . . therefore, largely govern his
progress." But, unlike Kidd, Roosevelt does not believe that natural selection
determines every aspect of human progress. In fact, he argues, natural selection is a much more complicated process than Kidd's study suggests.[4]

Kidd's *Social Evolution* was written as a way of reconciling competition,
natural selection, and the increasing demand for economic reform through
positive state action. Specifically, Kidd argues that, because progress results
from selection, and because selection involves competition, the central purpose of the modern state must be to sustain competition. At the same time, he
understands and sympathizes with the protests of the economic underdogs.
Why, he asks, would these lower classes, who have been exploited by the
competitive system, wish to maintain the existing social order?[5] Indeed, some
might say that the "great masses of people, the so-called lower class," have a
rational interest in abolishing competition and replacing it with Socialism.
Kidd concludes that there is a conflict between the economic interests of the

masses and continued progress through economic competition, and it cannot be resolved by reason. Rather than reason, he suggests that society look to the emotional qualities of religion as the most powerful expression of human feeling and the emotional side of man's nature. Religion, he believes, has the greatest potential for social good because, unlike science, it implores man to act in a socially responsible way. Yet, while this altruistic impulse runs counter to self-interest and has no rational basis, it is nonetheless the best possible defense against the abandonment of competition, because society is made more efficient and vigorous by the effect of charity and social legislation that equips members of the lower class with the means to compete in the free marketplace.[6] Thus, Kidd concludes, without going so far as to authorize government's management of industry or confiscation of private property, legislation can enable the masses to participate more energetically in economic competition.[7]

Roosevelt's reaction to Kidd lays the foundation for his thought on how individualism and social concern can be compatible. He acknowledges that social progress rests on biological laws but is unwilling to concede that natural selection monopolizes all aspects of human progress. Kidd had argued that the progress of a species was dependent upon its fertility, that selection appeared most rigid in those cases involving the most fertile species. Roosevelt agrees that, all things being equal, the species where "rivalry is keenest" will make the most progress, but adds that all things are hardly ever equal. TR argues that *selection* is most rigid where a species is most fertile, but it is also the case that the most fertile species are the ones that *progress* the least. He cites the guinea pig as an example of this paradox: it is a most fertile species and selection is quite rigid, but it has not progressed as markedly (or as rapidly) as the dog, which is less fertile.[8]

Furthermore, Roosevelt declares that, in associating the great progress of human societies with the great rigidity of competition, Kidd overlooks "certain very curious features in human society," namely that, where the struggle for life in human society is most intense, energy is spent on the mere effort to survive and national progress is inhibited. It is for this reason, Roosevelt argues, that the English and the Germans have progressed further than the Italians, Irish, and Poles. A society struggling "under conditions which make the competition for bare existence keenest," TR writes, "never progresses as fast as the race which exists under less stringent conditions." Competition may be necessary for progress, but Roosevelt maintains that, if competition is too severe, progress suffers. Indeed, in a highly competitive society, the population rate declines, thereby endangering the entire race. "No matter how large the number of births may be," he explains, "a race cannot increase if the number of deaths [due to competition] also grows at an accelerating rate."[9] Moreover,

TR adds, a society does not advance if the men who perform the great deeds must be struggling for mere survival. The great generals, admirals, poets, philosophers, historians, artists, musicians, statesmen, judges, legislators, and industrialists all come from classes "where the struggle for the bare means of subsistence is least severe." Roosevelt concludes that the rivalry associated with natural selection "works against progress" in civilized societies. In fact, he says, progress is made in spite of the competition for survival; it is the result of "the steady rise of the lower classes to the level of the upper class, as the latter tend to vanish, or at most barely hold their own."[10] In sum, the societies in which the happiness of individuals is highest, and where progress "is most real," are those in which "the grinding competition and struggle for mere existence is least severe." In societies where competition and the struggle for survival are most severe, misery and suffering are great, and these, TR holds, are the societies that make the least progress.[11]

While Roosevelt agrees that many of the plans proposed to ease the plight of oppressed individuals are destructive of social growth and progress, he denies that the interests of the individual and the society are, and must remain, antagonistic. Unlike Kidd, he argues that the individual has a rational interest in subordinating himself to the welfare of society. Roosevelt asks his readers to consider the men in a military regiment, police officers, or firefighters. All of these men willingly subordinate themselves to the needs of their brothers-in-arms as well as society-at-large. The soldier does not cower or desert, but instead takes pride in the organization of which he is a part and does not wish to disappoint the others with whom he serves. Roosevelt insists that the soldier has a rational interest in conduct that subordinates himself to the welfare of the whole, for in the process of social evolution, men have reached the stage where they feel "more shame and misery from neglect of duty, from cowardice or dishonesty," than can be offset by the gratification of any individual desires.[12] Reason, in other words, does not have to be rooted in a narrow self-interest. The woman who watches over a sick child, the soldier who dies at his post, and the man who risks his life for another are not acting unreasonably from Roosevelt's standpoint. To TR, these individuals are neither brutish nor unintelligent, for reason and intelligence do not preclude ethics and morality.[13] Both intellect and morality "will persistently war against the individuals in whom the spirit of selfishness . . . shows itself strongly."[14]

Roosevelt stresses that the development of intellect is necessary for evolution, but so too is the development of character. Indeed, he suggests, character is even more important than intellect, for the "prime factor" in social evolution is "the power to attain a high degree of social efficiency;" and social efficiency is derived from "love of order, ability to fight well and breed well, capacity to subordinate the interests of the individual to the interests of the community, . . .

and similar rather hum-drum qualities."[15] There is thus an interdependency between individualism and society. Roosevelt agrees with Kidd's attack on Socialism, arguing that the state should "make the chances of competition more even" but not abolish competition altogether. There must be competition, he maintains, and success in the race of life must go to the most meritorious; otherwise, progress is compromised. Roosevelt concludes that it is not wrong to pity the man who "falls or lags behind in the race," but it would be wrong to "crown" an undeserving individual "with the victor's wreath." But more important to TR is that everyone run the race on fair terms. He insists that a fair race will make it "more than ever a test of the real merits of the victor, and this means that the victor must *strive* heart and soul for success."[16]

In its rejection of Social Darwinism and the notion that any attempt by the state to assist the deficient will only prevent them from making the necessary adaptation to their environment, Roosevelt's critique of Kidd is a justification for using the institutional capacities of the state to eliminate the obstacles that prevent everyone from competing on a level economic playing field and thereby having the opportunity to realize their individual potential. It also reflects Roosevelt's belief that an individual's success depends on the efforts of that individual. For Roosevelt, who believed in the importance of both social obligation and individual effort, the salvation of society lay not only in individual discipline, strength, and self-reliance but also in compassion and service to others. Through certain economic regulations, as well as the power of rhetoric and the inspiration of his leadership, Roosevelt hoped to teach this lesson to the American people. It was a lesson dear to his heart, because he had learned it from his father.

LIKE FATHER, LIKE SON

Theodore Roosevelt Sr., or "Thee," as he was known, drew a clear and strict line of morality that he expected his children to walk. He did not tolerate cruelty, laziness, dishonesty, selfishness, or cowardice on the part of his sons and daughters. At the same time, he was described by all who knew him as kind, courteous, and strongly devoted to the idea of noblesse oblige, or the belief that privilege entails obligation to the less fortunate.[17] A former employee described Theodore Sr. as a "dignified, courteous man, who took a lively interest in the welfare of every employee, and was held in affectionate regard by all, from office boy upward." The co-proprietor of a plate glass importing firm, Thee visited his employees who were seriously ill and attended the funerals of those who died. He even paid for the medical expenses of those who could not afford them and regularly gave cash advances to struggling employees.[18] These acts are more impressive given the large number of workers available in the 1850s, 1860s, and 1870s. This was a time of massive immigration, and the new arrivals were desperate for work. Stated crudely, Thee did not have to be so kind to his employees, for they were easily replaceable. Rather, he was dedicated to taking an interest and lending a helping hand. Thee's generosity was not confined to his business. He also worked to build new mental asylums to reduce overcrowding and improve conditions at existing facilities, and actually took the time to visit insane asylums on Wards and Blackwell's islands, often inviting various city officials to join him and see for themselves the horrible conditions of the patients living there. His financial support also helped to create Roosevelt Hospital, the Bellevue Training School for Nurses, and the New York Orthopaedic Dispensary for the Deformed and Crippled, and owing to a deep concern with the rising rate of crimes committed by minors, he was dedicated to improving the lives of orphans.[19] Thee was vice-president of the State Charities Aid Association, a trustee of the Children's Aid Society, and a large contributor to the Newsboy's Lodging House. Every Thanksgiving and Christmas, he would join the orphaned newsboys for dinner.[20]

According to Charles Loring Brace, the founder of the Children's Aid Society, this willingness to sacrifice money, time, and energy was a sign that Roosevelt's work with orphaned boys, like all of his charity work, "was not perfunctory; it was not done as a duty." As Brace explained, Roosevelt "seemed to attract and win the sympathies of every boy in the house. He knew them by name, he knew their histories, and, whenever he came there, they would gather round him, and he would question each one as to what he was doing, and give him advice and sympathy and directions. . . . " He genuinely cared, and this generous spirit was rooted in Thee's firm Christian beliefs.[21] No doubt, these beliefs made a strong impression on his son, who writes in his autobiography, "My father, Theodore Roosevelt, was the best man I knew. He combined strength and courage with gentleness, tenderness, and great unselfishness. . . . With great love and patience, and the most understanding sympathy and consideration, he combined insistence on discipline."[22] This was how TR tried to live, and by personalizing the public offices that he held, especially the presidency, he intended to serve as a model for others to emulate. Indeed, TR hoped to be a source of inspiration for the American people, as his father was for him. "Get action!" and "Seize the moment!" were two of Thee's favorite phrases. Likewise, they became Theodore's mantra—and, ultimately, the nation's.

Perhaps the best example of Thee's influence and Theodore's eagerness to embrace the values and ways of his father came in the fall of 1870. After years of nursing his son and arranging special trips to alleviate his asthma,

Thee decided that Theodore should embrace a physical rehabilitation regime. "You have the mind, but you have not the body," he told young Theodore. "You must *make* your body." "I'll make my body," the boy vowed, and he lived up to the promise. To help his son, Thee bought him new exercise equipment and a membership at John Wood's gymnasium. Two years later, he bought Theodore eyeglasses and his first hunting weapon, a French pin-fire, double-barreled shotgun. He also hired hunting guides for his son as well as a professional taxidermist to teach the boy how to preserve the animals he killed. For the next several years, TR would spend a good portion of his summers in the Adirondack Mountains, where he would camp, hunt, canoe, hike, mountain-climb, gather all sorts of specimens, and study birds. This was the beginning of Roosevelt's devotion to "the strenuous life." It was in the Adirondacks that he relieved his asthma, strengthened his body, and learned to appreciate both nature and the rugged independence of his wilderness guides.[23] After the death of his father, "these outsized mountain men became mentors and important surrogate father figures for Theodore." They also influenced TR's political thinking, as well as his later efforts as a conservationist.[24]

Thee encouraged Theodore to make his body and overcome physical weakness by sheer force of will so that he might be able to withstand the temptations of the corrupt society around him.[25] This belief was central to the "muscular Christianity" of the day, which rejected the image of Jesus Christ as gentle, meek, and mild. Believing that Christianity had become too effeminate, muscular Christians like Thee reinterpreted Jesus as a vigorous and energetic crusader for righteousness. Moreover, they believed that teaching young men to view their bodies as temples to the Lord was the best way to protect them from sexual temptation and self-indulgence. For men like Thee, physical fitness and courage were signs of a true Christian faith, and he taught Theodore that Jesus Christ was not the emaciated Christ found in so much religious art. Jesus was instead strong, muscular, and fearless, the embodiment of moral purity, a man who welcomed all but never equivocated in his condemnation of sin. Thee's Jesus was the one who did not think twice about upsetting the tables of the moneychangers. This was the Jesus that Thee also brought to his interest in the welfare of newsboys. Not satisfied merely to preach the virtues of strength, manliness, and purity, he helped to equip the Newsboy's Lodging House and other missions with boxing gloves, horizontal bars, and all sorts of exercise equipment. Like Theodore, the orphaned newsboys could improve themselves and counter the "weakening of true masculine vigor" that would make them susceptible to contagious vice.[26]

TR's effort to "make his own body" led him to view both the flesh and fear as enemies to be conquered, and it gave him a greater appreciation for hard work and self-discipline. Taking boxing lessons from ex-prizefighter John Long, he impressed both his teacher and himself with his ability to take hard punches and keep fighting. Boxing, he believed, would help to "knock the sissy out of him." It also forced him into difficult and dangerous situations that pushed him beyond the limits of his fears.[27] Roosevelt forced his spirit to ignore the weaknesses of his flesh, and he urged others to learn from his experience that "man does in fact become fearless by sheer dint of practicing fearlessness when he does not feel it." In his autobiography, he admits, "There were all kinds of things of which I was frightened at first, ranging from grizzly bears to 'mean' horses and gun-fighters; but by acting as if I was not afraid I gradually ceased to be afraid. Most men can have the same experience if they choose."

As Roosevelt struggled to make himself into a man who could assert himself and hold his own in the world, his beloved books provided him with great models for emulation, and the more heroic, the better. The "Saga of King Olaf," which introduced him to the Vikings and their life of warfare and discovery, and the second part of *Robinson Crusoe*, in which the hero battles the wolves of the Pyrenees and wanders through the Far East, were just the kind of stories that suited young Roosevelt.[28] He also delighted in reading about the soldiers at Valley Forge and listening to the heroic deeds of his mother's southern forefathers and relatives, especially his uncles, who achieved great fame in the Confederate navy.[29] These stories and their romantic depiction of the world, as H. W. Brands explains, influenced TR's thought and actions throughout his life: "He cast himself as the romantic hero, battling natural and human odds in pursuit of nobler and glorious goals."[30] For him, life was all about struggle, and the point of it all was to persevere and triumph over all challenges, none more so than wrongdoing. Others could do the same, if they just followed his lead.

Theodore inherited a strict moral code from his father. As he left for college, Thee instructed him, "Take care of your morals first, your health next, and finally your studies." Theodore never once hesitated in following this advice. He did not smoke because of his desire to remain in peak physical shape, and he also regarded it as a vice. Similarly, he drank alcohol only occasionally and considered gambling to be a waste of both money and time. Finally, sex was to be reserved for marriage. All and all, Theodore refused to do anything he would be ashamed to admit to his father. He had an easy time distinguishing between right and wrong and was not shy about calling people to task for their misdeeds.[31] From his father, Theodore came to understand the threats posed by saloons, gambling halls, brothels, and pornographic bookstands, all of which preyed on human weakness and thereby weakened the moral fabric of the entire society.[32] At the same time, Thee taught his son the need to back rhetoric with action. Thee contributed money to Anthony Comstock's crusade against pornography and prostitution. Comstock not only used physical force, particularly an axe, to destroy the materials of pornographers; he also supported book burning and was responsible for a federal law that forbade brothels and pornographers from using the federal mail. Thee also organized prayer breakfasts for evangelist Dwight Moody. Kathleen Dalton suggests that TR's adult speaking style was probably influenced by his boyhood exposure to Reverend Moody's "chopping arm gestures" and "plain-talking moral sincerity."[33]

Beyond drinking, gambling, and pornography, Thee despised corruption in politics. Like other members of his class, he believed that politics was a dirty business and tried to steer clear of it. Then, in 1877, he found himself nominated to be New York collector of customs and caught in a political battle between President Rutherford B. Hayes and Roscoe Conkling, the boss of New York Republican politics. A United States senator with presidential aspirations, Conkling represented a new breed of Republican. Unlike an earlier generation of Republicans who had formed the party to oppose the spread of slavery, new Republicans like Conkling cared more about electoral survival and power than ideology and moral vision. Conkling thus sought to maintain control over the appointment of New York's collector of customs and other jobs at the Port of New York, which he hoped to distribute as political patronage in order to maintain his base of power.

Republican bosses like Conkling also used the protective tariff as another form of political patronage to retain the support of influential businessmen.[34] A group called Liberal Republicans attacked these practices in the administration of Ulysses S. Grant, disapproving of the protective tariff and endorsing civil service reform to establish a nonpartisan, merit-based staffing of certain government jobs.[35] Seeking to defeat Grant and end Reconstruction, they nominated their own candidate for President in 1872, Horace Greeley, the editor of *The New York Tribune*, who also won the Democratic nomination.[36] Greeley lost, but Liberal Republicans won the battle of ideas. More and more people supported civil service reform, and one of them was Thee Roosevelt, who joined the Republican reform movement in 1876, hoping to rescue his party from corrupt professionals like Conkling. There had been a great deal of fraud in nearly every department of the federal government during the second term of the Grant administration. What most concerned Roosevelt and men like William Graham Sumner, Charles Francis Adams, Brooks Adams, Carl Schurz, George William Curtis, and Henry Cabot Lodge was Conkling's interest in the Republican Party's presidential nomination.[37]

At the 1876 Republican National Convention in Cincinnati, Thee Roosevelt led a reform delegation, whose express purpose was "to fight Conkling at all events." On the floor of the convention hall, he delivered a blistering speech against Conkling, charging him with widespread corruption. The speech, which was carried in newspapers across the country, was "so persuasive that it proved to be the spoiler at the convention." This speech, coupled with the decision of Roosevelt and his fellow reformers to throw their support behind reform candidate Benjamin Bristow, effectively blocked Conkling's pursuit of the nomination and paved the way for the candidacy of Rutherford B. Hayes. After the election, Hayes nominated Thee to be New York collector of customs. The nomination was, in part, a reward for Roosevelt's hard work at the convention and, in part, a way of baiting Conkling for one final showdown.

The controversy over Roosevelt's nomination was national news, and the press was willing to portray Conkling as a corrupt political boss needlessly attacking an altruistic public servant. The *Nation*, for example, wrote that Roosevelt possessed "wealth above the temptations of any office, character, and great business experience." Despite widespread support, Thee hated being the pawn in the battle between Hayes and Conkling. Being in the political crossfire was an uncomfortable position for a man who had long avoided politics, but he used the controversy surrounding his nomination as an opportunity to continue the attack against patronage and to push for a meritocratic civil service, which would later become Theodore's "signature cause" as a legislator, administrator, and governor.[38] But Conkling fought back, urging the Senate to reject Roosevelt's nomination. He denied that the New York Custom House was part of a political machine and contended that Roosevelt's public attack against him was a personal vendetta. The Senate delayed Roosevelt's nomination, but after a long recess, Hayes resubmitted it. As the battle continued, so too did Thee's discomfort with the public ordeal.

The whole sordid experience left Thee physically ill. He lost weight, grew weak, and began to experience severe stomach pains, the result of an intestinal blockage. Ultimately, Conkling won the battle. The Senate rejected Roosevelt's nomination by a vote of 31 to 25 in favor of the current collector of customs, Chester A. Arthur (a Stalwart, or Conkling loyalist), who had acquired political power through the patronage practices that reformers deplored.[39] Thee ultimately recovered from his intestinal disorder, but "it set into motion a swift decline in the previously healthy and robust 46-year-old man." When Thee died in the winter of 1878, Theodore blamed his father's suffering and death on the disgraceful fight over his nomination as collector of customs.[40] As Brands suggests, Theodore "would have had to be a saint or an expert oncologist" not to have concluded that the customhouse battle had hastened Thee's death. For young TR, Conkling and Arthur became evil incarnate, yet if anything positive came from Thee's death, it may be that it in-

spired Theodore to dedicate himself to ridding politics of the corrupting influences that hurt his father. This was reinforced by the outpouring of emotion over Thee's death, which made Theodore even more aware of just how
much his father meant to all sorts of people, both rich and poor.[41] His increasing awareness of how Thee's public service improved the lives of others
strengthened TR's decision to pursue a similar career. Like Thee, he could be
a help to others and serve as an example to all.

Thee's actions during the Civil War also contained a lesson on public service, though it was a somewhat mixed message that pointed to the potential
conflict between public and private responsibilities. Only twenty-nine years
old when the war began, Thee was healthy and willing to enlist on the Union
side. But his wife, a southern belle whose heart and sympathies remained in
the South, begged him not to take up arms against her Confederate brothers.
TR's older sister later recalled, "Mother was very frail and felt it would kill
her for him to fight against her brothers." So Thee took advantage of a loop-
hole in the Conscription Act that allowed wealthy men to buy their way out
of military service. He paid $600 to hire two soldiers to take his place. He
joined a Home Guard Cavalry unit that drilled to defend New York City from
possible Confederate attack, but he remained haunted by his willingness to allow other men to fight for him.[42] Thee's decision not to fight also left
Theodore troubled for the rest of his life. His sister, Corinne, later suggested
that much of her brother's obsession with war stemmed from a desire to compensate for their father's failure to take up arms during the Civil War.[43]

Thee did serve the Union cause through a mission of charity that was vitally
important to the soldiers and their families. One problem was that soldiers' pay
was not sent home to their families, which led to millions of dollars being squan-
dered. Thus, Thee and two colleagues established an allotment commission that
enabled soldiers to send a portion of their pay home to support their wives and
children. With the help of President Abraham Lincoln, they lobbied Congress for
the passage of an allotment law and then traveled from camp to camp to regis-
ter troops for the program.[44] But Roosevelt's contribution "was more than orga-
nizational. He rolled up his sleeves and pitched in with the least glamorous
tasks." Upon witnessing the slaughter at Fredericksburg, for example, he took
command of evacuating the wounded, personally loading the bleeding men onto
hospital wagons.[45] Back home in New York, Thee also joined others in preaching loyalty to the Union and dispensing patriotic propaganda to promote wartime
loyalty. He even volunteered to work with the Women's Central Association of
Relief and the Sanitary Commission, which sent supplies and nurses to Union
hospitals.[46] As Kathleen Dalton writes, Thee was comfortable in these organizations that promoted nationalism, and his talk about the importance of service to
the nation heavily influenced TR's later political views.

During the war, Theodore was thrilled to learn that his father had become a friend of President Lincoln and was especially impressed to learn that Thee, sitting in the President's pew at one Sunday service, had been mistaken for the President. Indeed, TR would forever associate his father with Lincoln. In his heart and mind, the two men were united. When TR became President in 1901, Dalton notes, "he talked about Thee and Lincoln on his first night in the White House, for they always remained his two most important guiding spirits."[47] As for Lincoln, Roosevelt had the opportunity as President to hear John Hay, his secretary of state and former aide to Lincoln, tell tales about the 16th president, personalizing and making Lincoln an even more immediate presence in his life, and he listened to Hay as eagerly as he had read the letters that his father wrote about Lincoln during the war. The night before Roosevelt's inauguration, on March 4, 1905, Hay gave TR a ring that held a snip of Lincoln's hair, which Roosevelt wore the next day and treasured always. He also hung a large portrait of Lincoln above the mantel behind his desk, and when asked about it by a reporter, TR replied, "When I am confronted with a great problem, I look up to that picture, and I do as I believe Lincoln would have done. I have always felt that if I could do as he would have done were he in my place, I would not be far from right."[48]

THE INFLUENCE OF THE GREAT EMANCIPATOR

TR frequently referred to Lincoln as his hero but was by no means the only Progressive reformer who admired Lincoln. Jane Addams urged the immigrant children living in her settlement house to follow the example of Lincoln, and the Great Emancipator was used for a range of purposes that covered the political spectrum. Democrats like William Jennings Bryan and Woodrow Wilson, and even Socialist Eugene Debs, invoked Lincoln's memory to justify their demands for more positive state action to deal with the problems of the new social and economic order.[49] With some justification, the Progressives considered themselves to be the children of Lincoln. Lincoln had saved the Union and freed the slaves and was thus seen by Progressives as both a nationalist and a model of moral leadership. In addition, Lincoln embodied the Progressive ideal of democracy. He was, after all, a man of common origins who rose to greatness to save the nation. He was as well a Republican, as were most Progressives. Finally, for these predominantly Protestant reformers, the Lincoln presidency was "the defining moment in American/biblical history and prophecy."[50] Influenced by Lincoln and Protestant clergymen, who infused the Civil War with biblical meaning, Progressive reformers viewed the four-year conflict as an apocalyptic battle against the evil of slavery. They believed that, through the loss of life, the sins of the nation were purged; the war—and Lincoln's handling of it—had saved the very soul of the nation.

But, as Jerome Mileur suggests, Progressives embraced "a mythical Lincoln." Focused entirely on his expansions of national power, they used Lincoln not only to defend their attacks on trusts and party bosses but also to construct "a new democratic order in which government and politics served national purposes." The Lincoln who was a master of the political and patronage practices of his time and who made that politics work in the national interest was, more or less, lost on them. Furthermore, they ignored the reality that Lincoln, while a strong defender of the Union, was not an advocate of an expanded national state.[51] For him, Union had a special purpose "that could not be violated without making the Union something other than what the Founders intended." Linking Union to the proposition that "all men are created equal," he regarded slavery as an evil that the national government should deplore and place on the course of ultimate extinction. The Union, "born of the Declaration of Independence and institutionalized in the Constitution," embodied the founders' ideal of republican liberty and should be preserved at all costs, save the expansion of slavery.[52] In short, Lincoln called the American people to a renewed embrace of the *equality* that had been at the heart of the founding.

Lincoln believed that the Declaration's assertion that all men are created equal was the great objective of the nation, "but it was a goal to be pursued together with an equally important purpose—that of preserving republican liberty protected by the Constitution." As Mileur explains, "These two great principles—the equality of all in a regime of republican liberty—came together in his conception of Union and, indeed, gave moral purpose and direction to that Union and through it to the nation." Moreover, it was within this framework that Lincoln understood politics as a way of resolving differences through reasoned debate and accommodation, thereby securing the equal right of all to live in liberty. For Lincoln, politics was not without this moral purpose. It could be used to move the nation toward the achievement of this goal, but only if the Union endured and politics sacrificed neither human equality nor republican government. "Politics thus functioned to moderate differences, isolating extremists in both the North and the South as it sought accommodations that at once preserved the Union and moved the nation relentlessly, if incrementally, toward its larger purpose."[53]

Lincoln was the master of politics, yet most Progressive reformers despised politics, especially the corrupt politics of party bosses and their machines. Popular government was self-government, and the Progressives argued that this meant an engaged, active, and nationally-minded citizenry, not one that was limited to casting periodic votes for elected officials. Progressives sought a new kind of citizenship that was based on the direct participation of individuals. They held that representative institutions, which mediated public opinion, only thwarted the true will of the people. They believed instead in the virtues of direct democracy and championed ballot reforms and the democratic tools of initiative, referendum, and recall as necessary to promoting and strengthening the influence of the popular will. It is important to note that this popular will was not the same as majority rule, which the Progressives believed was influenced by nothing more than petty individual and local interests. The popular will that Progressives hoped would guide governmental decision-making was defined as rational, steeped in the collective conscience, and ever mindful of the common good.[54]

But the Progressives' general disdain for politics was rooted in more than the belief that politicos denied citizens "their democratic birthright." Most reformers simply hated the activity of politics itself (the bargaining, the trading, the deal-making). It entailed compromise and flexibility rather than principle and finding the best solution to a problem. For the majority of Progressives, there was no moral purpose to politics, no higher good served by it. It was corrupt, and those who participated in and controlled the activity were far more interested in satisfying their individual and local interests than in promoting the national good.[55] Roosevelt certainly sympathized with these sentiments, but he also knew how to play the game and respected others who could play it well. Thus, unlike other reformers, Lincoln's mastery of politics did not go unnoticed by TR. More than anything, his public celebrations of Lincoln emphasized the 16th President's political skill and moderation; his ability to strike a balance between extremist demands.

In various speeches and writings, such as the essay entitled "Lincoln," Roosevelt contends that no modern leader has faced a greater and more difficult task than Lincoln did during the Civil War. By the same token, he adds, no leader had ever met such "a fierce trial" more successfully than Lincoln. Lincoln managed to hold the Border States and unite northerners in defense of the Union, for he understood better than any that dissolution of the Union meant the victory of pro-slavery forces.[56] Among the qualities that enabled him to do this were practicality, shrewdness, tact, adaptability, flexibility, and a conciliatory approach. In addition, Roosevelt sees Lincoln as being guided and controlled by "a fine and high moral sense." Speaking to the reformers of his time, TR concludes that all could profit from understanding that Lincoln's greatness was rooted in his ability to combine "indomitable resolution with cool-headed sanity." This is why the Great Emancipator was able to succeed and also why both the timid denounced Lincoln as an extremist and the extremists denounced him for his timidity. TR explains, "He had continually to check those who wished to go forward too fast, at the very time that he overrode the opposition of those who wished not to go forward at all."[57]

Appreciative of how Lincoln used politics for moral purposes, Roosevelt repeatedly refers to Lincoln as a *statesman*. In both word and deed, he declares, Lincoln was "single-hearted in his devotion to the weal of his people." Lincoln called upon his fellow-citizens to see the truths that he saw and rallied them behind a cause that stood for the preservation of freedom. "With far-sighted vision," Roosevelt declares, Lincoln "could pierce the clouds that obscured the sight of the keenest of his fellows, could see what the future inevitably held." Moreover, he could inspire his countrymen to sacrifice themselves "for the good of mankind, for the betterment of the world."[58]

"Yet," Roosevelt writes in commemoration of Lincoln's 100th birthday, "perhaps the most wonderful thing of all, and, from the standpoint of the America of today and of the future, the most vitally important, was the extraordinary way in which Lincoln could fight valiantly against what he deemed wrong and yet preserve undiminished his love and respect for the brother from whom he differed." Lincoln, in other words, did not hate those with whom he differed. Such a sentiment was alien to his "strong, gentle nature." As Roosevelt explains, Lincoln understood clearly that both the men of the North and the men of the South possessed the same courage, the same patriotism, "the same willingness for self-sacrifice," and the same devotion to their beliefs in right.[59] What these celebrations of Lincoln reveal is that Roosevelt not only appreciates Lincoln's ability to move people through rhetoric but also understands that the most successful appeals for reform are those that gently persuade. An appeal must be rooted in understanding and the recognition of shared problems.

Indeed, Lincoln understood the limits of a moral politics. On the question of slavery, for example, self-interest threatened to preserve the horrid system, while overtly moral claims and demands, such as those that characterized the abolitionist movement, threatened to undermine both individual rights and democratic deliberation. Therefore, to preserve both the Union and democratic freedom, Lincoln had to use rhetoric to convince the American people to recommit themselves to the principle of equality upon which popular government is based. He had to remind the American people that, without a belief in the equality of all to support it, popular sovereignty means nothing and cannot endure. He would do so by disguising his moral appeals in the garb of patriotic sentiment and calculated self-interest.[60] Perhaps, Jeffrey Sedgwick suggests, Lincoln anticipated the coming Progressive movement, "with its explicit rejection of moderate, materially oriented politics in favor of morally invigorated leadership grounded in an energetic president addressing the nation from his 'bully pulpit.'"[61] Admittedly, this immoderate, energetic, and "morally invigorated" leadership from the "bully pulpit" sounds a great deal like TR. Yet Roosevelt at least understood, unlike most Progressive reformers, that rhetoric was often better than institutional reform and the force of law in reaching into the private lives of individuals and persuading them to support one another in a spirit of civic attachment. This was the essence of Lincoln's statesmanship, and Roosevelt's effort to emulate it demonstrates his sincere respect for individual freedom.

Lincoln used his words and example to befriend the nation and thereby attempt to change human behavior for the better, while Roosevelt, as will be shown, used the power of rhetoric and personal example to play the role of the kindhearted tough guy, who could inspire his countrymen to practice not only discipline, strength, and self-reliance but also compassion and service to others. Regardless, in their appeals to the better angels of self-interested individuals, both Lincoln and Roosevelt were concerned about infringing upon individual rights. As a result, each offered a distinctive "third way" that transcends dichotomous thinking—a middle path between a self-interested individualism and a moral zeal that abandons individual freedom and rights for the sake of "the social good."

Roosevelt put his faith in people and in the belief that his words and deeds could persuade them to act in the public interest. This appreciation for the capacity of people to improve themselves was rooted in his earlier success in transforming himself, both physically and mentally, through sheer will and iron self-discipline. As Edmund Morris writes, Roosevelt "plotted every day with the Methodism of a Wesleyan minister." Every bit of his free time was packed with mental, physical, and social activity. At night, he could go to bed "satisfied that he had wasted not one minute of his waking hours."[62]

CELEBRATING INDIVIDUALISM: *THE NAVAL WAR OF 1812*

In his autobiography, Roosevelt observes that success comes in two forms. First, there is the success that results from a man's natural talents. But a more common type of success, available to nearly every person in every endeavor, is that which comes from determination, self-reliance, and hard work. "This kind of success is open to a large number of persons, if only they seriously determine to achieve it. It is the kind of success which is open to the average man of sound body and fair mind, who has no remarkable mental or physical attributes, but who gets just as much as possible in the way of work out of the aptitudes that he does possess." Roosevelt modestly attributes his success to the second type, writing that he "never won anything without hard labor and the exercise of my best judgment and carefully planning and working long in advance."[63]

Such sentiments are not much different from many of Roosevelt's early letters. Traveling with his brother in the summer after graduating from Harvard, Roosevelt stayed with a farm family in western Illinois. "The farm people are pretty rough," he wrote, "but I like them very much," adding that "like all rural Americans they are intensely independent."[64] Similarly, Roosevelt wrote of his 1881 honeymoon trip through Europe, "This summer I have passed traveling through Europe, and though I have enjoyed it greatly, yet the more I see, the better satisfied I am that I am an American; free born and free bred, where I acknowledge no man as my superior, except for his own worth, or as my inferior, except for his own demerit."[65]

But perhaps none of Roosevelt's early writing better exemplifies his celebration of individualistic values—self-reliance, hard work, discipline, and merit-based achievement—than *The Naval War of 1812*. The book was a labor of love, as well as quite an achievement for a young man of twenty-three, and has proven to be one of Roosevelt's most popular works. Over a century after its publication, it is still "a standard work on the subject."[66] Most scholars focus only on the book's argument for preparedness and a strong navy, but another thesis pervades the work: the idea that American victories on the sea were, in no small part, due to "free American institutions" that "developed self-reliance" and encouraged advancement based on merit. According to TR, a life of adventure and hardship on the high seas only strengthened this self-reliance.

Roosevelt argues that, while the American navy was prepared to fight the British, this preparation was more the result of *individual effort* than government foresight. "Without the prudence to avoid war or the foresight to prepare for it," the administrations of Thomas Jefferson and James Madison "drifted helplessly" toward war with Britain. TR contends that it was only because of earlier Federalist efforts to strengthen the navy and the unique characteristics of American sailors that the United States was spared a "complete and shameful defeat."[67] At the start of the war, the British navy had thousands of ships, while the American navy numbered only half a dozen frigates, and six or eight sloops and brigs. Furthermore, the American seamen themselves were unknown to the British; the small skirmishes in which they had been involved could hardly be expected to attract attention in a time that saw mighty battles involving British and French fleets. Yet Roosevelt finds that these "petty wars" provided the Americans with excellent training opportunities. He argues that a steady stream of victories had made British sailors overconfident and thus inattentive to matters of maneuvering and gunnery, while at the same time, the Americans were learning how to receive and give "hard knocks." In addition, the American sailors belonged to a branch of the military service that was "too young" to be overconfident.

Coupled with its youth was the small size of the American navy, but Roosevelt finds its ships and crews were both strong and efficient. To TR, strong ships and powerful artillery were important to the success of the American navy, but they were not the whole story. Poor ships, he notes, and "impotent artillery" led to the devastation of nearly the entire Dutch navy. On the other hand, "fine ships and heavy cannon" did not save the French and Spanish navies from similar devastation. In Roosevelt's view, efficient crews are at least as important as efficient ships, and the United States owed a great deal of its naval successes to its sailors.[68] Roosevelt contends that the American sailors, in contrast to the British, were better trained and enjoyed the added advantage of greater self-reliance. Where British officers owed their commands to favoritism and bureaucracy, nearly every American officer owed his rank to the fact that he had "proven worthy of it." Having achieved his rank through hard work and discipline, Roosevelt continues, the American officer saw to it that his men were similarly skilled and disciplined, and these sailors proved to be worthy of their leaders' expectations. "There was no better seaman in the world," Roosevelt concludes, "than the American Jack."

Roosevelt attributes much of the discipline, skill, and self-reliance of the American sailors to the fact that many of them had been put to work on merchant or whaling ships at an early age.[69] By engaging French picaroons, Spanish buccaneers, and Malay pirates, they learned to be skillful and self-reliant. It was also the case that a large portion of America's entire population was engaged in "seafaring pursuits." In Salem, Baltimore, New York, and Long Island, Americans were experienced in sailing, fishing, whaling, trading, and ship building. Commerce was the American way of life, Roosevelt writes, and bold people could not resist its call. He concludes that this "stern school in which the American was brought up forced him into habits of independent thought and action which it was impossible that the more protected Briton could possess." The American sailors were as intelligent as the British and "perfectly obedient," but they could depart from routine, judge for themselves, and adapt more quickly in an emergency.[70]

Roosevelt concedes that nothing the American navy did in the War of 1812 materially affected the outcome of the war; however, while the material results were not that significant in their effect on Great Britain, "whose enormous navy did not feel in the slightest degree the loss of a few frigates and sloops," the naval war was of enormous moral benefit to the United States. TR explains that the American victories at sea rallied the spirits of the American people, who had grown accustomed to hearing news about defeat on land. Moreover, these victories also decided in favor of the Americans the major question in dispute: Great Britain's self-proclaimed right to search American ships and impress their crews. The U.S. owed much to the excellent design and make of its ships, but it owed even more to the well-trained, disciplined, and self-reliant men who were sailing on them. Basically of "the same stock," the American sailors differed from the Britons, and while this difference could be overcome by training, many British captains were too overconfident to train. In Roosevelt's view, it was the freer institutions of the United States, coupled with "the peculiar exigencies" of the American sailor's life, that made the American sailor "more intelligent and self-reliant."[71]

The Naval War of 1812 was published in 1882, but its emphasis on the value of independence, discipline, and hard work would reappear in nearly all of Roosevelt's subsequent public writings, including his 1913 autobiography. All the laws in the world, TR writes in his postpresidential memoirs, "will never make a man a worthy citizen unless he has within himself the right stuff, unless he has self-reliance, energy, courage, the power of insisting on his own rights." What TR did not stress in *The Naval War of 1812*, but which had become a staple of his myriad works by 1913, was his belief that these important individualistic qualities needed to be balanced with a strong regard for the welfare of others. While "a man must be respectful for what he made of himself," he has an obligation "to join with others in trying to make things better for the many by curbing the abnormal and excessive development of individualism in a few."[72] These remarks reveal TR's devotion to both individualism and collective action for the social good. Unlike most Progressives, he never abandoned individualism as a value to be celebrated and promoted; he simply rejected individualism in its most radical form—that which used Darwinian ideas as an excuse to ignore the plight of other humans.

NOTES

1. Herbert Spencer, *Principles of Ethics*, vol. 2 (New York: D. Appleton and Company, 1895–1898), 6–7, 17; Spencer, "Sins of Legislators," in *The Man versus the State* (New York: D. Appleton and Company, 1885), 64–66; Spencer, *The Study of Sociology* (New York: D. Appleton and Company, 1896), 315.

2. John Morton Blum, *The Republican Roosevelt* (Cambridge: Harvard University Press, 1981), 24–25.

3. Theodore Roosevelt, *Autobiography*, vol. 20 of *The Works of Theodore Roosevelt*, National Edition (New York: Charles Scribner's Sons, 1926), 16.

4. Theodore Roosevelt, "Social Evolution," in *American Ideals*, vol. 13 of *The Works of Theodore Roosevelt*, National Edition (New York: Charles Scribner's Sons, 1926), 224. For concise summaries of Roosevelt's article, see Richard Hofstadter, *Social Darwinism in American Thought* (Boston: Beacon Press, 1992), 101–02 and Blum, *Republican Roosevelt*, 26–27.

5. Hofstadter, *Social Darwinism*, 99. See also Benjamin Kidd, *Social Evolution* (New York: Macmillan and Company, 1894), 68.

6. Hofstadter, *Social Darwinism*, 100. See also Kidd, *Social Evolution*, chap. iv.

7. Hofstadter, *Social Darwinism*, 100. See also Kidd, *Social Evolution*, chap. viii.

8. Roosevelt, "Social Evolution," 225.

9. Roosevelt, "Social Evolution," 226.

10. Roosevelt, "Social Evolution," 227.

11. Roosevelt, "Social Evolution," 228.

12. Roosevelt, "Social Evolution," 230–31.

13. Roosevelt, "Social Evolution," 233.

14. Roosevelt, "Social Evolution," 234.

15. Roosevelt, "Social Evolution," 240.

16. Roosevelt, "Social Evolution," 239–40.

17. Roosevelt, *Autobiography*, 9–10.

18. Paul Grondahl, *I Rose Like a Rocket: The Political Education of Theodore Roosevelt* (New York: Free Press, 2004), 14.

19. Grondahl, *I Rose Like a Rocket*, 25.

20. Grondahl, *I Rose Like a Rocket*, 24.

21. Quoted in Grondahl, *I Rose Like a Rocket*, 25. See also Charles Loring Brace, "Theodore Roosevelt Memorial Meeting of the State Charities Aid Association," New York, February 15, 1878, 24.

22. Roosevelt, *Autobiography*, 9, 10.

23. Grondahl, *I Rose Like a Rocket*, 27–28.

24. Grondahl, *I Rose Like a Rocket*, 29.

25. Kathleen Dalton, *Theodore Roosevelt: A Strenuous Life* (New York: Vintage Books, 2002), 50.

26. Dalton, *Strenuous Life*, 18–19.

27. Dalton, *Strenuous Life*, 52.

28. H. W. Brands, *T.R.: The Last Romantic* (New York: Basic Books, 1997), 27. See also Roosevelt, *Autobiography*, 18–19.

29. Brands, *The Last Romantic*, 28. See also Roosevelt, *Autobiography*, 14.

30. Brands, *The Last Romantic*, 28.

31. Brands, *The Last Romantic*, 73–74.

32. Dalton, *Strenuous Life*, 18.

33. Dalton, *Strenuous Life*, 49.

34. Lewis L. Gould, *Grand Old Party: A History of the Republicans* (New York: Random House, 2003), 63.

35. Gould, *Grand Old Party*, 62.

36. Gould, *Grand Old Party*, 65–66.

37. David McCullough, *Mornings on Horseback: The Story of an Extraordinary Family, A Vanished Way of Life, and the Unique Child Who Became Theodore Roosevelt* (New York: Simon and Schuster, 2003), 150–51.

38. Grondahl, *I Rose Like a Rocket*, 34.

39. Grondahl, *I Rose Like a Rocket*, 35.

40. Grondahl, *I Rose Like a Rocket*, 36.

41. Brands, *The Last Romantic*, 80–81.

42. Dalton, *Strenuous Life*, 27.

43. Dalton, *Strenuous Life*, 19.

44. Grondahl, *I Rose Like a Rocket*, 31; Dalton, *Strenuous Life*, 27.

45. Grondahl, *I Rose Like a Rocket*, 32; Dalton, *Strenuous Life*, 27–28.

46. Dalton, *Strenuous Life*, 28.

47. Dalton, *Strenuous Life*, 28.

48. Merrill D. Peterson, *Lincoln in American Memory* (New York: Oxford University Press, 1994), 164.

49. Peterson, *Lincoln in American Memory*, 158,164–67.

50. Jerome M. Mileur, "The Legacy of Reform: Progressive Government, Regressive Politics," in *Progressivism and the New Democracy*, ed. Sidney M. Milkis and Jerome M. Mileur (Amherst: University of Massachusetts Press, 1999), 260–61.

51. Mileur, "The Legacy of Reform," 261–62.

52. Mileur, "The Legacy of Reform," 263.

53. Mileur, "The Legacy of Reform," 263–64.

54. Mileur, "The Legacy of Reform," 271.

55. Mileur, "The Legacy of Reform," 271–72.

56. Theodore Roosevelt, "Lincoln," in *Hero Tales from American History*, vol. 10 of *The Works of Theodore Roosevelt*, National Edition (New York: Charles Scribner's Sons, 1926), 160.

57. Theodore Roosevelt, "Abraham Lincoln: Centenary Address," in *Men of Action*, vol. 11 of *The Works of Theodore Roosevelt*, National Edition (New York: Charles Scribner's Sons, 1926), 212.

58. Theodore Roosevelt, "Lincoln's Word and Lincoln's Deed," in *Men of Action*, vol. 11 of *The Works of Theodore Roosevelt*, National Edition (New York: Charles Scribner's Sons, 1926), 208.

59. Roosevelt, "Centenary Address," 213–14.

60. Jeffrey Leigh Sedgwick, "Lincoln and the Character of Liberal Statesmanship," in *Legacy of Disunion: The Enduring Significance of the American Civil War*, eds. Susan-Mary Grant and Peter J. Parish (Baton Rouge: Louisiana State University Press, 2003), 100–101.

61. Sedgwick, "Lincoln and the Character of Liberal Statesmanship," 115.

62. Edmund Morris, *The Rise of Theodore Roosevelt* (New York: The Modern Library, 2001), 64.

63. Roosevelt, *Autobiography*, 54–56.

64. Theodore Roosevelt to Anna Roosevelt, 22 August 1880, *The Years of Preparation: 1868 1898*, vol. 1 of *The Letters of Theodore Roosevelt*, ed. Elting Morison (Cambridge: Harvard University Press, 1951), 46.

65. Quoted in Brands, *The Last Romantic*, 118.

66. Nathan Miller, *Theodore Roosevelt: A Life* (New York: William Morrow and Company, 1992), 116.

67. Theodore Roosevelt, *The Naval War of 1812*, vol. 6 of *The Works of Theodore Roosevelt*, National Edition (New York: Charles Scribner's Sons, 1926), 373.

68. Roosevelt, *Naval War*, 21–22.
69. Roosevelt, *Naval War*, 25.
70. Roosevelt, *Naval War*, 26–27.
71. Roosevelt, *Naval War*, 367–68.
72. Roosevelt, *Naval War*, 27–28.

Chapter Three

The "Dude" Emerges

In the fall of 1880, Roosevelt began to attend meetings of the 21st District Republican Association. The meetings were held at Morton Hall, a shabby room over a 59th Street store and saloon, and while the drinking, gambling, and coarse language of many members offended Roosevelt's moral sensibilities, the vigorous young man could not help but be attracted to the rugged masculinity of the place. When Theodore's family learned of his extracurricular activity, they registered strong objections. Not only did many members of Roosevelt's class consider politics to be a dirty business that was beneath their station in life, but the Roosevelt family blamed politics for Thee's early death. This, however, did not stop Roosevelt from agreeing, in the fall of 1881, to accept the nomination of district leaders Jake Hess and Joe Murray to run for the New York Assembly.[1] Hess and Murray had known Roosevelt's father through their work on the City Commission of Charities and Corrections and believed that Thee's son was the one Republican who could hold the party's seat in the state legislature. Manhattan was then, as now, a Democratic city, and the reasons for this preceded TR's political emergence by some forty years.

In the mid-19th century, the Democratic Party had taken power away from a predominantly Republican upper class that was more concerned with building business and accumulating wealth. By the time these wealthy elites refocused their attention on New York City politics, following the Civil War and Reconstruction, it had become "a venal free-for-all," led by Tammany Hall, the Democratic machine that maintained its grip on elective office by harnessing the ever-increasing votes of new immigrants and the lower class. In addition to rewarding party loyalists with jobs and public services, Tammany ingratiated itself with Irish gangs, such as the Dead Rabbits, Bowery Boys,

Roach Guards, and Plug Uglies, by nominating for elected office gang members, saloon keepers, and gambling operators. Believing that the Tammany Democrats perpetuated poverty, ignorance, violence, gambling, alcoholism, and other assorted vices, Republicans were determined to get control of the state government in order to override corrupt local governments like New York City and to counter municipal corruption with reform legislation. As Paul Grondahl explains, "Roosevelt fit the bill." His new-found interest in politics "coincided fortuitously with stepped-up efforts of Republican leaders trolling for electable candidates to send to Albany."[2]

Sensing that the 21st District's voters had turned against the incumbent Republican representative, who had opposed a popular non-partisan street-cleaning bill for fear that it might undermine the power of the Republican machine, Hess believed that he had an ideal candidate in TR. Roosevelt, after all, possessed great energy, his family's socially prominent name, and his father's reputation for morality and charity. Most important, he had the support of his father's former associates, the wealthiest men in Manhattan. Running on a platform of clean streets and clean government, Roosevelt promised to "obey no boss and serve no clique;" his campaign was a mixture of the values that both he and his father promoted throughout their lives: honesty, energy, courage, self-reliance, and sympathy for the rights of others. Theodore won handily, receiving 3,490 votes to 1,989 for the Democratic candidate—nearly twice the margin of victory for previous Republican candidates.[3] After the election, he wrote Charles Washburn, a Harvard friend, "Too True! Too True! I have become a 'political hack'. . . . I accepted the nomination to the assembly and was elected by a 1,500 majority, heading the ticket by 600 votes. But don't think I am going into politics after this year, for I am not."[4]

When he left for Albany, Roosevelt took with him his father's letters, which he referred to as "talismans against evil." In one letter, dated December 16, 1877, just after the defeat of his nomination as collector of customs, Thee wrote, "The 'Machine politicians' have shown their colors. . . . I feel sorry for the country however as it shows the power of partisan politicians who think of nothing higher than their own interests, and I feel for your future. We cannot stand so corrupt a government for any great length of time." With these words in mind, Roosevelt was ready to continue his father's crusade against corruption.[5]

Unlike Thee, however, Theodore would not have to deal with Roscoe Conkling, who had resigned from the Senate when President James Garfield rejected two of his top appointees to key cabinet posts. After his resignation, Conkling watched his political power gradually wither away and grew increasingly embittered, ultimately dropping out of politics and refusing a Supreme Court nomination.[6] Yet, even with Conkling off the political stage, plenty of selfishness and corruption remained for Roosevelt to fight. As Grondahl explains, "Albany was a bottomless feeding trough in literal as well as figurative ways." Champagne, food, and cash were lavished upon state legislators to influence their votes on important legislation, and such "goodies" were especially abundant in 1882, when the division of power between Republicans and Democrats was more or less even.[7]

ACQUIRING A REPUTATION

From the moment he entered the state legislature, Roosevelt stood out among his fellow-law makers. At his first Republican caucus meeting, he bounded into the room, walked confidently to the front table and took the seat next to the chairman of the conference. He was there to be noticed and paid no attention to such norms as seniority, long apprenticeship, courtesy, reciprocity, and restrained participation for younger members.

The first issue he chose to address was the initial order of business that session: electing a new Assembly Speaker. The 128 members of the Assembly were divided between 67 Democrats and 61 Republicans, and 64 votes were needed to win the speakership. Eight Tammany-backed Democrats were delaying the vote until the conditions of the Tammany machine were met. These demands essentially involved the leadership of powerful committees. Roosevelt had no patience for these shenanigans, and the eight men responsible "were fuel for [his] morally righteous fires."[8] "Not even one of them [the Democrats] can string three intelligible sentences together to save his neck," he later wrote.[9] At the same time, he was not blind and unquestioning in his devotion to the Republicans. He did not hesitate in calling longtime Republican Speaker Tom Alvord "corrupt" and a "bad old fellow." In response, Alvord dismissed Roosevelt as a pest and fringe character. "He is just a damn fool," Alvord charged. "There are sixty and one-half [Republican] members in the Assembly," he continued. "Sixty plus that damned dude."[10]

Roosevelt's first days in the Assembly were slow but not entirely uneventful. Because the Tammany leaders refused to support any of the candidates for Speaker, the house rules were inoperative, and the Assembly was paralyzed. To pass the time, Roosevelt boxed and took long walks around Albany. Such exercise kept him in shape and helped him to hold his own in the rough and tumble world of New York politics. Some of Roosevelt's new enemies, in an attempt at intimidation, hired "Stubby" Collins to assault him. As the freshman assemblyman left his room at the Delavan House, Collins bumped into him and angrily demanded to know why Theodore had run into him. Collins took a swing, but the punch never reached its mark. Within moments, Stubby was on the ground.[11]

While in the Assembly, Roosevelt was involved in a few such altercations, and unlike the "Stubby" Collins incident, he was often the aggressor. When a fellow legislator ridiculed him on the floor of the Assembly for grandstanding and monopolizing the debate, Theodore responded, "Mr. Speaker, I appreciate the fact that this is neither the proper place nor the time to make an adequate reply to the remarks of the gentleman from Brooklyn, but if the gentleman will step outside of the Capitol, I will give him the only kind of reply that his remarks deserve." The other legislator looked away and made no reply.[12] It was only a matter of time before Roosevelt did hit another assemblyman, however. When J. J. Costello, Tammany's candidate for Speaker, made fun of Roosevelt's outfit, Roosevelt punched Costello and proceeded to hit him each time he struggled to his feet. After the third knockdown, Costello remained on the floor, and Roosevelt instructed him to wash up, adding, "When you are in the presence of gentlemen, conduct yourself like a gentleman."[13]

Such stories of tough guy behavior spread among the other assemblymen and became part of Roosevelt lore. But no incident better captured the imagination than Roosevelt's action on a bill to assist the construction of additional terminals for Jay Gould's Manhattan Elevated Railway. As acting chairman of the Cities Committee, Roosevelt expected to pass the legislation without any hint of scandal, but other legislators expected payoffs for their support. So, when Roosevelt moved that the railway bill be reported to the full Assembly for a vote, most of his committee's members refused. They wanted to stall the legislation and give Gould time to "sweeten the pot." In response to the rejection of his first motion, Roosevelt moved that the bill be reported unfavorably but was refused yet again. As he writes in his autobiography, "I then put the bill in my pocket and announced that I would report it anyhow."[14] This almost started a riot, but there was no riot, because Roosevelt reached under the table and pulled out the leg of a broken chair. Simply displaying this potential weapon calmed the other legislators and allowed Roosevelt to prevail, at least temporarily. Once on the floor of the Assembly, the bill was given to an older assemblyman and quietly became law. The appropriate legislators received envelopes full of cash, and the citizens of New York footed the bill in the form of higher taxes. As Grondahl observes, to fight corruption, Roosevelt needed something stronger than a chair leg and soon discovered the power of the media. Not only did he make himself readily available for interviews, but his quotable nature, quirky displays of physical fitness, and tough guy exploits captured both the attention of the reporters and the imagination of the public.[15]

THE CRUSADE AGAINST CORRUPTION

Roosevelt was becoming a star, and he would use this star power to fight for reform. "Almost single-handedly," Grondahl writes, "Roosevelt injected a spirit of reform into the 1882 session."[16] One of the most famous examples of this was his investigation of Jay Gould's acquisition of Manhattan Elevated Railway. It had been alleged that, in buying the company, Gould had acted on insider information and with the cooperation of corrupt government officials to drive down its stock price by ninety-five percent. Essentially, critics charged, Gould had cheated Manhattan Elevated Railway's regular share-holders of some $15 million by forcing the company into bankruptcy. More-over, when State Attorney General Hamilton Ward sued Gould's railway as an illegal and fraudulent corporation, Gould's operatives bribed Ward, and the suit was dropped. The attorney general declared that Manhattan Elevated was guilty only of being broke. To add insult to injury, Judge Theodore Westbrook also found nothing wrong with the acquisition, declaring the company solvent and handing it over to Gould. In fact, the court proceedings regarding Gould's acquisition of the railway company were held in Gould's private office, and it was learned that Westbrook had written to Gould, "I am willing to go to the very verge of judicial discretion to protect your vast interests."[17]

Roosevelt charged that Westbrook assisted Gould in the illegal stock ma-nipulation and was rewarded with a financial kickback. On March 29, TR launched a campaign to impeach the judge. In a speech before the Assembly, he charged that Westbrook placed "the whole road in the hands of swindlers," adding that, "We have a right to demand that our judiciary should be kept be-yond reproach, and we have a right to demand that if we find men against whom there is not only suspicion, but almost a certainty that they have been in collusion with men whose interests were in conflict with the interests of the public, they shall, at least, be required to bring positive facts with which to prove there has not been collusion; and they ought themselves to have been the first to demand such an investigation."[18]

Most of the newspapers, except those owned by Gould, heartily approved of Roosevelt's bold attack on Gould and Westbrook. He was earning a repu-tation as a true reformer and was even given a new nickname: "the Scotch Terrier."[19] In the meantime, Gould's forces attempted to stall a vote on Roo-sevelt's impeachment resolution by calling for an investigation, but the pub-lic outcry was too strong. Eventually, the Assembly approved the resolution, although the subsequent investigation by the Judiciary Committee was a sham. After being bribed by Gould, the majority of committee members con-cluded that Westbrook had been "indiscreet and unwise" but had committed nothing more grievous than an act of "excessive zeal" in trying to save Manhattan Elevated from financial destruction.[20]

Roosevelt was utterly disgusted with the Judiciary Committee's report. "I cannot believe that the Judge had any but corrupt motives in acting as he did in this case," he declared to his fellow legislators. "He was in corrupt collusion with Jay Gould. . . . There cannot be the slightest question that Judge Westbrook ought to be impeached. He stands condemned by his own acts in the eyes of all honest people. All you can do is to shame yourselves and give him a brief extension of his dishonored career. You cannot cleanse the leper. Beware lest you taint yourself with his leprosy." Westbrook had declared that his actions were legitimate, because all parties to the affair were satisfied with his ruling and because no one had appealed his decision to a higher court. But Roosevelt countered that, while the parties to the action were satisfied with the outcome, "the great mass of people who were not parties to the action, but who suffered by it, [were] not satisfied." Furthermore, TR said, the decision was not appealed because the people could not appeal it. Their representatives, "by whom they could appeal," betrayed them, choosing to line their own pockets rather than fight for the public good.[21]

The Westbrook case only fueled Roosevelt's belief that the relationship between business and government should not be abused, either by government officials extorting corporations, or by corporations bribing the servants of the people. Years later, TR noted that Westbrook might not have been corrupt, but there was a serious problem with his obvious reverence for men of great fortune, as well as his sincere belief that business could do no wrong. Of Westbrook, Roosevelt writes in his autobiography, "He sincerely believed that business was the end of existence, and that judge and legislator alike should do whatever was necessary to favor it; and the bigger the business the more he desired to favor it." For its part, Roosevelt adds, big business "thoroughly appreciated" the usefulness of officials like Westbrook and fought hard to protect them.[22]

These remarks suggest that, although Roosevelt's anti-corruption crusade was waged to rid the government of certain undue influences, it may also be seen as the beginning of a larger effort to fight the abuses of big business. According to most scholars, however, TR's early efforts focused on eliminating corruption in government, not on addressing economic and social ills. In fact, Roosevelt initially opposed both legislating eight-hour workdays and bills that prohibited prisons from selling for profit the forced labor of inmates.[23] Even Roosevelt admitted that he went through "various oscillations" on these matters before finding himself politically.[24] In his autobiography, he explains that he fought for honesty, decency, and efficiency in government but had yet to understand the need for "more genuine social and industrial justice." But, TR notes, by the time he was governor of New York (1899–1901), he understood that political corruption was directly related to social and economic in-security: when and where big business interests were improperly favored or discriminated against by public officials, the political boss was almost sure to arise, and his power was only enhanced by the unwillingness of many politi-cal reformers to improve the social and industrial conditions around them. Roosevelt explains that, while many political reformers opposed economic reform, as well as the extension of the franchise to blacks and immigrants, the political bosses were quite willing to reach out to the poor and immigrant masses, offering social services in exchange for continued political support. In many places, political bosses acted as both the friend and the protector of their constituents. They used influence to get jobs for young men who needed them, provided cash or credit to struggling widows and the unemployed, or-ganized picnics and other forms of local entertainment, and consulted with lo-cal labor leaders. Many voters, Roosevelt concludes, probably preferred clean and honest government, but they were struggling against poverty and were not about to support attacks on those men who were willing and able to make their lives easier. Therefore, to strike effectively at the base power of corrupt party bosses, reformers needed to couple their calls for honest government with human understanding and sympathy.[25]

By his own admission, TR's outlook as an assemblyman was not as broad as it would become, but he does note that it was consistent with his later agenda in a crucial way. Throughout his entire public career, Roosevelt openly opposed "crookedness" and vicious self-interest. Sometimes he fought the wrongdoing of capitalists, while other times he railed against the sins of labor. Always, though, he decided cases "with impartial justice on grounds of con-duct and not on grounds of class." Just as he never denounced a man as wicked simply because he was rich, he never insisted that labor was always right. "The loud-mouthed upholder of popular rights who attacks wickedness only when it is allied with wealth, and who never publicly assails any misdeed, no matter how flagrant, if committed nominally in the interest of labor, has either a warped mind or a tainted soul, and should be trusted by no honest man."[26] Roosevelt spent his entire career resisting the efforts of *all* dishonest men— politicians, capitalists, and workers alike. Admittedly, his autobiography draws some distinction between the fight for honesty in government and his battle against the kind of corruption that defends privilege and thereby undermines individual opportunity, but it also stresses that his early efforts to eliminate corruption in government share with his later economic and industrial reforms a similar intent to use government to help ordinary individuals combat the cor-ruption of powerful elites whom they could not otherwise control. At its most basic level, then, Roosevelt's anti-corruption campaign was, as he says, "part of the eternal war against the Powers that Prey."[27]

Moreover, TR did support an early attempt by his state's government to regulate the economic marketplace and control the behavior of the business class. As a member of the City Affairs Committee, Roosevelt had to consider a bill introduced by the Cigar-maker's Union that would outlaw the making of cigars in tenement apartments. At that time, one-third of the 670 million cigars rolled and packaged in New York City each year were produced in tenements. Workers, most of whom were new immigrants, labored up to eighteen hours a day in poorly lighted, crowded rooms—and for very little money. Even children worked. Initially, Roosevelt had doubts about this reform legislation. Writing in his autobiography, he admits, "As a matter of fact, I had supposed I would be against the legislation and I rather think I was put on the committee with that idea. For the respectable people I knew were against it; it was contrary to the principles of political economy of the *laissez-faire* kind." But, when Samuel Gompers pleaded with Roosevelt to inspect the conditions of the tenement houses himself, he agreed, and even returned twice more. Recalling what he saw, Roosevelt states, "There were several children, three men, and two women in this room. The tobacco was stowed about everywhere, alongside the foul bedding, and in a corner where there were scraps of food. The men, women, and children in this room worked by day and far on into the evening, and they slept and ate there." Roosevelt decided to support a bill to increase wages, limit the workweek, and improve the sanitary conditions of the tenements. As he explains in his autobiography, "Whatever the theories might be, as a matter of practical common sense I could not conscientiously vote for the continuation of the conditions which I saw." Roosevelt even persuaded Governor Grover Cleveland to throw his support behind the bill.[28]

Despite his initial reservations about the regulation of cigar manufacturing, Roosevelt's political thought was beginning to solidify. Some of his early votes were not consistent with the Roosevelt the American people would later come to know. Nevertheless, TR was beginning to supplement his commitment to self-reliance and individual freedom with a belief that it was the responsibility of the entire community to use its collective power, and even the institutions of the government, to help individuals do what they could not do for themselves. As he argues in the 1895 review of Benjamin Kidd's *Social Evolution*, a widespread concern for the public good allows individuals to compete in the economic marketplace and thereby remain self-sufficient. But, as TR was beginning to see a need for governmental regulation to improve economic, industrial, and social conditions, he was also developing a *noninstitutional* means of promoting the collective good in an individualistic society.

A MODEL OF PROPER LIVING

It was Roosevelt's experience in the Badlands that enabled him to create a romantic image of himself that would capture the hearts and minds of his countrymen and inspire them to appreciate the importance of discipline, hardiness, honor, duty, and service to the larger community—qualities that, taken together, are both individualistic and collectivistic but, for Roosevelt, not at all contradictory. Theodore left public office and set out for the American West in 1884. Like the journey of the Puritans to New England, Kathleen Dalton observes, TR moved to the Badlands not only to achieve a more fulfilling life for himself but also to provide a model of proper living for others to follow.[29] This model can be found in his writings on hunting and ranch life. These volumes are celebrations of certain individualistic values like self-mastery and hard work as well as the spirit of cooperation and camaraderie.

According to Roosevelt, the western frontier was a place of "rugged and stalwart democracy," where every man stands for what he actually is and can prove himself to be.[30] It was, he said, a place of freedom, new beginnings, and equal opportunity to remake oneself. Yet, as TR stressed, the frontier was closing. Unless he could bring the pioneer spirit to Americans of all regions, classes, and ethnicities, people had little hope of experiencing the kind of transformation he did. Like Roosevelt, they had to learn how to balance those individualistic values that are healthy and vital to a society (discipline, personal responsibility, and a strong work ethic) with such positive collectivistic values as an appreciation for mutual support and concern for the good of the community.

In *Hunting Trips of a Ranchman*, Roosevelt stresses that the value of ranch life lay in its freedom and the particular lifestyle it requires men to lead. The work is hard and constant, but it is also "the pleasantest part of a cowboy's existence."[31] Roosevelt explains that ranchmen do not have much free time, but whatever time they can spare is spent hunting. Cattlemen are intensely devoted to sport, and Roosevelt intends "to give some description of the kind of sport that can be had by the average ranchman who is fond of the rifle." TR understands that most civilized men have limited opportunity to hunt and cannot expect to rival the skill of the ranchman, whose work offers more chance "to get sport" than is the case with other occupations. Still, he adds, those who are willing to learn from the experiences of a ranchman like Roosevelt are apt to become more self-reliant, resolute, spirited, and adventurous in life.[32] Unlike most people, TR explains, the frontiersman possesses "iron nerve and will," yet he will soon be displaced. "The ground over which he so gallantly rides his small, wiry horse will soon know him nowhere, and in his stead there will be the plodding grangers and husbandmen." Roosevelt hopes that he will not live to see this occur, but he is determined to tell of this lifestyle, a phase of American life that is "as fascinating as it is evanescent."[33] The message seems to be that the spirit of the frontiersman will not be lost if other Americans can embrace his many positive attributes.

In a passage that connects him to the average reader, Roosevelt admits that he is not, and will never be, a great shot; however, he has killed every kind of game on the plains, and the reason for this is practice and perseverance. Time and again he has heard men claim to have practiced sufficiently with a target, yet they are unsuccessful, even when the game is plentiful. He suggests that the problem, more often than not, is lack of perseverance—both when training and when hunting. According to Roosevelt, even the best sportsmen miss their targets (sometimes by a great deal), but the secret to their success is continued practice, persistence, and a good acquaintance with the nature of the animals they pursue. "With practice," he assures readers, "an amateur will become nearly as good a shot as the average hunter," and he uses stories of his encounters with various game to underscore this point. A good shot may be a poor hunter, and a rather successful hunter may be only an average shot. Shooting well with a rifle requires the highest skill and is a difficult art to learn. Fortunately, Roosevelt says, "other qualities go to make up the first-class hunter"—he must be watchful, patient, resolute, and energetic. It also helps to be a good judge.[34] These are, of course, the same qualities that TR believed led to success in daily life.

It is significant that, in addition to celebrating the self-reliance and solitary practices of the frontier hunter, Roosevelt also emphasizes the advantages of hunting with a companion. His valued companion is the foreman of his ranch, William Merrifield, who TR describes as both daring and self-reliant, "a good rider and a first-class shot, and a very keen sportsman." In fact, Roosevelt freely admits that he kills more game with Merrifield than he can alone. More important, though, he stresses that a companion like Merrifield is just about indispensable when hunting on the plains. As Roosevelt explains, "It frequently happens that a solitary hunter finds himself in an awkward predicament from which he could be extricated easily enough if there were another man with him. His horse may fall into a washout or may get stuck in a mud hole or quicksand in such a manner that a man working by himself will have great difficulty in getting it out; and two heads often prove better than one in an emergency. . . ." He concludes, "The first thing that a Western plainsman has to learn is the capacity for self-help, but at the same time he must not forget that occasions may arise when the help of others will be most grateful."[35] Thus, years before the introduction of his Square Deal and New Nationalism, Roosevelt's western experience has taught him that mutual support can be critical to individual well-being.

In *Ranch Life and the Hunting Trail*, Roosevelt builds on this lesson about the importance of mutual support, noting that, despite their firm devotion to self-reliance, ranchmen are learning more and more to act together. He explains that they have united and formed themselves into associations like the great Montana Stock Growers' Association. Among the "countless benefits" they have derived from this wise decision, "not the least has been the way in which the roundups of member ranches work with and supplement one another." Each spring, Roosevelt explains, before the cattle are driven to market, the association maps out cattle roundup districts and affixes the time and place that each district's roundup will begin. The spring roundup is "the great event of the season, as it is then that the bulk of the calves are branded." It usually lasts about six weeks, Roosevelt adds, and the Stock Growers' Association is careful to make sure that none of the district roundups conflicts with the others. This allows the ranches in each district to send representatives to two or three roundups in neighboring districts, where some of their cattle might have strayed. Roosevelt explains that, as there are no fences in the West, cattle are allowed to wander free throughout the winter. Having previously been branded with the unique marker of their respective owners, these grown cows can easily be gathered and taken back to the appropriate ranges during the spring roundup. But this is only made possible by the staggered scheduling of the Stock Growers' Association.

Roosevelt emphasizes that a larger outfit can spare many cowboys to represent its interests in nearby districts, but many smaller outfits must band together to send outside representatives, or else "go along with their stronger neighbors" and pay part of the expenses. Put simply, it is in the individual interests of all ranchmen to work with their neighbors' consent and assistance.[36] Elsewhere Roosevelt adds, "In the cow country a man is peculiarly dependent upon his neighbors, and a small outfit is wholly unable to work without their assistance when once the cattle have mingled completely with those of other brands." Yet, even a larger outfit, which "is much more master of its destiny," must worry about those selfish men, "who for the sake of the chance of gain . . . are willing to jeopardize the interests of their neighbors by putting on more cattle than the land will support." According to TR, it is against such individuals that all ranch owners—large and small—must unite. Suggesting that individual self-interest and collective good are not necessarily mutually exclusive, Roosevelt concludes, "To protect ourselves completely is impossible, but the very identity of interest that renders all of us liable to suffer for the fault of a few also renders us as a whole able to take some rough measures to guard against the wrongdoing of a portion of our number; for the fact that the cattle wander intermixed over the ranges forces all the ranchmen of a locality to combine if they wish to do their work effectively."[37]

Although ranch life is the subject of *Ranch Life and the Hunting Trail*, Roosevelt is teaching lessons on every page, and his lessons have universal implications. He is the central figure in these various accounts of herding, riding, Indian attacks, and game hunting, so when the book is finished, Roosevelt's teachings and personal examples are what have made the most indelible impression on the reader. The theme of this volume is that much of life entails struggle, and success requires hard work, toughness, decency, loyalty, duty, and, as the discussion of the Montana Stock Growers' Association shows, a willingness to cooperate and rely on the assistance of others. *Ranch Life* celebrates the manly qualities of the ranchman "that are invaluable to a nation." At various points, Roosevelt makes clear that these "manly qualities" include bravery, hardiness, hospitality, cooperation, and camaraderie. Unlike many people in other parts of the country, most frontiersmen do not tolerate meanness, cowardice, dishonesty, or selfishness. Roosevelt writes, "There is a high regard for truthfulness and keeping one's word, intense contempt for any kind of hypocrisy, and a hearty dislike for a man who shirks his work."[38] Like *Hunting Trips*, the underlying message of *Ranch Life* is that the rest of the country can learn much from the West, and in particular from TR's experience there.

In introducing ranch life to civilized people, Roosevelt emphasizes the cowboy's strong and vigorous nature as well as the ranch owner's shrewdness, thriftiness, patience, bravery, hardihood, and self-reliance. TR was both a cowboy and a ranch owner. In 1883, he invested heavily in the Dakota Territory's growing open-range cattle industry, purchasing a ranch and 400 head of beef cattle. A year later, he bought another ranch and more cattle. But, as his book suggests, the most successful ranchmen invest more than their money in cattle; they also devote serious time and energy to their work. Roosevelt stresses that he insisted on putting in the same number of hours in the saddle as the other cowboys. He also tackled the toughest and most dangerous jobs on the ranch, such as branding duty. By his own admission, he never became more than a mediocre roper and rider, but what he lacked in natural ability, he made up for with sheer determination. He soon found that ordinary men, who do not shirk tasks simply because they are disagreeable or bothersome, soon earn their place. As a matter of fact, TR says that he wholly embraced the life of grueling work, hardship, monotony, and exposure to the elements. There are few ranchmen, he writes, "who do not look forward to [this rough life] and back to it with pleasure." The men with whom he lived and worked are "good-humored, bold, and thoroughly interested in their business, continually vying with one another in an effort to see which can do the work best."[39]

Clearly, Roosevelt wholeheartedly respects the ranchmen and their way of life, but he also describes the less noble side of these men. For much of the same reason they are self-reliant, bold, honest, and loyal, he explains, frontier-types can also be wild, reckless, rough, and vindictive. On the frontier, violence is a normal part of life, and personal qualities "take on very pronounced colors." As Roosevelt notes, "A man who in civilization would be merely a backbiter becomes a murderer on the frontier; and on the other hand, he who in the city would do nothing more than bid you a cheery good morning, shares his last bit of sun-jerked venison with you when threatened by starvation in the wilderness."[40] But, for all their undesirable characteristics, Roosevelt regards most frontiersmen as better than the men he has known in the New York Assembly. In his view, while the latter are corrupt, the behavior of the former is straightforward and easy to understand: a cowboy will not take an insult lightly and is "ever ready to avenge his own wrongs."[41] Besides, Roosevelt cautions, it is unfair to judge a whole class of men according to what a few characters do in the course of a couple of days spent in town. Judge these men, instead, by their many months of "weary, honest toil."[42] He concludes that no one traveling through or living in western lands "need fear molestation from the cowboys unless he himself accompanies them on their drinking-bouts, or in other ways plays the fool."[43]

Roosevelt advises that a key to survival on the western frontier, as in life, is a willingness to stand up to all varieties of ruffians and bullies, none of whom respects the rights of others. As he opines in his autobiography, a man should "walk warily and fearlessly, and while he should never brawl if he can avoid it, he must be ready to hit hard if the need arises."[44] In the same manner that he had defied the corrupt political bosses in the Assembly and would ultimately attack corporate abuse, Roosevelt took on a whole host of frontier characters and, as *Ranch Life* makes clear, is only too eager to share these experiences with readers so that they might do the same with the thoughtless and tyrannical thugs in their own lives.

One story, which Roosevelt mentions briefly in *Ranch Life* but details more in his autobiography, involves a barroom lout. While TR was reading in the saloon of the hotel where he was staying, a man staggered to the bar and ordered drinks for the house. The other patrons eagerly went to the bar for their drinks, but Theodore remained seated and buried in his book. When the offended man demanded that Roosevelt accept his drink and fired his gun at the barroom's clock, Roosevelt stood up and punched the man in the face. He then pinned the belligerent to the floor, threw his pistol aside, and sneered, "When I intimate that I don't care to drink with you, just understand that I don't care to drink." According to Roosevelt, this was the only time in his life that he was "shot at maliciously."[45]

Similarly, *Ranch Life* describes the time that Roosevelt faced down a band of five Sioux Indians. When the five men spotted Theodore riding across the plateau near his ranch, they whipped out their guns and galloped toward him. Roosevelt recalls that he dismounted his horse, raised his rifle, and drew a bead on his target. The whole party scattered and doubled back on their tracks. They gathered again, consulted, and one of them rode toward him. When he came within fifty yards, TR warned him not to come any closer. When his companions began to draw near, Roosevelt raised his rifle to the first and "made him move." He explains that the Indians probably intended nothing more than to scare him, but he remained confident and cool, making it clear that he was not afraid to shoot, if necessary.[46]

Continuing to illustrate his refusal to be bullied, Roosevelt also recounts how he led a posse to capture a band of thieves who stole his boat. It was necessary to have a boat on the Little Missouri River, and as deputy sheriff of the northern-end of his county, Roosevelt was determined to find and apprehend the perpetrators. After a few days of chasing them downriver, and in frigid winter conditions, Theodore and his gang caught up with the thieves. But the adventure was only half over, for there still remained the 100 mile return trip—upriver and against the current. At night, Roosevelt and two friends took turns watching the prisoners, and once they made it back to the ranch, he and another ranch hand continued on to Dickinson, the nearest town, where they presented the thieves for arraignment.[47] Fully appreciating how inspiring this story was, Roosevelt posed for photographs during a staged reenactment of the arrest. He was becoming something of a local celebrity, which was due, in no small part, to the good press that he cultivated.[48] It was Theodore, for example, who encouraged Arthur T. Packard, a friend and editor of the *Bad Lands Cow Boy*, to use the name "Teddy" when referring to him in articles that were carried across the country. Roosevelt had initially despised this nickname, which was given to him affectionately by the other ranch hands, but he soon came to appreciate its folksy appeal.[49]

As tales of his adventures spread across the plains and throughout the country, Roosevelt's popularity only grew. In fact, he was asked to be the orator of the day during Dickinson's Fourth of July festivities. After the Declaration of Independence was read and the crowd sang "America the Beautiful," the local hero spoke to the values and virtues of being an American, as he would often in his subsequent political career:

> Much has been given to us, and so, much will be expected of us; and we must take heed to use aright the gifts entrusted to our care. . . . So it is peculiarly incumbent on us here today to act throughout our lives as to leave our children a heritage, for which we will receive their blessing and not their curse. . . . If you fail to work in public life, as well as in private, for honesty and uprightness and virtue, if you condone vice because the vicious man is smart, or if you in any other way cast your weight into the scales in favor of evil, you are just so far

corrupting and making less valuable the birthright of your children . . . It is not what we have that will make us a great nation; it is the way in which we use it. . . . I do not undervalue for a moment our material prosperity; like all Americans, I like big things; big prairies, big forests and mountains, big wheat fields, railroads—and herds of cattle, too—big factories, steamboats, and everything else. But we must keep steadily in mind that no people were ever yet benefited by riches if their prosperity corrupted their virtue. It is of more importance that we should show ourselves honest, brave, truthful, and intelligent, than that we should own all the railways and grain elevators in the world. We have fallen heirs to the most glorious heritage a people ever received, and each one must do his part if we wish to show that the nation is worthy of its good fortune. Here we are not ruled over by others, as in the case of Europe; we rule ourselves. . . . When we thus rule ourselves, we have the responsibilities of sovereigns, not of subjects. We must never exercise our rights either wickedly or thoughtlessly. . . . I am, myself, at heart as much a Westerner as an Easterner; I am proud, indeed, to be considered one of yourselves, and I address you in this rather solemn strain today, only because of my pride in you, and because your welfare, moral as well as material is so near my heart.[50]

Contained within this speech are the seeds of the Square Deal and the New Nationalism, and with only minor alterations, these words might have been spoken by Thee Roosevelt to his oldest son. Certainly, Theodore revealed his father's influence by supporting with real action and personal example these sentiments about the need for more communal concern and service to others. Not only did TR organize funerals for neighbors and advise young boys on healthy living, but he cashed in on his hero status and used the power of his personality to organize the Little Missouri Stockmen's Association, a smaller version of the great Montana Stock Growers' Association.[51] Thus, he continued the effort to collectivize the most rugged individualists in the United States, and he did so successfully.

Proving that collective action could serve the individual interests of all cattlemen, Roosevelt's organization devised and enforced new range regulations, fired the region's incompetent livestock inspector, and united against cattle rustlers.[52] Without a doubt, this organization, and Roosevelt's leadership of it, was a harbinger of even greater things to come. Through his writings, and because of various "Teddy" tales, Roosevelt was already beginning to broaden his local hero status beyond the borders of his small frontier community. Ultimately, he would become the nation's superhero and rely on both personal example and governmental coercion to show all Americans the advantages of incorporating communal habits into their individual lives. Indeed, Roosevelt's use of personal experience to make the case for a connection between individualism and collectivism shows his belief that, in dealing with real life, philosophical tensions can be resolved in practical ways; that actions

speak louder than words, a belief that was to inform his presidency and produce the bully pulpit.

Despite what his western writings might suggest, Roosevelt devoted only
a portion of his time in the Badlands to ranching. In fact, he made regular trips
back to New York City, kept his hand in New York politics, and published
speeches that urged his fellow Republicans to defeat the Democrats in the
midterm elections of 1886. As Paul Grondahl notes, Roosevelt "was more
successful as a politician than a businessman." Due to severe summer
droughts and winter snowstorms, Roosevelt lost about 60 percent of his cattle by the spring of 1887. "The losses are crippling," he wrote. "For the first
time I have been utterly unable to enjoy a visit to my ranch. I shall be glad to
get home." In all, Roosevelt lost about $40,000 in the Badlands. This was ap-
proximately half of his initial investment and a quarter of the entire inheritance his father had left him. He did not sell out completely until 1898, but he
had come to understand that his future lay elsewhere.[53] He returned to New
York and tried to make more of a literary career for himself by continuing to
work on a biography of Thomas Hart Benton, which he had promised to write
for the distinguished "American Statesman" series.

TWO TREATISES OF ROOSEVELT'S THOUGHT

Thomas Hart Benton is less a biography than a declaration of Roosevelt's nationalism. Through discussions of the rise of Jacksonian democracy, the spoils
system, slavery, nullification, and the war on the Second Bank of the United
States, Roosevelt interprets himself and his political thought better than could be
done by anyone else. At times, TR even seems to identify with his subject, writing that Benton "was a faithful friend and a bitter foe, and quite unable to com-
prehend such emotions as are expressed by the terms of despondency and yield-
ing. . . . He was very courteous, except when provoked; his courage was proof
against all fear, and he shrank from no contest, personal or political. He was
sometimes narrow-minded, and always willful and passionate; but he was honest and truthful. At all times and in all places he held every good gift he had
completely at the service of the American Federal Union." As H. W. Brands observes, this is as much a description of Roosevelt as it is of Benton.[54]

Writing of the Jacksonian spoils system, Roosevelt declares that Jackson's
administration "derives a most unenviable notoriety as being the one under
which the 'spoils system' became, for the first time, grafted on the civil service of the nation; appointments and removals in the public service being
made dependent upon political qualifications, and, not, as hitherto, upon
merit or capacity." Roosevelt notes that, in the first month after Andrew Jack-

son assumed the presidency, more people were removed from the federal civil service than during all the previous administrations combined. According to TR, the best and most faithful servants, who had been appointed by Presidents Washington, Adams, and Jefferson, were "unceremoniously and causelessly dismissed." New appointments were then made with little or no regard for fitness, or even honesty. As Roosevelt stresses, the only thing that mattered was party loyalty. Similarly, he says, subsequent removals were not made in accordance with any standard. In fact, "the most frivolous pretexts were sufficient, if advanced by useful politicians who needed places already held by capable incumbents."[55]

On the other hand, Roosevelt's appreciation for the value of party loyalty explains why he criticizes the exaggerated nonpartisanship of John Quincy Adams' administration. "Indeed," he writes, "Adams certainly went altogether too far in his nonpartisanship when it came to appointing Cabinet and other high officers, his views on such points being not only fantastic, but absolutely wrong." TR adds, "The colorless character of his administration was largely due to his having, in his anxiety to avoid blind and unreasoning adherence to party, committed the only less serious fault of paying too little heed to party, for healthy party spirit is prerequisite to the performance of effective work in American political life." Roosevelt continues, declaring that Adams was elected on account of ideology and the principles that he was supposed to represent. When he decided to surround himself with men of opposite principles, he betrayed his supporters and "rightly forfeited much of their confidence."[56]

Notwithstanding his point about the disastrous nonpartisanship of Adams' administration, TR praises Benton's strong opposition to the spoils system. Benton had argued that spoils undermined public service, as well as the harmony and union of the people. Roosevelt wholeheartedly agrees, suggesting that the political bosses of this era were concerned with nothing more than acquiring and maintaining power. TR believes that, in rewarding their loyalists, political bosses advanced candidates for whom the people at large would never have voted otherwise. As for those Presidents and public men who had widespread popular support, Roosevelt regards them as nothing more than figureheads. They answered, he says, not to the American people, but to party bosses, "who held no public position, and yet devoted their whole time to politics, and pulled the strings in obedience to which the apparent public leaders moved." Of course, Roosevelt stresses, the most important cogs in the party machines were the countless officeholders, who cared more for job preservation than serving the public good. He concludes that a political machine "can only be brought to a state of high perfection in a party containing very many ignorant and uneducated voters; and [Jackson's Democratic Party] held in its ranks the mass of the ignorance of the country."[57] Yet, Roosevelt is certain to add, it is not simply that patronage politics undermines public service, specifically honesty and efficiency in government: because of patronage practices, Jacksonian era politics revolved primarily around concerns about money, power, and advantage, not such moral questions as union and slavery. Put simply, TR charges that matters of vital national importance were sorely neglected during this period.

Due to the materialism of the Jacksonian era, Roosevelt declares, slavery "lowed like a thunderstorm on the horizon; and though sometimes it might seem for a moment to break away, yet in reality it had reached that stage when, until the final all-engulfing outburst took place [the Civil War], the clouds were found forevermore to return after the rain."[58] From Roosevelt's standpoint, slavery was a transgression of God's law and therefore compromise upon compromise could not solve the problem. Influenced by the speeches and writings of Lincoln, TR believes that the whole nation had to pay for this sin by enduring the bloodshed of a long civil war, and it found redemption only by reaffirming and recommitting to the principle of equality. At the same time, Roosevelt cannot mask his contempt for the "professional abolitionists," who, like all inflexible extremists, insisted that their particular views were wholly inspired and exalted by God. Their cause, Roosevelt asserts, "has had such a halo shed round it by the after-course of events which they themselves in reality did very little to shape, that it has been usual to speak of them with absurdly exaggerated praise." No doubt, he continues, their "tendency toward impracticable methods" was well shown in the attitude with which they regarded Lincoln, the greatest of Americans. Throughout the Civil War, while he worked and suffered for all Americans, the "sad, strong, patient" Lincoln "had to dread the influence of the extreme abolitionists only less than that of the Copperheads." Roosevelt concludes that most abolitionists possessed no good qualities other than fearlessness and moral certitude, yet he finds that the southern slave owners possessed the same qualities.[59]

Roosevelt admires Lincoln's championship of Union every bit as much as his moral opposition to slavery; therefore, it is not surprising that he praises both Jackson and Benton for their opposition to the nullification movement. The nullification movement was South Carolina's call for the right of a state to declare null and void any federal law (in this case, the existing federal tariff) that it deemed improper and contrary to its interests. The doctrine of nullification was proclaimed, not as a right of revolution, but rather as a constitutional privilege, and the Nullifiers counted on Jackson's support. Jackson was a southerner, but he was also a strong Unionist, who, Roosevelt asserts, "correctly" believed that the United States had "the same right to protect itself from death by nullification, secession, or rebellion that a man has to protect himself from death by assassination."[60] Benton, Roosevelt adds, also "threw himself in, heart and soul, with the Union party, acting as Jackson's right-hand man throughout the contest with South Carolina, and showing an even more resolute and unflinching front than Old Hickory himself."[61] Taking a deep and personal pride in his country—North, South, East, and West—Benton declared that the founders "established a Union instead of a League—to be sovereign and independent within its sphere, acting upon persons through its own laws and courts. . . ." This interpretation of the Constitution, Roosevelt concludes, was sound and, thankfully, the one that the course of events has made "universally accepted."[62]

Nevertheless, Roosevelt continues, if the struggle with the Nullifiers shows Benton at his best, then the war against the National Bank places him in a less favorable light. Both Jackson and Benton opposed the Bank for the same reason that many of their followers did. This opposition was, according to Roosevelt, "partly from honest and ignorant prejudice and partly from a well-founded feeling of distrust as to some of its actions." Certainly, TR explains, the Bank had many faults. Not only did it possess enormous power, but its president, Nicolas Biddle, was conceited, untruthful, and unscrupulous in how he used the political influence of his institution.[63] Benton assailed the Bank "as having too much power over the people and the government, over business and politics, and as too much disposed to exercise that power to the prejudice of the freedom and equality which should prevail in a republic, to be allowed to exist in our country." Because Benton saw the Bank as favoring eastern capitalists to the disadvantage of smaller western capitalists and farmers, he added that the institution aggravated "the inequality of fortunes," making the rich richer and the poor poorer. In short, Jacksonians like Benton were concerned that the Bank, by favoring certain economic interests over others, was creating artificial elites, and Benton's words were meant to evoke moral outrage against special privilege. Roosevelt admits that the force of such rhetoric in popular politics is acknowledged by all practical politicians, but he maintains that Benton should not have opened the discussion of a great financial matter with a demagogic appeal to "caste prejudices."

As Roosevelt observes, Benton was a firm believer in Jeffersonian principles regarding the will of the majority as "always right" and therefore did not appear to understand that the majority could use its power to violate the rights of the minority. Roosevelt says that, unlike Benton and Jackson, he shares Lincoln's realization that the will of the majority can be just as mischievous and tyrannical as "the divine right of kings." For this reason, he concludes, certain individual freedoms must be placed beyond the reach of majority opinion, and public servants like Benton need to exercise greater restraint when making public addresses and electoral appeals. Roosevelt contends that much of Benton's speech regarding the National Bank was pompous and "sheer declamation." In his view, such speech should not be mistaken for "genuine oratory," which uplifts an audience by challenging them to listen to the better angels of their nature and thereby fulfill the promise of America's greatest ideals.[64]

Recall that Roosevelt understood, in contrast with most Progressive reformers, that rhetoric was often better than institutional reform and the force of law in reaching into the private lives of individuals and persuading them to support one another in a spirit of civic attachment. This was the essence of Lincoln's statesmanship, and Roosevelt's effort to emulate it demonstrates a sincere respect for individual freedom. Of course, Lincoln used his words and example to befriend the nation and thereby work to change human behavior for the better, while Roosevelt, in both word and deed, created an inspirational persona—an American ideal—that was essentially the ultimate action hero—a larger-than-life, self-driven tough guy, whose superior ability and devotion to good compelled him to pursue his morally righteous goals, even in the face of powerful opposition.

Much like *Thomas Hart Benton*, TR's biography, *Gouverneur Morris*, offers readers insights into Roosevelt's character and political ideas. First of all, Roosevelt praises Morris' defense of strong executive leadership. On the whole, he concludes, Morris' views regarding the proper power and functions of the American President were sound, and the United States is fortunate to have most of these views embodied in the Constitution. Roosevelt explains that Morris wished to have the national executive hold office during good behavior, and while this proposal was defeated, he did succeed in making the President eligible for reelection to the position. Morris, TR adds, was also instrumental in giving the President a qualified veto over legislation, in making him commander-in-chief of America's armed forces, and in allowing him to appoint lesser governmental officers. But Morris' greatest contribution, in Roosevelt's opinion, was in successfully opposing the plan whereby the President was to be selected by Congress. According to Roosevelt, Morris was right to argue that this plan would "take away greatly from the dignity of the Executive, and would render his election a matter of cabal and faction."[65]

Roosevelt stresses that, during the American Revolution and well into the early years of the republic, Morris served the nation in a variety of ways, but he also devoted his vision and energy to the people of New York. TR adds that Morris was unique among most New Yorkers in that he did not allow the past wrongdoings of that state's royal governors to blind him to necessity. In short, Roosevelt explains, Morris saw that the problem with New York's past executives lay, "not in the power that they held, but in the source from which that power came." Once that source of power was changed, the power itself would benefit, not harm, the state. Thus, during New York's constitutional convention, Morris defended the power of the governor to appoint the civil servants of the state. The New York convention ultimately rejected this proposition and adopted in its place what Roosevelt refers to as "the cumbrous and foolish plan of a 'council of appointment' to consist of the governor and several senators." Roosevelt concludes, "As might have been expected, this artificial body worked nothing but harm, and became simply a peculiarly odious political machine."[66] Note that statements like these reveal what will later attract Roosevelt to the Progressive camp: a firm belief that effective and dynamic leadership depends on releasing chief executives (governors and Presidents) from the clutches of corrupt and parochial political bosses. Still, as stressed above, this should not be taken to suggest that TR advocated strict nonpartisanship.

Roosevelt certainly saw a place in the American political system for political party organizations, which is as evident in *Gouverneur Morris* as in *Thomas Hart Benton*. Much as he criticizes the extremely nonpartisan character of John Quincy Adams' administration, TR faults the appointment practices of James Monroe as "an excellent example of the folly of trying to carry on a government on a non-partisan basis." In his view, even George Washington was "gradually weaned" from this theory "by bitter experience." "It goes without saying," Roosevelt writes, "that in a well-ordered government the bulk of the employees in the civil service, the men whose functions are merely to execute faithfully routine departmental work, should hold office during good behavior, and should be appointed without reference to their politics." On the other hand, he asserts, the heads of departments and foreign ministers should be in complete ideological accordance with the President. Otherwise, Roosevelt reasons, the government will be marked by "halting indecision and vacillation."[67]

Roosevelt praises Morris' devotion to the entire national community, rather than to the narrow interests of his state. Like so many of his generation, TR writes, Morris saw the "absolute need" of establishing a National Union, not a mere league or confederation.[68] In Roosevelt's opinion, Morris did all he could to bring into combination those varied interests that were favorable to the formation of a strong, responsible, and free government. For this reason, he suggests, states' rights advocates in Jefferson's party were hostile to Morris. Fortunately, Roosevelt concludes, these destructive forces did not prevail, for if the separatists and states' rights men had obtained the upper hand, either in 1787 or 1861, the United States would have fallen apart, leaving the rest of the world to conclude that the American people were not fit for republican self-government.[69] In a passage that perfectly summarizes his political thought,

Roosevelt asserts that the United States has succeeded like no other nation because the American people are able "to preserve the largest possible individual freedom on the one hand, while showing an equally remarkable capacity
for combination on the other."[70]

According to TR, while most Americans originally favored the laxness of
confederation, they had the good sense to learn the lessons taught by the weakness and lawlessness that they witnessed around them. In other words, they came
to realize that they needed a stronger central government, and once they reached
that decision, neither demagogues nor extreme states' rights doctrinaires could
sway them from it. Even Jefferson, Roosevelt concedes, "learned to acquiesce"
to some of the strong government and nationalist principles of the Federalists,
and his administration was good when it adhered to the theories of the Hamilto-
nians. Unfortunately, Roosevelt continues, Federalists like Hamilton and Morris
refused to learn the one great truth taught by Jefferson—"that in America a
statesman should trust the people, and should endeavor to secure to each man all
possible individual liberty, confident that he will use it aright."[71] Roosevelt believes that, if the Federalists had trusted the people and stood staunchly for individual liberty, the party might have survived. But, he concludes, there is no hope
for leaders who ignore the people. These observations, written in 1888, antici-
pate the central argument of Roosevelt's New Nationalism—that Hamiltonian
means (a strong central government that is focused on the collective good) can
be used to achieve Jeffersonian ends (more freedom and equality for all).

In these biographies, Roosevelt makes clear his belief in an energetic national government, a strong executive, civil service reform, and a strong party
government. He also voices his dislike for ideologues and his attraction to
those—like Benton, Morris, and Lincoln—who combined idealism with
pragmatism, as expressed in their actions and not simply their ideas. Finally,
as with the cowboy tales and western narratives, Roosevelt celebrates the man
who manages, in both his thought and his behavior, to ease the tension between the competing values of individualism and collectivism.

NOTES

1. Paul Grondahl, *I Rose Like a Rocket: The Political Education of Theodore Roosevelt* (New York: Free Press, 2004), 63. See also Theodore Roosevelt, *Autobiography*, vol. 20 of *The Works of Theodore Roosevelt*, National Edition (New York:
Charles Scribner's Sons, 1926), 59.

2. Grondahl, *I Rose Like a Rocket*, 61–63.

3. Grondahl, *I Rose Like a Rocket*, 65–66.

4. Quoted in Grondahl, *I Rose Like a Rocket*, 66. See also Theodore Roosevelt to
Charles Grenfill Washburn, 10 November 1881, *The Years of Preparation:*

1868–1898, vol. 1 of *The Letters of Theodore Roosevelt*, ed. Elting Morison (Cambridge: Harvard University Press, 1951), 55.

5. Grondahl, *I Rose Like a Rocket*, 68–69.

6. Grondahl, *I Rose Like a Rocket*, 70.

7. Grondahl, *I Rose Like a Rocket*, 75.

8. Grondahl, *I Rose Like a Rocket*, 79.

9. Quoted in Grondahl, *I Rose Like a Rocket*, 79. See also Theodore Roosevelt, "Diary of Five Months in the New York Legislature," in *The Years of Preparation: 1898–1900*, vol. 2 of *The Letters of Theodore Roosevelt*, ed. Elting Morison (Cambridge: Harvard University Press, 1951), 1471.

10. Grondahl, *I Rose Like a Rocket*, 80.

11. Grondahl, *I Rose Like a Rocket*, 82. See also Alvin F. Harlow, *Theodore Roosevelt: Strenuous American* (New York: Julian Messner, 1943), 84.

12. Quoted in Grondahl, *I Rose Like a Rocket*, 82. See also Nathan Miller, *Theodore Roosevelt: A Life* (New York: William Morrow, 1992), 125.

13. Quoted in Grondahl, *I Rose Like a Rocket*, 83. See also Will M. Clemens, *Theodore Roosevelt: The American* (New York: F. Tennyson Neely, 1899), 65.

14. Quoted in Grondahl, *I Rose Like a Rocket*, 85. See also Roosevelt, *Autobiography*, 76–77.

15. Grondahl, *I Rose Like a Rocket*, 85.

16. Grondahl, *I Rose Like a Rocket*, 89.

17. Quoted in Grondahl, *I Rose Like a Rocket*, 91. See also Miller, *Theodore Roosevelt*, 132; Roosevelt, *Autobiography*, 78–79.

18. Quoted in Grondahl, *I Rose Like a Rocket*, 92. See also Miller, *Theodore Roosevelt*, 133–34; Theodore Roosevelt, "The Investigation of Judge Westbrook," in *Campaigns and Controversies*, vol. 14 of *The Works of Theodore Roosevelt*, National Edition (New York: Charles Scribner's Sons, 1926), 11.

19. Grondahl, *I Rose Like a Rocket*, 92.

20. Grondahl, *I Rose Like a Rocket*, 96. See also Miller, *Theodore Roosevelt*, 136.

21. Quoted in Grondahl, *I Rose Like a Rocket*, 96. See also Miller, *Theodore Roosevelt*, 136–37.

22. Roosevelt, *Autobiography*, 79.

23. Kathleen Dalton, *Theodore Roosevelt: A Strenuous Life* (New York: Vintage Books, 2002), 83.

24. Roosevelt, *Autobiography*, 88.

25. Roosevelt, *Autobiography*, 152–55.

26. Roosevelt, *Autobiography*, 81–82.

27. Roosevelt, *Autobiography*, 95.

28. Roosevelt, *Autobiography*, 82–83.

29. See Dalton, *Strenuous Life*, 97–101. According to Dalton, TR used his western writings to "reinvigorate [civilized society] along more elemental and primitive masculine lines." That is, he portrayed western life as a life of freedom that taught men to be tough and manly. While I do not disagree, I am arguing that, in addition to qualities like discipline, hardiness, and self–reliance, Roosevelt's frontier writings emphasize the need for empathy, communal concern, and an individual's willingness to rely

on the assistance of others. In this way, then, TR encourages his readers to embrace both individualism and collectivism in their everyday lives.

30. Quoted in Dalton, *Strenuous Life*, 98. See also Theodore Roosevelt, *The Wilderness Hunter*, vol. 2 of *The Works of Theodore Roosevelt*, National Edition (New York: Charles Scribner's Sons, 1926), xxix.

31. Theodore Roosevelt, *Hunting Trips of a Ranchman*, vol. 1 of *The Works of Theodore Roosevelt*, National Edition (New York: Charles Scribner's Sons, 1926), 14.

32. Roosevelt, *Hunting Trips*, 24.

33. Roosevelt, *Hunting Trips*, 25–26.

34. Roosevelt, *Hunting Trips*, 29–30.

35. Roosevelt, *Hunting Trips*, 33–34.

36. Theodore Roosevelt, *Ranch Life and the Hunting Trail*, vol. 1 of *The Works of Theodore Roosevelt*, National Edition (New York: Charles Scribner's Sons, 1926), 317–18.

37. Roosevelt, *Ranch Life*, 291–92.

38. Roosevelt, *Ranch Life*, 325–26.

39. Roosevelt, *Ranch Life*, 340. See also Grondahl, *I Rose Like a Rocket*, 149–50.

40. Roosevelt, *Ranch Life*, 351.

41. Roosevelt, *Ranch Life*, 326.

42. Roosevelt, *Ranch Life*, 369.

43. Roosevelt, *Ranch Life*, 280.

44. Roosevelt, *Autobiography*, 88.

45. Roosevelt, *Autobiography*, 125–26. See also Grondahl, *I Rose Like a Rocket*, 148–49.

46. Roosevelt, *Ranch Life*, 371–73. See also Grondahl, *I Rose Like a Rocket*, 162.

47. Roosevelt, *Ranch Life*, 379–98. See also Grondahl, *I Rose Like a Rocket*, 162–63.

48. Grondahl, *I Rose Like a Rocket*, 163–64.

49. Grondahl, *I Rose Like a Rocket*, 160.

50. Quoted in David McCullough, *Mornings on Horseback: The Story of an Extraordinary Family, A Vanished Way of Life, and the Unique Child Who Became Theodore Roosevelt* (New York: Simon and Schuster, 2003), 349–50.

51. Dalton, *Strenuous Life*, 101.

52. Grondahl, *I Rose Like a Rocket*, 165.

53. Grondahl, *I Rose Like a Rocket*, 167.

54. H. W. Brands, *T.R.: The Last Romantic* (New York: Basic Books, 1997), 213–14. See also Theodore Roosevelt, *Thomas Hart Benton*, vol. 7 of *The Works of Theodore Roosevelt*, National Edition (New York: Charles Scribner's Sons, 1926), 232–33.

55. Roosevelt, *Thomas Hart Benton*, 52, 54.

56. Roosevelt, *Thomas Hart Benton*, 53–54.

57. Roosevelt, *Thomas Hart Benton*, 119–20.

58. Roosevelt, *Thomas Hart Benton*, 149–52.

59. Roosevelt, *Thomas Hart Benton*, 102–04.

60. Roosevelt, *Thomas Hart Benton*, 62–64.

61. Roosevelt, *Thomas Hart Benton*, 65.

62. Roosevelt, *Thomas Hart Benton*, 71.

63. Roosevelt, *Thomas Hart Benton*, 75–76.

64. Roosevelt, *Thomas Hart Benton*, 78–80.

65. Theodore Roosevelt, *Gouverneur Morris*, vol. 7 of *The Works of Theodore Roosevelt*, National Edition (New York: Charles Scribner's Sons, 1926), 336–37.

66. Roosevelt, *Gouverneur Morris*, 279–80.

67. Roosevelt, *Gouverneur Morris*, 429–30.

68. Roosevelt, *Gouverneur Morris*, 302.

69. Roosevelt, *Gouverneur Morris*, 321–22.

70. Roosevelt, *Gouverneur Morris*, 323.

71. Roosevelt, *Gouverneur Morris*, 323, 327.

Chapter Four

Hero Tales

As early as 1888, Roosevelt argued that Alexander Hamilton's advocacy of strong central government had to be united with broad popular participation and individual liberty ("the one great truth taught by Jefferson"). An American statesman, Roosevelt explained, had to trust the people and make it his top priority to use the powers of a strong government to secure the rights of all. In the United States, he said, it was "a foregone conclusion" that any party that did not believe in the people would sooner or later lose power and vanish from the political landscape. Thus, Roosevelt criticized the extent to which elites like those represented by Hamilton and Gouverneur Morris alienated the majority of Americans, who did not share the same "habits of refinement and ways of looking at life." Roosevelt declared that the American people may have owed their present form of government to the Federalists, as opposed to the Jeffersonian Republicans, but Jefferson's party offered certain "articles of faith" that were "essential to our national well-being." Once he proved willing to acquiesce to some principles of Federalism, it was inevitable that Jefferson would lead his party to victory, and his government was best, TR argued, when it adhered to Hamiltonian theories of nationalism. Still, Roosevelt concluded, the fact was that Jefferson supported nationalistic principles like a loose interpretation of the Constitution only when it suited his immediate purposes, and Jeffersonian adherents continued to believe in "a strong people and a weak government." It was Abraham Lincoln, Roosevelt believed, who was the first to show "how a strong people might have a strong government and yet remain the freest on earth."[1]

Considering TR's own aristocratic background, it is interesting that he accepted broader democratic participation as early as the 1880s, and this attitude is even better appreciated by comparing Roosevelt with his friend, Henry

Cabot Lodge. Lodge detested corrupt businessmen as much as Roosevelt, but he could not overcome his distaste for the common man. As John Milton Cooper suggests, this difference lay in their contrasting personalities as well as "the breadth of perspective each brought to bear on national problems." While Roosevelt personified exuberance and optimism, Lodge was detached and critical, the epitome of New England cultivation and intellectualism. Undoubtedly, they made "a political odd couple." Still, Roosevelt and Lodge remained close throughout their long political careers, and this is a testament not only to their friendship and mutual respect but also to the basic assumptions about man and government that they shared.[2] As Kathleen Dalton explains, "Both men had had their manhood challenged by working-class toughs in their youth, and both grew up with a fighting edge and a hatred of the effeminacy and 'decrepit dilettantism' they saw in abundance in their own upper class." They were strong nationalists, who admired military might and sought to strengthen America's naval power. Both also admired history's "men of action," especially the heroes of the Civil War generation.[3] Indeed, with the hope of motivating their generation to prove that it was just as patriotic and self-sacrificing as the men of the blue and gray, Roosevelt and Lodge collaborated on a collection of articles entitled *Hero Tales from American History*.

THE HERO TALES

Like *Hunting Trips* and *Ranch Life*, *Hero Tales* is intended to inspire the American people to embrace those moral qualities that Roosevelt sees as indispensable to the good health and survival of a nation. As Lodge himself explains in the Preface, their book is not meant to contribute anything new or novel to historical scholarship. Each article is much too brief, too condensed, to offer anything in the way of original research. Nor is it intended to serve as a text book, for the disconnected subject matter lacks the continuity and completeness necessary to instruct students in the subject of history. Without overtly preaching or moralizing, Roosevelt and Lodge simply allow their descriptions of heroic men and events to speak for themselves, not only to awaken the patriotism of readers but also to inspire them to practice personal discipline, self-reliance, courage, loyalty, and self-sacrifice.[4] The message of the book is simple: because men like George Washington, Stonewall Jackson, Abraham Lincoln, Andrew Jackson, and Daniel Boone embodied all of these virtues, they contributed positively to the development of the United States. Boone, for example, surveyed the country, tilled the soil, cleared forests, built settlements, fought Indians, hunted for his food, and even represented his people in the Virginia House of Burgesses.[5] In short, he was both independent and community-oriented, and Roosevelt suggests that those modern Americans who care for the future prosperity and survival of their country would do well to emulate behavior like his.

As Roosevelt and Lodge understand, merely to assert that it is noble to live honestly, work hard, love one's country, and care for both friend and stranger is not likely to make an indelible impression on the heart and spirit of the reader. Such statements, while recognized by most as truth, will spark only ephemeral attention and interest. On the other hand, the soul of the individual might be transformed by telling of how Captain Craven, aboard his sinking ship in Mobile Bay, threw open the door of the pilothouse and said to his companion, "After you, pilot." The same might be said of Davy Crockett's decision to fight for Texan independence.[6] As Roosevelt writes, Crockett arrived in Texas just when the Mexican army was marching toward San Antonio, and he slipped through the Mexican lines to join the 150 freedom fighters who had gathered in the Alamo. Recognizing that the Alamo was "a mere shell" and "utterly unable to withstand either a bombardment or a regular assault," Crockett knew the risks but nonetheless never wavered in his devotion to freedom and the needs of his fellow Americans. Similarly, Roosevelt adds, the other men who lost their lives there were "wild and ill-disciplined," but also possessed great skill and "iron courage." Never once did they complain about their plight and "whatever doom fate might have in store for them." All were killed, but none surrendered.[7]

During the Civil War, Roosevelt writes, northerner and southerner alike performed many heroic deeds. Certainly, he acknowledges, that great conflict offers many examples of cowardice, treachery, and "barbarous brutality," which "should be set forth by every historian and learned by every statesman and soldier," but its most valuable lessons are the tales of heroism. At Fredericksburg, Roosevelt notes, the Fifth New Hampshire regiment, having lost 186 men out of 300, fell back behind a fence that was within easy range of Confederate rifle fire. When the color guard was shot and the flag fell to the ground, Captain Perry ran out to rescue it. As he reached Old Glory, he was shot through the heart. At that point, Captain Murray made the same attempt and was also killed; so was a third man. Several privates succumbed to the same fate. Roosevelt writes that all of the men were killed close to the flag, and their dead bodies fell across one another. Finally, Lieutenant Nettleton crawled from behind the fence, seized the flag, and brought it back to his men.[8] Like the other subjects of *Hero Tales*, Nettleton and his brothers-in-arms personified patriotism, courage, and concern for a higher good. In TR's view, these are the virtues required for the advancement of civilization. In fact, the Rough Rider remained devoted to them throughout his life.

Men of Action is another example of Roosevelt's belief that the fortunes of great nations are determined by both individual effort and devotion to the common good. Like *Hero Tales*, the book is a collection of sketches that focus upon the notable figures and events in American history. Also included are essays on some of TR's most eminent contemporaries. The papers were written at various points throughout Roosevelt's life, examining the deeds of soldiers, statesmen, explorers, hunters, judges, artists, and naturalists. But all of them suggest that the reader would be wise to adopt the noble qualities that make these different subjects so worthy of attention and veneration.

In the Preface, Roosevelt explains that the public men described in the book were virtuous in both public and private life. While conceding that the private life of a man is "of secondary importance" to his public deeds, Roosevelt hastens to add that the lack of private virtues like fidelity in marriage, punctuality in the payment of debts, and concern for one's neighbors should establish a presumption against a public servant. Perhaps only half-consciously referring to his past, present, and future attempts to lead by setting an inspirational personal example, Roosevelt writes, "One function of any great public leader should be to exert an influence upon the community at large, especially among the young men of the community; and therefore it is idle to say that those interested in the perpetuity of good government should not take into account the fact of a public man's example being something to follow or avoid, even in matters not connected with his direct public services."[9]

Roosevelt writes that Washington and Lincoln were strong, forceful, self-made, and self-sacrificing. According to the Rough Rider, both men recognized a higher law and moral obligation that bound them not only in their relations to their fellow countrymen but also in their relations to all mankind. "Each was willing to pour out the blood of the bravest and best in the land for a high and worthy cause, and each was a practical man, as far removed as possible from the sentimentalist and the doctrinaire. But each lived his life in accordance with a high ideal of right which forbade him to wrong his neighbor, and which when he became head of the state forbade him to inflict international wrong, as it forbade him to inflict private wrong." Roosevelt concludes that, because each left his countrymen "an ennobling memory of a life which achieved great success through rendering far greater service," Washington and Lincoln are the two greatest Presidents the United States has known.[10]

At the same time, Roosevelt argues that one can do a great deal of public good yet hold no public office of any kind, citing George William Curtis as an example. Curtis was a private citizen who took an active and indispensable part in public affairs as a civil service reformer. Not content merely to criticize and talk about the conditions that needed to be changed, he did not shirk the "raw, rough work" associated with "practical politics." For this reason, Roosevelt says, Curtis' criticisms are more worthy of respect than those of overzealous reformers, "who have never themselves tried to do the things that they criticize other people for doing less perfectly than they should." Like TR, Curtis appreciated that there are times when it is necessary to act as a party man, and there are times when it is necessary to work independent of a political party. But, Roosevelt stresses, Curtis' independence was never "malevolent neutrality" or inaction in the face of evil.[11]

In the middle of his Curtis narrative, Roosevelt directs attention toward his own efforts on behalf of civil service reform. Roosevelt proclaims that he has set himself to the task of working for fair play and justice in appointments to government offices, adding that his efforts, like those of Curtis, have been challenged and countered by "the brigades of trained mercenaries," who use money and resources from the public chest to remain entrenched in power. Hoping that readers will join him in his effort to do away with a system that is based on the self-interest of the office-holder, rather than the true needs and interests of the people, Roosevelt reminds them that Curtis never lost sight of the moral imperative to promote merit above spoils in government. Those who admire Curtis' public career, Roosevelt contends, can best pay tribute to his memory by joining in the ongoing effort to perfect the great work that he began.[12]

But, as Roosevelt stresses in other articles, reformers must be careful to couple high-mindedness and determination with practicality and flexibility. Determined to show that it is possible to strike such a balance between idealism and pragmatism, TR discusses the character and accomplishments of the soldiers who fought at Gettysburg. He explains that the Gettysburg battlefield is considered hallowed ground because the soldiers who fought there "combined the power of fealty to a lofty ideal with the power of showing that fealty in hard, practical, common-sense fashion." He adds, "They stood for the life of effort, not the life of ease. They had that love of country, that love of justice, that love of their fellow men, without which power and resourceful efficiency but make a man a danger to his fellows. Yet, in addition thereto, they likewise possessed the power and the efficiency; for otherwise their high purpose would have been barren of result." These men knew not only how to act for themselves but also how to act in cooperation with one another. In his view, they fought not to destroy, but to save liberty; not to overthrow, but to establish the supremacy of the law.[13] Most of all, he concludes, their actions prove that freedom is not a gift that can be enjoyed by those who do not show themselves worthy of it. Freedom enables the intelligent and good man "to do better things than he could do without it," but it also entails responsibility.

Roosevelt advises his readers to recognize the close connection between liberty and responsibility "in every domain of human thought and action." He declares, "Those who desire to be considered fit to enjoy liberty must show that they know how to use it with moderation and justice in peace, and how to fight for it when it is jeopardized by malice of domestic or foreign levy." This, TR says, was the view taken by Lincoln and all of those who participated in the Civil War, and it remains as applicable in an individual's daily life as in a nation's time of great turmoil and stress.[14] Thus, Roosevelt concludes, modern Americans can preserve both their liberty and their greatness only by exercising the virtues of common sense, honesty, fairness, self-restraint, loyalty, and devotion to the common good. Like the men of the Civil War generation, today's Americans must learn how to use liberty "temperately."[15]

As both *Hero Tales* and *Men of Action* demonstrate, Roosevelt possessed a keen understanding of history's inspirational lessons; however, he had not forgotten how to use himself and the experiences of his acquaintances to highlight the ways of proper living, as his book *The Rough Riders* attests. In this work, TR recounts his exploits in the Spanish-American War, and while he does not give the impression that he is a braggart, the tone of the book is so authoritative that it is easy to forget the tens of thousands who also participated in the war.[16] In fact, Roosevelt himself could not help but laugh at humorist Finley Peter Dunne's suggestion that the book be renamed *Alone in Cuba*.[17] Nevertheless, Roosevelt's portrayal of himself as a rugged and courageous leader is well-balanced by a great deal of praise for his gallant and selfless regiment, to whom the volume is dedicated.

It is obvious from various anecdotes that the reader is supposed to feel as much respect and admiration for the Rough Riders as for Roosevelt. Harry Heffner, for example, was mortally wounded through the hips, but he fell without uttering a sound. After his companions propped him up against a tree trunk, Heffner asked to be given his canteen and rifle. He then began shooting and continued to shoot until the line moved forward and he was left alone to die in "the gloomy shade." Roosevelt also discusses the time that he dispatched three of his men to locate part of his wing command. The three men had to expose themselves to severe fire, "but they were not men to whom this mattered." One was killed, but the other two were able to report back to Roosevelt. After they resumed their places on the firing line, Roosevelt noticed that one of the men, Rowland, had blood pouring from his side. Roosevelt ordered him to the hospital, but fifteen minutes later he was back on the firing line, claiming that he could not find the hospital. Roosevelt doubted his story but allowed him to stay until the end of the fight.[18] Later, the doctors decreed that Rowland's wound was serious and ordered him back to the United States.

Rowland waited until nightfall, escaped from the hospital, and made his way back to camp. Roosevelt again decided to let him stay, and Rowland went on to distinguish himself in the fight at San Juan.[19] But perhaps the most heroic was Thomas Isbell, a Cherokee man shot *seven* times in the course of a half an hour (three times in the neck, once in the left thumb, once in the right hip, once in the left hand, and once along his head). Despite his sufferings and the risk to his own life, Isbell refused to leave the firing line.[20]

In addition to these individual vignettes, Roosevelt tells of the many hardships that his entire regiment endured together. Upon being deployed to Cuba, for instance, they were packed tight into troop ships and, for several days, endured heat, "steaming discomfort," cramped space, and forced inaction. Making the best of the situation, the men focused only on improving themselves by rereading books of tactics.[21] After landing on the southern coast of Cuba, Roosevelt led his Rough Riders on a long march to Santiago. The searing temperatures were especially tortuous for the soldiers: "The men were not in very good shape for marching, and moreover they were really horsemen, the majority being cowboys who had never done much walking. The heat was intense and their burdens very heavy. Yet there was very little straggling." In fact, to some of the men, the entire march seemed like "nothing but an enjoyable outing." It was not long until they were attacked at Las Guasinas, and despite the fact that they faced an entrenched and invisible enemy, Roosevelt and his men prevailed. TR suggests that their success was due to courage, hardihood, individual initiative, and mutual support.[22]

For about a week, Roosevelt and his men camped near Las Guasinas, awaiting an assault on Santiago planned for July 1. At 6:30 that morning, the Americans opened fire on the Spanish. Enemy mortars exploded over the Rough Riders, wounding four men. Roosevelt led his regiment down the hillside and took cover in the jungle foliage at the base of Kettle Hill, beyond which stood San Juan Hill and Santiago. During the battle, Roosevelt lost several men but stayed in the saddle of his horse, continuing to be harassed by sniper fire, so that his regiment could see him and know which way he was headed. Finally, Roosevelt received the order "to move forward and support the regulars in the assault on the hills in front." The instant he got the order, TR sprang on his horse, and his "crowded hour" began.[23]

TR explains that, as he was getting the men to move forward, "a curious incident" occurred. "Always," he admits, "when men have been lying down under cover for some time, and are required to advance, there is a little hesitation, each looking to see whether the others are going forward." But, as he rode down the line, shouting the order to move forward, he encountered a man hiding behind a little bush. When Roosevelt ordered him to jump up, the man looked up with hesitation and did nothing. Roosevelt again bade him to rise, jeering him and saying, "Are you afraid to stand up when I am on horse-back?" As Roosevelt spoke, the man suddenly fell forward on his face, a bul-let having just struck him "and gone through him lengthwise." Roosevelt sup-poses that the bullet was intended for him. At any rate, he concludes, "I, who was on horseback in the open, was unhurt, and the man lying flat on the ground in the cover beside me was killed."[24] The implicit lesson is clear: be-cause life is full of ironic twists and turns, there is no guarantee that cow-ardice will assure self-preservation. For this reason, at least, one might as well resign himself to the expectation that he will sacrifice for the sake of others.

Once the Rough Riders reached the top of Kettle Hill, Roosevelt led an ef-fective attack against the Spanish forces on San Juan Hill. After the battle of San Juan, Roosevelt notes, his men trusted each other implicitly and knew that he was ready and willing to share with them every kind of hardship and danger. For his part, Roosevelt "felt utter confidence in them, and would have been more than willing to put them to any task which any crack regiment of the world, at home or abroad, could perform." According to him, the Rough Riders were natural fighters and men of great intelligence, courage, and hardihood.[25] At the same time, he adds, these tough and resolute men were extremely caring and especially determined not to see Roosevelt suffer any hardship at all. TR proudly records, "Whether I had any food or not myself made no difference, as there were sure to be certain troopers, and, indeed, cer-tain troop messes, on the lookout for me. If they had any beans they would send me over a cupful, or I would suddenly receive a present of doughnuts from some ex-roundup cook who had succeeded in obtaining a little flour and sugar, and if a man shot a guinea-hen it was all I could do to make him keep half of it for himself."[26]

In Roosevelt's account, the Rough Riders had learned to cooperate and care for one another, but they never lost their self-reliant spirit. As a whole, he writes, the men disbanded and returned home; "gaunter than when they had enlisted, sometimes weakened by fever or wounds." Still, they were "just as full as ever of sullen, sturdy capacity for self-help; scorning to ask for aid, save what was entirely legitimate in the way of one comrade giving help to another." Examining surgeons marveled at how different the Rough Riders were from so many other regiments. Ordinarily, Roosevelt notes, the surgeons had to be on the lookout for soldiers who faked disability to get out of ser-vice. In the case of the Rough Riders, however, the surgeons had to resist men who, at great risk to their own health and lives, belittled their bodily injuries and refused pensions.[27]

In sum, *The Rough Riders* is a story of how a number of individuals over-came their differences in geography, race, ethnicity, religion, class, education, and experience and learned to work together as one disciplined unit with one selfless purpose: the liberation of a persecuted people. Roosevelt stresses that the regiment included college graduates, cowboys, hunters, soldiers, farmers, miners, Indians, blacks, whites, northerners, southerners, easterners, and westerners. Some of the men were professional gamblers, while others were devout clergymen. Despite their many differences, Roosevelt declares, all of them possessed a similar hardihood and thirst for adventure—they were physically fit, tough, patriotic, and loyal.[28] Most were accustomed to rugged conditions, fighting, and exploring the unknown. In these respects, Roosevelt explains, they were "ready made" soldiers. What they lacked originally was the ability to take orders and work together. Before long, though, they came to understand that commanders like TR did not insist upon discipline to humiliate them but were as anxious to learn their own duties as they were to have the soldiers learn theirs.[29]

All of TR's hero tales, from the volume of that name through *The Rough Riders*, are lessons in democratic citizenship. Actions should be principled as well as practical. They should be guided by a higher purpose, one larger than the individual—saving the Union, securing freedom, restoring popular control of government. Roosevelt saw no heroism in the reformer who criticized but refrained from action, just as there was no heroism in simply amassing a great personal and private wealth (especially if it came at the expense of the public interest). Heroism—and the hope for America's future—lay in men acting on principle for high purpose in the public realm. It was an enduring connection to which Roosevelt returned repeatedly in the public "sermons" that marked his life and career.

THE FRONTIER SPIRIT

Like *The Rough Riders*, *The Wilderness Hunter* is another example of how Roosevelt uses stories of his and others' personal experiences to promote his particular conception of the ideal American citizen. The theme of this book, the third of Roosevelt's western accounts, is the nobility of hunting, which permits the development of the heroic qualities that are, in TR's opinion, essential to a nation's survival. On the hunt, TR says, a man has the opportunity to test and develop his nerve reactions, muscular coordination, observation, judgment, hardiness, indifference to fatigue and all sorts of environmental discomforts, endurance, determination, patience, and optimism about his chances for success. Roosevelt emphasizes that the successful hunter must possess all of these qualities, and their perfection is solely dependent upon practice. Moreover, TR claims that he tries to exemplify this kind of sportsmanship in both the wilderness and everyday life, and he hopes that other

Americans will as well. In short, *The Wilderness Hunter* is not simply an account of game pursued and killed. Rather, it is a collection of lessons about
what it takes to be a valuable member of society. In TR's view, the cultivation of *the frontier spirit* is essential to both individual and national progress.

According to Roosevelt, the greatest leaders in American history—
Washington, Lincoln, and Jackson—all tested themselves first as hunters.
Because hunting entails "the exercise of daring, and the endurance of toil
and hardship," it taught these men to lead and gave them the qualities
needed to be national heroes.[30] Washington, in particular, was quite fond of
hunting. Of Washington, Roosevelt writes, "Essentially the representative
of all that is best in our national life, standing high as a general, high as a
statesman, and highest of all as a man, he could never have been what he
was had he not taken delight in feats of hardihood, of daring, and of bodily process."[31] Hunting offered Washington "the best possible training for
war," and the founding father did not undervalue either the pleasure or the
real worth of outdoor sport. Roosevelt concludes, "The qualities of heart,
mind, and body which made him delight in the hunting-field, and which he
there exercised and developed, stood him in good stead in many a long
campaign and on many a stricken field; they helped to build that stern capacity for leadership in war which he showed alike through the bitter woe
of the winter at Valley Forge, on the night when he ferried his men across
the half-frozen Delaware to the overthrow of the German mercenaries at
Trenton, and in the brilliant feats of arms whereof the outcome was the de-
cisive victory of Yorktown."[32]

Throughout his book, Roosevelt frequently mentions the kind of men with
whom he was "intimately thrown" during his life on the frontier. Specifically,
he writes that most of those he had known in the Dakota Territory were "good
fellows, hard-working, brave, resolute, and truthful." They were usually tol-
erant and not inclined to inquire too much about a man's past or criticize him
too harshly for failing to "discriminate in finer ethical questions." The cowboy "saw nothing out of the way in the fact that he had himself been a road-
agent, a professional gambler, and a desperado at different stages of his career. On the other hand, he did not in the least hold it against any one that he
had always acted within the law." Roosevelt adds that most neither boasted of
nor apologized for their past misdeeds. At the same time, he observes, these
were stern men who had an uncompromising sense of right and wrong and
were quick to punish such vile offenses as rape, robbing a friend, and "murder under circumstances of cowardice and treachery." They were both hos-
pitable and humorous and "put unlimited faith in the unknown and untried."
Roosevelt concludes that they possessed "an admirable mixture of adventur-
ousness, frugality, and ready adaptability to circumstances."[33]

Still, he laments, the life of the cowboy is evanescent, "and when it has vanished there can be no real substitute." In his opinion, private game preserves hardly simulate the experience of hunting and frontier life. As a result, they offer an individual little or no chance to cultivate the noble qualities. This is why Roosevelt suggests the need to pass a rigid system of game laws and establish, under state control, great national forest reserves, which would also be breeding grounds and nurseries for wild game. As much as possible, he maintains, the American people should save their frontier and thereby preserve a way of life that offers all individuals the chance for a fresh start because of its "rugged and stalwart democracy" where "every man stands for what he actually is and can show himself to be."[34] Roosevelt's message is simply that America needs more western vigor, for the way of the West tends to enhance the very best personal qualities, as it did in his case.

Without a doubt, the advice given by Roosevelt in *The Wilderness Hunter* is based on a belief that the American frontier, specifically the pioneers' self-reliant struggle to conquer the wilderness, has given the entire nation its distinct and exceptional character. It is a theme to be found also in *Hunting Trips*, *Ranch Life*, and even the first chapter of *Thomas Hart Benton*. But a fourth book, *The Winning of the West*, is the most ambitious and comprehensive effort to define and explore the pioneering spirit that makes America so unique. According to Edmund Morris, the introduction alone shows Roosevelt's "breadth of mind" more clearly than anything else written prior to his presidency. "All of his previous books had been, in a sense, sketches for this one, just as his subsequent books were postscripts to it."[35]

In the first chapter of the first volume, Roosevelt chronicles the centuries-long colonization of America, differentiating between the English and Spanish conquests. While the English either exterminated or assimilated the Indians of America, the Spaniards "simply sat down in the midst of a much more numerous aboriginal population." Roosevelt notes that there was little displacement of the indigenous population, and the Indians of Peru and Mexico, while keeping certain customs and habits of their own, learned the language and adopted the laws, religion, customs, and governing system of the Spanish. Roosevelt also distinguishes between the English conquest of India and Africa and its conquest of the United States and Canada. In the latter two cases, he contends, large tracts of fertile land, a temperate climate, and a thinly peopled country ensured more successful settlement.[36]

Of course, he adds, the Indians of North America presented a formidable resistance to the settlement of the United States and Canada, but the coming of the whites could not be prevented. Once the Americans won their independence from Great Britain, they began a rapid movement across the American continent, from the Alleghenies to the Pacific. In doing so, they not only dispossessed the Indian tribes but also won the land from its European occupiers.[37] Roosevelt suggests that the rapidity with which the American people settled the West in the decades after the Revolutionary War was aided by the fact that the American people acted as a nation rather than "a loose assemblage of petty seaboard communities." Only as a united people were the Americans able to conquer the western lands, and Roosevelt believes all other matters, except the preservation of the Union and the emancipation of slaves, "have been of subordinate importance when compared with the great question of how rapidly and how completely they were to subjugate that part of their continent lying between the eastern mountains and the Pacific."[38]

Roosevelt, however, stresses that the manner in which the American people extended their borders differed depending on where the territory was located. On the one hand, he explains, the Northwest Territory was acquired and opened by the national government, which defeated many Indian tribes, surveyed the land, issued grants, and organized the new communities. Because the title to the land and the power to rule over it belonged to Congress, the northwestern settlers did not engage in long disputes over land rights. In contrast, Roosevelt continues, the southwestern settlements were opened by self-reliant individuals and without the assistance and supervision of either the national government or their parent states. For over a quarter of a century, the southwestern frontiersmen cleared their own land, supplied themselves, raised their own armies, fought for their soil, and governed themselves.[39] After years of hard fighting with the Indians, French, and Spanish, they managed to conquer the Southwest. Roosevelt concludes, "They were led by no one commander; they acted under orders from neither King nor Congress; they were not carrying out the plans of any far-sighted leader. In obedience to the instincts working half blindly within their breasts, spurred ever onward by the fierce desires of their eager hearts, they made in the wilderness homes for their children, and by doing so wrought out the destinies of a continental nation."[40]

In chapter after chapter, Roosevelt details the combat between the white settlers and their Indian foes, acknowledging the virtue and savagery of both sides. He writes that the frontier settlers were "a stern race of freemen who toiled hard, endured greatly and fronted adversity bravely, who prized strength and courage and good faith, whose wives were chaste, who were generous and loyal to their friends." But, he adds, these admirable qualities are "interspersed by deeds of the foulest and most wanton aggression, the darkest treachery, the most revolting cruelty."[41] Elsewhere, he says of the white settlers: "A grim, stern people, strong and simple, powerful for good and evil, swayed by gusts of stormy passion, the love of freedom rooted in their very hearts' core. Their lives were harsh and narrow, they gained their bread by their blood and sweat in the unending struggle with the wild ruggedness of nature. They suffered terrible injuries at the hands of the red men and on their foes they waged a terrible warfare in return. They were relentless, revengeful, suspicious, knowing neither truth nor pity, they were also upright, resolute, and fearless, loyal to their friends and devoted to their country."[42]

Despite their many failings, Roosevelt concludes that the white American settlers were the best suited to conquer the wilderness, and the former cowboy cannot help but convey his belief in the dignity and heroism of their western way of life. The lesson of his book is difficult to miss: a free land can only be developed and sustained by a free-spirited people. As he declares, "The whole character of the westward movement, the methods of warfare, of settlement and government, were determined by the extreme and defiant individualism of the backwoodsmen, their inborn independence and self-reliance, and their intensely democratic spirit." Reluctant to give too much comfort to the champions of rugged and unrestrained individualism, however, Roosevelt reminds his readers that "a sound common sense and capacity for combination" tempered the individualism of the frontiersmen. He stresses, "The first hunters might have come alone or in couples, but the actual colonization was done not by individuals, but by groups of individuals."[43] These collectivist sentiments shaped Roosevelt's political thought and actions in the years preceding, during, and after his presidency.

Any discussion of *The Winning of the West* cannot ignore the fact that Roosevelt sees the brutal warfare between the whites and Indians as "elemental in its consequences to the future of the world." Though savage and barbaric (the kind of war that was waged "in the ages of bronze and iron"), the white man's war with the Indians was "ultimately righteous." "The rude, fierce settler who drove the savage from the land lays all civilized mankind under a debt to him," Roosevelt declares. "American and Indian, Boer and Zulu, Cossack and Tartar, New Zealander and Maori," he writes, "in each case the victor, horrible though many of his deeds are, has laid deep the foundations for the future greatness of a mighty people, [and] it is of incalculable importance that America, Australia, and Siberia should pass out of the hand of their red, black, and yellow aboriginal owners, and become the heritage of the dominant world races."[44] For Roosevelt, then, the white man's victory over the Indians laid the foundation necessary to refine the aborigine, so that he can partake in every opportunity available to the superior race. In other words, the Indian, once conquered and civilized, is free to challenge and beat the white man in any field of endeavor. Edmund Morris suggests that nothing gave TR more satisfaction "than to see such a reversal, for he admired individual achievement above all things." In *The Winning of the West*, Roosevelt makes clear his belief that any black man or Indian who is willing to try, work hard, and persevere is superior to the white man who either refuses to try or fails.[45] It is in this way that Roosevelt envisions the steady betterment of America's minority population. Still, TR's emphasis on race, specifically his talk of superior and inferior races, troubles many modern readers—and rightfully so. Fortunately, subsequent studies of the West, such as those of Frederick Jackson Turner, contain more nuance, explaining how environment continually forced the American settlers to adapt themselves to new opportunities and various dangers that included, among other things, Indian warfare.[46]

Roosevelt's focus on racial distinctions and race warfare cannot be ignored, but it should not obscure the main thesis of his work: America's rugged and individualistic identity is the direct result of its western experience. Moreover, the relevant point for a discussion of TR's views on the relationship between individualism and collectivism is that the book reveals a strong faith in progress, a pragmatic belief that American institutions and ideals are the result of experience, a preference for nationalism over sectionalism, an emphasis on the transformative power of individualism, and a certainty that unchecked and reckless individualism can be tempered by a larger communal awareness and concern. In short, *The Winning of the West* not only fit the individualistic temper of the late nineteenth century but also gave support to the growing forces of Progressivism.

THE STRENUOUS LIFE

For their part, the essays and addresses collected under the title *The Strenuous Life* magnify Roosevelt's view that the interests of the individual and the community need not be opposed to one another. In it, he contends that individualism and collectivism are two halves of the same whole; each is incomplete without the other. Roosevelt explains that, unless it is backed by such individualistic values as hard work, personal responsibility, and self-restraint, the spirit of compassion can all too easily excuse idleness and irresponsibility. On the other hand, he stresses that an excessive individualism, unrestrained by a feeling of brotherhood and obligation to the rest of the community, breeds selfishness and permits the exploitation of the weak.[47] By themselves, then, both "hard-headed" individualism and "soft-headed" collectivism undermine social stability. It is a point that Roosevelt unwaveringly repeats through most of the articles in *The Strenuous Life*.

Specifically, Roosevelt argues that "fellow-feeling, sympathy in the broadest sense, is the most important factor in producing a healthy political and social life. Neither our national nor our local civic life can be what it should be unless it is marked by the fellow-feeling, the mutual kindness, the mutual respect, the sense of common duties and common interests, which arise when men take the trouble to understand one another, and to associate together for a common object."[48] Roosevelt asserts that the great political, economic, and social problems faced by this country stem from the failure to appreciate one another's point of view. Men, he says, cannot afford to remain isolated and view the majority of their fellow-citizens with indifference. Roosevelt is certain that, if people of all races, classes, and creeds have the opportunity to realize their common motives, by working together for a common good, there will be more respect and fair play for all.

Using himself as an example that might inspire his audience, Roosevelt recalls the men with whom he interacted in cattle country. Initially, in working with other ranch-hands, he was impressed by the absence of such devoted workers in the eastern parts of the country. Later, he got to know some of the local farmers, after which it was not long before he viewed them as favorably as his "beloved cowmen." It was this, Roosevelt says, that made him conclude that the farmers formed the real backbone of the country. Later, he was "thrown into intimate contact with railroad men" and formed a favorable impression of this group. Eventually added to the pedestal were carpenters, blacksmiths, and mechanics. "By that time," Roosevelt observes, "it began to dawn on me that the difference was not in the men but in my own point of view, and that if any man is thrown into close contact with any large body of our fellow-citizens it is apt to be the man's own fault if he does not grow to feel for them a very hearty regard and, moreover, grow to understand that on the great questions that lie at the root of human well-being, he and they feel alike." TR suggests that his fellow citizens must likewise realize that all Americans have the same fundamental needs, aspirations, and interests. For Roosevelt, it is imperative that individuals work in combination for a common good, and when individuals are unable to effect needed change, it becomes the responsibility of the state to act on behalf of the public interest.[49]

Of course, Roosevelt stresses, one cannot help a man who is unwilling to help himself. "The greatest possible good can be done by the extension of a helping hand at the right moment, but the attempt to carry anyone permanently can end in nothing but harm."[50] Roosevelt asserts that, unless the individual is permitted to exercise his own intelligence, thrift, energy, and self-mastery, he will know nothing of self-respect. The best that government can do is "provide against injustice, and then let the individual rise and fall on his own merits." Thus, the gross misconduct of individuals and corporations must be countered by the regulatory powers of the state, but once every individual has been saved from the tyranny and exploitations of other men, his own qualities of body and mind must determine success or failure in life.[51] As Roosevelt observes, "The fundamental law of healthy political life in this great republic is that each man shall in deed, and not merely in word, be treated strictly on his worth as a man; that each shall do full justice to his fellow, and in return shall exact full justice from him."[52]

Roosevelt sees life as work, but work, far from being a hardship, can be "a great blessing," provided it is experienced under conditions that preserve a man's self-respect by allowing him to develop his character and receive rewards in proportion to his merit. In Roosevelt's eyes, the idle man—rich or poor—is a useless and "noxious" member of the community, and no one should be excused for failing to give his or her full service to the rest of society. This service, TR explains, can be rendered in a variety of ways—in art, in literature, in philanthropy, as a statesman, or as a solider. Regardless, he says, all citizens, but especially the wealthy and educated, to whom much has been given, are "honor bound" to work not only for themselves but also for others. Roosevelt stresses that each and every American has a duty to himself as well as to his family, his community, and his country. Simply put, self-help and self-sacrifice are not mutually exclusive.[53]

The great social and industrial developments of the last half-century may have made the conditions of life more complex and puzzling, but the only way to weather such change, according to Roosevelt, is to cling to such "hum-drum" qualities as honesty, fairness, courage, thrift, industry, common sense, sympathy, and "fellow-feeling." He regards a nation as the aggregate of all the individuals comprising it, and each individual improves the nation when he wrongs no other, tolerates no injustice on the part of others, and demonstrates both a capacity for self-help and a readiness to give assistance to those who stumble on the path of life.[54] "On the whole," Roosevelt declares, "we shall all go up or go down together. Some may go up or go down further than others, but, disregarding special exceptions, the rule is that we must all share in common something of whatever adversity or whatever prosperity is in store for the nation as a whole." We can best help ourselves, Roosevelt maintains, not at the expense of others, but by working together for the values of justice and fair play.[55] With mass industrialization and the concentration of wealth, TR explains, the forces of evil have been strengthened; therefore, it is necessary for our self-preservation that we should cooperate so as to strengthen the forces for good. No one can do everything necessary to achieve social and economic reform, "but each of us can do something, and the aggregate of these somethings will be very considerable." Most Americans, Roosevelt believes, do not seek either charity or sentimentality; rather, they simply wish to strike some sort of balance between individuality and cooperation—that is, to give and receive support without having to sacrifice their independence and self-respect.[56]

As TR argues in "The City in Modern Life," it is not desirable to have either unrestricted individualism or "untempered" collectivism. The demands on modern government call for "a system of mixed individualism and collectivism." Furthermore, he suggests, the decision of whether to increase or decrease the power of the state at the expense of individual activity is less a matter of theory than of practical expediency. Roosevelt contends that paid police and fire departments are manifestations of state Socialism, but the absolute necessity of these public services allows us to overlook this fact. "The fact that such departments are absolutely necessary is sufficient to show that we need not be frightened from further experiments by any fear of the dangers of collectivism in the abstract; and on the other hand, their success does not afford the least justification for impairing the power of the individual where that power can be properly exercised." In Roosevelt's opinion, all that can be said regarding how to reconcile individualism with the responsibility of the government to act in certain aspects of life is that the individual must be left free to pursue happiness as he sees fit, so long as he does not infringe upon the lives and rights of others; however, economic reward should be proportional to effort and ability, as this encourages enterprise, thrift, industry, and sobriety. Of course, he concludes, wherever it is found, by practice and experimentation, or by the failure of individualistic methods, that collectivism and state interference are both wise and necessary, then this course of action must be pursued.[57]

The lessons implicit in Roosevelt's nonpolitical writings are thus basic to and inform his more explicitly "political" thought. Among these is the importance of individualism and the moral responsibility for one's self and one's achievements. Roosevelt's writings also emphasize community and the importance of joint endeavors with one's fellows. He clearly uses himself and the experiences of his acquaintances to highlight the ways of proper living. *The Rough Riders* and *The Wilderness Hunter* are good examples of this. Recall that the former book is a story of how a number of individuals overcame various differences and learned to care for one another. At the same time, they never lost their self-reliant spirit. But TR also had a keen understanding of history's inspirational lessons. Writings like *Hero Tales* and *Men of Action* are intended to inspire the American people to embrace the independent and community-oriented qualities that he regards as indispensable to the good health and survival of a nation. Even *The Winning of the West*, which stresses that the pioneers' self-reliant struggle to conquer the American wilderness gave this nation its independent character, suggests that individualism must be tempered by a larger communal concern. This leads to Roosevelt's most important lesson: the need for a mixed society. For him, neither individualism nor collectivism alone will achieve the good society. While individual success ultimately depends on one's intelligence, thrift, energy, and self-mastery, Roosevelt believes that society has an obligation to assure equal opportunity by removing economic obstacles and protecting individuals from the gross misconduct and exploitations of others. Roosevelt's experiences on the frontier—its ever-changing and multidimensional development—made him more receptive to the idea that American industrialism must also evolve, and that the people acting collectively through government could play a constructive role and be a positive force in that evolution.

Roosevelt maintained that "the sphere of the state's action should be extended very cautiously, and so far as possible only when and where it will not crush out healthy individual initiative," but at the same time, he believed that positive state action was sometimes needed.[58] Where individual solutions to political, economic, and social problems proved insufficient, a reformer had to be willing to extend or strengthen the regulatory powers of government. TR's advocacy of statutory and regulatory approaches to dealing with problems that seemed beyond the reach of private solutions was the other part of his attempt to redefine American individualism. As the governor of New York, he had a brief opportunity to give some tangible expression to this vision, and references to these public actions will be made in the next chapter. Nevertheless, Roosevelt quickly alienated conservative leaders like Thomas Platt, the boss of New York's Republican organization and former Roscoe Conkling ally, who used the vice presidency to get the young reformer out of New York after only two years. It appeared that Roosevelt was destined for political irrelevance. In less than a year, however, the assassination of President William McKinley placed the full power of the presidency at TR's disposal, giving him the ultimate opportunity to lead the entire nation toward his distinctive third way.

NOTES

1. Theodore Roosevelt, *Gouverneur Morris*, vol. 7 of *The Works of Theodore Roosevelt*, National Edition (New York: Charles Scribner's Sons, 1926), 323, 327, 443.

2. John Milton Cooper, *The Warrior and the Priest: Woodrow Wilson and Theodore Roosevelt* (Cambridge: Belknap Press, 1997), 41–42.

3. Kathleen Dalton, *Theodore Roosevelt: A Strenuous Life* (New York: Vintage Books, 2002), 94.

4. See Henry Cabot Lodge, "The Hero Tales," in *Hero Tales from American History*, vol. 10 of *The Works of Theodore Roosevelt*, National Edition (New York: Charles Scribner's Sons, 1926), xv–xvi.

5. Theodore Roosevelt, "Daniel Boone and the Founding of Kentucky," in *Hero Tales from American History*, vol. 10 of *The Works of Theodore Roosevelt*, National Edition (New York: Charles Scribner's Sons, 1926), 13–17.

6. See Lodge, "The Hero Tales," xvi–xvii.

7. Theodore Roosevelt, "Remember the Alamo," in *Hero Tales from American History*, vol. 10 of *The Works of Theodore Roosevelt*, National Edition (New York: Charles Scribner's Sons, 1926), at 85–87.

8. Theodore Roosevelt, "The Flag–Bearer," in *Hero Tales from American History*, vol. 10 of *The Works of Theodore Roosevelt*, National Edition (New York: Charles Scribner's Sons, 1926), 97–98.

9. Theodore Roosevelt, "Preface," in *Men of Action*, vol. 11 of *The Works of Theodore Roosevelt*, National Edition (New York: Charles Scribner's Sons, 1926), 183.

10. Roosevelt, "Preface," 184–85.

11. Theodore Roosevelt, "George William Curtis," in *Men of Action*, vol. 11 of *The Works of Theodore Roosevelt*, National Edition (New York: Charles Scribner's Sons, 1926), 227–29.

12. Roosevelt, "George William Curtis," 232–34.

13. Theodore Roosevelt, "The Men of Gettysburg," in *Men of Action*, vol. 11 of *The Works of Theodore Roosevelt*, National Edition (New York: Charles Scribner's Sons, 1926), 327.

14. Roosevelt, "The Men of Gettysburg," 326.

15. Roosevelt, "The Men of Gettysburg," 328.

16. H. W. Brands, *T.R.: The Last Romantic* (New York: Basic Books, 1997), 374.

17. Brands, *The Last Romantic*, 376.

18. Theodore Roosevelt, *The Rough Riders*, vol. 11 of *The Works of Theodore Roosevelt*, National Edition (New York: Charles Scribner's Sons, 1926), 60–61.

19. Roosevelt, *The Rough Riders*, 70.

20. Roosevelt, *The Rough Riders*, 68–69.

21. Roosevelt, *The Rough Riders*, 41–42.

22. Roosevelt, *The Rough Riders*, 49–51, 71.

23. Paul Grondahl, *I Rose Like a Rocket: The Political Education of Theodore Roosevelt* (New York: Free Press, 2004), 269; Roosevelt, *The Rough Riders*, 81.

24. Roosevelt, *The Rough Riders*, 82.

25. Roosevelt, *The Rough Riders*, 116–17.

26. Roosevelt, *The Rough Riders*, 126–27.

27. Roosevelt, *The Rough Riders*, 160–61.

28. Roosevelt, *The Rough Riders*, 14–15.

29. Roosevelt, *The Rough Riders*, 20, 22.

30. Theodore Roosevelt, *The Wilderness Hunter*, vol. 2 of *The Works of Theodore Roosevelt*, National Edition (New York: Charles Scribner's Sons, 1926), 358–59.

31. Roosevelt, *The Wilderness Hunter*, 361.

32. Roosevelt, *The Wilderness Hunter*, 366.

33. Roosevelt, *The Wilderness Hunter*, 326, 330–31.

34. Roosevelt, *The Wilderness Hunter*, 353–54.

35. Edmund Morris, *The Rise of Theodore Roosevelt* (New York: The Modern Library, 2001), 474. For a thoughtful and concise summary of *The Winning of the West*, which I found helpful, see Morris, *The Rise of Theodore Roosevelt*, 474–79.

36. Theodore Roosevelt, *The Winning of the West I*, vol. 8 of *The Works of Theodore Roosevelt*, National Edition (New York: Charles Scribner's Sons, 1926), 10–12.

37. Roosevelt, *The Winning of the West I*, 14–15.

38. Roosevelt, *The Winning of the West I*, 16–18.

39. Roosevelt, *The Winning of the West I*, 19–20.

40. Roosevelt, *The Winning of the West I*, 21–22.

41. Roosevelt, *The Winning of the West I*, 76–77.

42. Roosevelt, *The Winning of the West I*, 108.

43. Theodore Roosevelt, *The Winning of the West II*, vol. 9 of *The Works of Theodore Roosevelt*, National Edition (New York: Charles Scribner's Sons, 1926), 12–13.

44. Roosevelt, *The Winning of the West II*, 57–58.

45. Morris, *The Rise of Theodore Roosevelt*, 477.

46. Morris, *The Rise of Theodore Roosevelt*, 478. See also Frederick Jackson Turner, *The Frontier in American History* (New York: Henry Holt and Company, 1953); Ralph Henry Gabriel, *The Course of American Democratic Thought* (New York: Ronald Press Company, 1956), 318–23.

47. Theodore Roosevelt, "Christian Citizenship," in *The Strenuous Life*, vol. 13 of *The Works of Theodore Roosevelt*, National Edition (New York: Charles Scribner's Sons, 1926), 495.

48. Theodore Roosevelt, "Fellow–Feeling as a Political Factor," in *The Strenuous Life*, vol. 13 of *The Works of Theodore Roosevelt*, National Edition (New York: Charles Scribner's Sons, 1926), 355.

49. Theodore Roosevelt, "The Labor Question," in *The Strenuous Life*, vol. 13 of *The Works of Theodore Roosevelt*, National Edition (New York: Charles Scribner's Sons, 1926), 482–84.

50. Theodore Roosevelt, "Civic Helpfulness," in *The Strenuous Life*, vol. 13 of *The Works of Theodore Roosevelt*, National Edition (New York: Charles Scribner's Sons, 1926), 380.

51. Theodore Roosevelt, "Promise and Performance," in *The Strenuous Life*, vol. 13 of *The Works of Theodore Roosevelt*, National Edition (New York: Charles Scribner's Sons, 1926), 398.

52. Roosevelt, "The Labor Question," 481.

53. Roosevelt, "The Labor Question," 487–88.

54. Roosevelt, "The Labor Question," 489.

55. Roosevelt, "The Labor Question," 491.

56. Roosevelt, "Christian Citizenship," 494–95.

57. Theodore Roosevelt, "The City in Modern Life," in *Literary Essays*, vol. 12 of *The Works of Theodore Roosevelt*, National Edition (New York: Scribner's Sons, 1926), 225–26.

58. Roosevelt, "Christian Citizenship," 494.

Chapter Five

The Square Deal

The "Square Deal" is the label given to the presidential program of Theodore Roosevelt. At its most general level, the Square Deal was a series of decisions and policies that increased the administrative power of the national government. It was rooted in Roosevelt's belief that the entire community should use its collective power, including the institutions of the government, to help individuals do what they were unable to do for themselves. In TR's view, the public had no responsibility to carry the man who chose to give up, but it was obligated to assure that the worthy man had a chance to show his worth. It was obvious to Roosevelt that American workers in the early twentieth century faced different conditions from those that greeted their counterparts in the eighteenth and nineteenth centuries. In those earlier times, individual fortunes were smaller, wealth was not combined to create business monopolies, the majority of the people lived in rural areas, and individual employees bargained with individual employers, not with gigantic corporate entities. But, by the twentieth century, society was much more complicated and interdependent, and the nation needed new laws and new approaches to deal with these changes. Thus, Roosevelt sought to assure that the national government had the regulatory power to control for corporate misconduct. He also promoted the conservation of natural resources for the benefit of all people and supported the right of American workers to organize and engage in collective bargaining. Put simply, the Square Deal was TR's view of what the government should do to serve the public interest. At the same time, he clearly believed that the government could not and should not do it all. Beyond the Square Deal was the responsibility of the individual to take initiative and work for his own success in the race of life.

THE "AGE OF COMBINATION"

The problems posed by large-scale industrialization were the central issues of Theodore Roosevelt's presidency. By the time he assumed office, in September 1901, many American businessmen had created "vertically integrated firms" that controlled every aspect of their respective industries, from the extraction of raw materials to the production of finished goods, marketing, sales, and service. "Captain" Frederick Pabst, for instance, not only brewed beer and had temperature-controlled cars to transport his product all over the United States but also owned his own timberlands, barrel plants, and saloons. In addition, these vast corporations began to join together in interlocking directorates by assigning the voting rights of a majority of stockholders in each corporation to a single group of trustees. Their intent was to reduce, even eliminate, economic competition, which had been devastating to them during the depression of the 1890s. In the decade prior to 1900, many large firms, desperate to cover extremely high costs of production, had cut their prices to unprecedented levels. Forbidden from joining together in pools and selling agencies to stop such harmful competition, they decided to merge.

Between 1897 and 1904, 1,800 companies merged into 157. As Michael McGerr explains, vertical integration, coupled with this "horizontal integration" of firms in the same business, "changed the face of the American economy." To be sure, small businesses were not completely eliminated by the giant corporations, nor did the latter dominate every part of the economy. Nevertheless, the trusts commanded key sectors of the economy, including food products, petroleum, fabricated metals, and lumber. And, as McGerr notes, "no one knew whether or not the merger movement would stop."[1]

While most Americans were impressed by the size and efficiency of these new corporations, they could not help but fear their growing power. If corporations could create monopolies that restrained competition, then they could overcharge consumers to make larger profits. This was, after all, the major reason for the creation of trusts in the first place, though the defenders of these combinations argued that consolidation meant greater efficiency, lower prices, and a higher standard of living, and to some extent, this was the case. Not only did the combinations provide an assortment of new goods and services, often at lower costs, but they also offered greater opportunities and prosperity to investors, managers, and even some wage earners. Yet the fact was that these large-scale corporations had it within their power to hurt consumers by raising the price of goods; to eliminate small business by reducing the price of goods and services; to undermine the prosperity and independence of farmers and businessmen by raising both railroad rates and the cost of raw materials; and to increase the despair of the working class by cutting wages and demanding more work.[2]

The new economic system had produced a massive industrial work force, but this had not meant prosperity and greater freedom for more people. The depression of the 1890s kept most of the working class in or near poverty. In addition, while skilled craftsmen in certain industries retained some control over some aspects of production, such as work rules, output quotas, and the training of apprentices, this economic freedom applied to only a small portion of the industrial workforce. Most workers were unskilled, easily expendable, and therefore with little or no autonomy. Low pay and poverty was known to drive women to prostitution; child labor was becoming a more serious problem than ever; industrial accidents were common; and workplace conditions were commonly dark, hot in the summer, cold in the winter, and unsanitary. Moreover, American laborers were forced to compete with unrestricted immigration, which meant lower wages for all but greater profits for the millionaires, who not only had a total income equal to that of the bottom half of the population but also owned more property than the remaining ninety-nine percent. In 1900, for example, Andrew Carnegie earned an estimated $23 million. During the previous five years, his income had averaged $10 million a year, but neither he nor anyone else paid taxes on income, because there was no direct tax of income.[3]

Many businessmen, politicians, economists, and social scientists saw the concentration of wealth and capital as a natural by-product of an ever-expanding mass market in which "the modern corporation has replaced the independent producer as the driving force of economic change." Attempting to justify the new order, economists maintained that wages were determined by the iron law of supply and demand and that wealth rightly belonged to those with the vision and ability to satisfy the needs and demands of consumers. Language adapted from the science of Charles Darwin—"natural selection," "the struggle for existence," and "the survival of the fittest"—reinforced the laissez-faire (or "let it be") outlook of the time. Theories like Social Darwinism appealed to American notions of individualism but were regarded by many as incapable of meeting the challenges posed by the industrial age.[4]

But laissez-faire was only one of five approaches to the problem of big business in the early twentieth century. Many advocated *Socialism*, or public ownership of the means of production. Like laissez-faire, Socialism was an extreme solution to the problem of big business, and despite their obvious differences, these two schools of thought shared some interesting similarities: both accepted large-scale business, and both were likely to lead to the end of competitive capitalism. By 1900, some municipalities even permitted the public ownership of so-called natural monopolies like water works and gas plants. Never in American history was the Socialistic ideal more popular, yet it was ultimately deemed too radical by a society that valued individual liberty, and whose governing institutions were rooted in a respect for the sanctity of private property.[5]

Between the extremes of laissez-faire and Socialism were three Progressive solutions: antitrust, regulation, and compensation. *Antitrust* would limit the power of big business and preserve competition by using the power of the federal government, under the Sherman Act of 1890, to break up big corporations. The problem with the Sherman Act, however, was that the Supreme Court had weakened its antitrust provisions by applying them only to those instances in which it could be demonstrated that businesses combined with the clear intent of restricting competition unreasonably. Moreover, most Americans, like the Court, were concerned about the extent to which the government's antitrust actions infringed on personal freedom and private property rights. The same could be said for *regulation*, which would permit the continued existence of the trusts but rely on governmental standards and oversight to assure that these combinations did not harm society. Finally, *compensation* accepted the existence of large-scale businesses but would tax them and use the revenue to counter their harmful effects on society. In the end, compensation proved to be too limited in its effects, for most Americans were unwilling to support the kind of taxes that would effectively break up big businesses, or at least alter their practices. As McGerr notes, the first corporate tax, adopted in 1909, "claimed only a tiny portion of corporate revenues."[6]

ROOSEVELT'S BELIEF IN CORPORATE REGULATION

Roosevelt came to be known as the "trust buster," but he was, in principle, no enemy of the trusts. There were, in his view, good trusts and bad trusts, the latter being those that ignored the public interest. He worked to strengthen the regulatory power of the federal government to make it a coequal force in the economic arena. This, he believed, was the most effective way to assure that big business did not ignore or undermine the public interest.[7] As he explains in his Fifth Annual Message to Congress, "I am in no sense hostile to corporations. This is an age of combination, and any effort to prevent all combination will be not only useless, but in the end vicious, because of the contempt for law which the failure to enforce law inevitably produces." The American people, he agrees, should recognize that corporations do a great deal of good, for they attract to their service many intelligent, energetic, and devoted individuals. Still, he adds, absent any restraint by government, some corporate officers and directors might use their energies "not in ways that are for the common good, but in ways that tell against this common good." Roosevelt believes that both corporations and trade unions are here to stay. "Each can do and has done great good. Each should be favored so long as it does good. But each should be sharply checked where it acts against law and justice."[8]

Roosevelt insists that the national government is the only true representative of the people, and that it has both the right and the responsibility to supervise the activities of the great trusts and, when necessary, to prevent and punish them for acting in ways that undermine the health of social and industrial life. It is his belief that all of the great corporations should be held responsible by, and be accountable to, some sovereign strong enough to check their conduct. For TR, experience has shown that the states are incapable of regulating and supervising the activities of the great corporations. Moreover, he observes, most of the trusts do not even operate within the jurisdiction of a single state; rather, they engage in interstate commerce, and interstate commerce is within the constitutional jurisdiction of the national government. "The makers of our National Constitution," Roosevelt explains, "provided especially that the regulation of interstate commerce should come within the sphere of the Central Government. The arguments in favor of their taking this stand were even then overwhelming. But they are far stronger today, in view of the enormous development of great business agencies, usually in corporate form."[9]

Roosevelt acknowledges in his address to the Harvard Union that there has been "a curious revival" of the doctrine of states' rights but argues that this is just a cover for people who wish to see governing authority exercise no control over business. States' rights, he charges, is a means of sweeping current economic problems under the rug, for the states have shown time and again that they do not possess the capacity or, in many cases, the will to curb the power of predatory wealth. For more than a decade, Roosevelt continues, some states have attempted to control corporate abuses, yet the problems persist. Many more states have been content to do nothing. TR notes also that states' rights advocates are quick to criticize every suggestion that the federal government should exercise proper and adequate supervision, but they fail to offer any constructive alternative. "I have watched for six years these men, both those in public and those in private life, and though they are prompt to criticize every affirmative step taken, I have yet to see one of them lift a finger to remedy the wrongs that exist." He concludes that the doctrine of states' rights should be employed only on behalf of the people's rights; it should never be used to suppress or obstruct the rights of the people.[10]

In his Fifth Annual Message, TR notes that many Americans want action to restrain the powerful and potentially dangerous trusts, and that needed regulation can be obtained by the passage of a simple congressional statute. If such legislation is declared unconstitutional by the courts, then Roosevelt suggests that the Constitution be amended to give this power to the national government. It would be hasty and unwise, he concedes, to seek the adoption and ratification of such an amendment, until it has been shown that these aims cannot be achieved under the present constitutional order.[11] "Great corporations are necessary," Roosevelt stresses, "and only men of great and singular mental power can manage such corporations successfully, and such men must have great rewards. But these corporations should be managed with due regard to the interests of the public as a whole. Where this can be done under the present laws it must be done. Where these laws come short, others should be enacted to supplement them."[12]

As for the proponents of antitrust, Roosevelt expresses his preference for *regulation*. Unfortunately, he says, the federal government's response to the problems posed by big business has been too negative. In seeking to prevent what cannot effectively be prohibited, Roosevelt contends, both the federal government and the states have passed impotent and meaningless laws. In his view, the aim should be to assert the sovereignty of the national government "by affirmative action." "It is generally useless," he explains, "to try to prohibit all restraint on competition, whether this restraint be reasonable or unreasonable; and where it is not useless it is generally hurtful." In short, antitrust can do more harm than good. Furthermore, TR maintains that antitrust fails to account for the realities of the modern age. Throughout his first term, he concedes, the Department of Justice devoted more attention to the enforcement of antitrust legislation than to anything else, and much good was accomplished. Indeed, the "moral effect" of his prosecutions cannot be underestimated. But TR argues frankly that these actions led to little in the way of constructive economic change. "The successful prosecution of one device to evade the law immediately develops another device to accomplish the same purpose. What is needed is not sweeping prohibition of every arrangement, good or bad, which may tend to restrict competition, but such adequate supervision and regulation as will prevent any restriction of competition from being to the detriment of the public, as well as such supervision and regulation as will prevent other abuses in no way connected with restriction of competition."[13]

This position on corporate regulation was not new. In fact, it had been central to Roosevelt's thought for well over a decade. In *The Strenuous Life*, TR argues that, although "the sphere of the state's action should be extended very cautiously, and so far as possible only when and where it will not crush out healthy individual initiative," positive state action is sometimes needed.[14] Moreover, as governor of New York, Roosevelt had his first great opportunity to strengthen the regulatory powers of the government to make it a coequal force in the economic arena. This was the institutional side of his attempt to reconcile individualism and collectivism. When bills granting rights to the Long Island Railroad and the Consolidated Gas Company were accused of being "grabs" for power, he rejected unlimited grants and instead limited these privileges to fifty years, renewable for twenty-five years. He also proposed legislation that required mandatory public reporting of corporate profits as well as strict reviews of corporate tax returns.[15] As early as the first six months of his term as governor, TR worked with the United Garment Workers to pass an eight-hour-day law that protected workers on public contracts. The law was eventually extended to cover women and all employees of the state. He supported the Costello Anti-Sweatshop Act, which provided for the inspection and regulation of working conditions in tenement houses, and he signed various consumer protection laws that, among other things, required the labeling of dairy products as well as goods that had been produced in sweatshops.[16] Likewise, as a candidate for Vice President, Roosevelt argued that the American people could not engage in reckless attacks on the whole industrial system; nonetheless, the state, acting in its collective capacity, could and should compel businesses to publicize their capital, profits, and any other pertinent information. "The mere fact of this publicity," he reasoned, "would in itself remedy certain evils, and, as to others, it would in some cases point out the remedies, and would at least enable us to tell whether or not certain proposed remedies would be useful." Much could be done by taxation, but much more could be done by regulation "and the unsparing excision of all unhealthy, destructive, and antisocial elements."[17] The worst enemies of property, TR added, were those men who, "whether from unscrupulousness or from mere heedlessness and thoughtlessness," took the position that property was sacrosanct and that responsibility was inversely related to wealth and privilege.[18]

TR's views on corporate regulation derived from a mix of sources. He relied on a combination of Darwinian theory and induction to argue that, while competition was necessary for progress, it could be too aggressive, too severe, and harmful to the ends it sought to serve. He pointed specifically to the fact that intense competition undermined population growth and thus endangered a nation. No matter how great the number of births may be, he declared, a nation or society could not increase if the number of deaths due to competition also grew at an accelerated rate. According to TR, the men who performed the great deeds that advanced society were not struggling for mere survival. The great generals, admirals, poets, philosophers, historians, artists, musicians, statesmen, judges, legislators, and industrialists came from classes where the struggle for basic subsistence was least severe. In his view, the rivalry associated with natural selection worked against progress in civilized societies.

In addition, TR repeatedly denied that the interests of the individual and the group were, and had to remain, antagonistic. He argued that the individual had a rational interest in subordinating his interests to the needs of the larger community. Both intellect and morality would "persistently war against the individuals in whom the spirit of selfishness . . . showed itself strongly." Roosevelt pointed to the soldier who took pride in the organization of which he was part and subordinated himself to the needs of his brothers-in arms. Such selflessness, Roosevelt maintained, was the essence of good character, and the development of character was even more important than the development of intellect. Indeed, he saw good character as the "prime factor" in social evolution.[19] In all likelihood, TR based these thoughts on his experiences with Badlands cowboys and his beloved Rough Riders. He had nothing but praise for these strong, brave, loyal, and selfless individuals. Indeed, writings like *Ranch Life*, *Hunting Trips*, *The Wilderness Hunter*, and *The Rough Riders* were intended to arouse similar respect and admiration on the part of his fellow citizens.

The combination of biological study, inductive reasoning, and personal experience permitted Roosevelt to conclude that the state had both the right and the responsibility to make competition more even. There had to be competition, Roosevelt stressed, and success in the race of life should belong to the most meritorious. He always believed it was not wrong to pity the man who stumbled or fell, but it was wrong to "crown" an undeserving individual "with the victor's wreath." By relying on its police powers, the state could assure that everyone competed on a relatively equal basis, for this was a better guarantee that the economic marketplace remained a true test of individual merit. It was possible, Roosevelt concluded, for the state to extend its sphere of activity without diminishing individual liberty and the happiness of the people. As a solution to economic problems, Roosevelt saw Socialism as improbable, unnecessary, and even dangerous. Laissez faire was equally deficient in his mind; it was at once inadequate and radical. Roosevelt concluded that the only alternative seemed to be responsible and moderate supervision of the economy in the interest of the public good.[20]

There were other sources upon which Roosevelt drew for his belief in public responsibility and the need for corporate regulation, and particularly regulation by a strong national government. His father, Thee Roosevelt, had been a patriotic and nationally minded man, whose talk about the importance of service to the nation greatly influenced Theodore's later political views. TR's father was also an advocate of *noblesse oblige*, or the idea that privilege entailed an obligation to the less fortunate. Abraham Lincoln had recognized a similar moral obligation that bound him to his fellow countrymen. For this reason, the Great Emancipator was willing to give his energy, his happiness, and his life for a cause greater than himself. TR was convinced that Lincoln's national outlook and positive use of presidential power pointed the way to solving the social and economic challenges of the twentieth century. In particular, Roosevelt believed that the problems of the early twentieth century closely resembled those of the Civil War era. Not only did Americans of both periods lack a strong sense of unity, but they faced the same challenge to eliminate artificial privilege and thereby equalize opportunity for all. Roosevelt's devotion to Lincoln inspired him to adopt the Great Emancipator's concept of positive liberty as well as his willingness to use the national government to ensure that all Americans had a chance to realize their potential.[21]

TR AS (RELUCTANT) TRUSTBUSTER

While Roosevelt had no wish to eliminate large corporations from the economic marketplace, and thought most antitrust measures ineffective, he was willing to use antitrust prosecutions to strengthen the executive power of the national government. The most famous instance was the federal suit to dissolve the Northern Securities Company, a giant railroad trust. During the spring of 1901, railroad magnates James J. Hill, E. H. Harriman, and J. P. Morgan combined to form the Northern Securities Company, which held the stock of the Great Northern and Northern Pacific railroads and of their subsidiary line, the Chicago, Burlington and Quincy Railroad. An investigation by the Interstate Commerce Commission (ICC) led Attorney General Philander C. Knox to conclude that the merger was illegal under the Sherman Act. Roosevelt ordered a lawsuit to be filed to stop the merger and announced his decision to Wall Street on February 19, 1902. The statement released by the Office of the Attorney General said the suit was intended "to prevent violent fluctuations and disaster in the market." But the effect of the announcement frightened the market. It also brought Morgan to Washington.

"If we have done anything wrong," Morgan told Roosevelt during a meeting on February 22, "send your man to my man and they can fix it up." "This can't be done," Roosevelt responded, and Knox added, "We don't want to fix it up, we want to stop it." Morgan next asked whether Roosevelt intended to attack his other interests, such as the Steel Trust. Roosevelt said not, "unless we find out that in any case they have done something that we regard as wrong." After Morgan left, Roosevelt turned to Knox and said, "This is a most illuminating illustration of the Wall Street point of view. Mr. Morgan could not help regarding me as a big rival operator who either intended to ruin all his interests or else could be induced to come to an agreement to ruin none." Roosevelt's conversation with Morgan illustrates the larger point that Morgan missed: Roosevelt refused to allow the President of the United States and the federal government to be treated as a mere rival business.[22] The suit proceeded and, while Roosevelt did not regard it as a permanent answer to the problem of corporate trusts, he believed litigation important and necessary to establish the authority of the federal government to intervene in business matters. In his autobiography, he describes the Northern Securities case as a critical event of his administration, explaining that the issue was not about how large corporations should be controlled. "The absolutely vital question was whether the government had the power to control them at all." This question had not yet been decided in favor of the national government. Indeed, the Supreme Court's decision in *United States v. E.C. Knight Corporation* (1895) had severely limited the government's power to regulate interstate corporations. But Roosevelt concludes that the Northern Securities case "annulled" that decision of the Court, "and the present power of the National Government to deal effectively with the trusts" is due solely to the success of the Administration in securing a reversal of *Knight*.[23]

In 1904, the Supreme Court backed Roosevelt's position, ruling in a five-to-four decision that the Northern Securities Company had violated the Sherman Act. The case was a clear victory for Roosevelt, and the same may be said for both the administration's 1902 suit to prevent the "beef trust" from conspiring to fix prices and its 1906 action against the Standard Oil Company. In the latter instance, John D. Rockefeller's company was accused of at least 1,462 violations of federal law. Roosevelt had clearly stated his preference for regulation over antitrust, but he could not afford to ignore the grassroots sentiment against Standard Oil. A federal investigation revealed that the company "has habitually received from the railroads, and is now receiving, secret rates and other unjust illegal discriminations." Moreover, it exercised "monopolistic control . . . from the well of the producer to the door step of the consumer." Thus, in November 1906, the Roosevelt administration filed suit under the Sherman Act to dissolve the Standard Oil Company of New Jersey as well as its subsidiary corporations. A federal circuit court ruled against the company in 1909, and the Supreme Court upheld this judgment in 1911, ordering that Rockefeller's company must go out of business and allow its subsidiary corporations to function freely and independently. When he learned of the verdict, while on safari in Africa, Roosevelt declared that the ruling was "one of the most signal triumphs for decency which has been won in our country."[24]

THE SPECIFICS OF CORPORATE REGULATION

As mentioned previously, Roosevelt, despite winning great acclaim as a "trustbuster," spent his presidency working primarily to strengthen the *regu-*

latory powers of the national government. In his Second Annual Message to Congress, he calls for the creation of a Department of Commerce, with "large powers" to oversee "the whole subject of the great corporations doing an interstate business," arguing that "corporations, and especially combinations of corporations, should be managed under public regulation." "Our aim," he continues, "is not to do away with corporations; on the contrary, these big aggregations are an inevitable development of modern industrialism, and the effort to destroy them would be futile unless accompanied in ways that would work the utmost mischief to the entire body politic." The aim, instead, is to prevent evil. From Roosevelt's standpoint, the government is not justified in discriminating on the basis of wealth, but it can and should draw the line against misconduct. Roosevelt suggests that creating a secretary of commerce, and giving him a seat in the Cabinet, would constitute a great advance toward preventing abuses by those corporations that engage in interstate activity. Moreover, he adds, the creation of this position is justified by the ever-increasing growth and complexity of business and labor organizations as well as the great strides that the United States has made in improving its trade with other nations.[25] After debate, the Congress created a Department of Commerce and Labor, which included a bureau that would "report such data to the President from time to time as he shall require; and the information so obtained or as much as the President may direct shall be made public." Roosevelt signed the legislation and appointed George B. Cortelyou as secretary of commerce and labor. James R. Garfield, the son of the martyred President, was made commissioner of corporations.[26]

"The preliminary work of the Bureau of Corporations in the Department [of Commerce]," Roosevelt reports in his Third Annual Message to Congress, "has shown the wisdom of its creation." "Publicity in corporate affairs," he asserts, "will tend to do away with ignorance, and will afford facts upon which intelligent action may be taken. Systematic, intelligent investigation is already developing facts the knowledge of which is essential to a right understanding of the needs and duties of the business world." Roosevelt assures his fellow Americans that the corporate executives who deal honestly and fairly with their stockholders, their competitors, and the public have nothing to fear from the investigative powers of the Bureau. He stresses that the purpose of the Bureau is not to embarrass or attack legitimate business, but rather to promote better conditions in the marketplace, such as obedience to the law and "recognition of public obligation by all corporations, great or small." To Roosevelt, the legislation creating the Bureau is both sane and moderate. While nothing revolutionary was attempted, he explains, a common-sense effort was made to assure that corporations remained mindful of the public good. TR's intent is not to attack good business but rather to stop gross misconduct. After all, the President observes, a great deal of good has been done by those capitalists who alone, or in combination with one another, engage in proper and legitimate business. Supervision, then, is meant only to prevent good businessmen from veering off the path of righteousness.[27]

Two years after the creation of the Department of Commerce and Labor, Roosevelt managed to win passage of the Hepburn Act, which granted the Interstate Commerce Commission the power to set the rates that railroads could charge to shippers. Evidence that the railroads gave special advantages to favored shippers led TR to call for the ICC to be given this power. "The Government," Roosevelt argues in his Fourth Annual Message to Congress, "must in increasing degree supervise and regulate the workings of the railways engaged in interstate commerce; and such increased supervision is the only alternative to an increase of the present evils on the one hand or a still more radical policy on the other." Thus, TR concludes, when a particular rate is challenged and subsequently found to be unreasonable, the ICC should be permitted to set a more reasonable rate, which would remain in effect until a federal court ruled on it.[28] This stance, Lewis Gould explains, "put the President among those who believed that the burden of challenging an ICC decision about rates should fall on the railroads, rather than on the shippers."[29]

When the railroad rate legislation stalled in the Senate, TR made a trip through the Midwest and Southwest, calling on the federal government to increase its control over corporations. His speech before the Iroquois Club of Chicago is a good example of what he said repeatedly in defense of reform. He begins by declaring, "Personally, I believe that the Federal Government must take an increasing control over corporations. It is better that that control should increase by degrees than it should be assumed all at once. But there should be, and I trust will be, no halt in the steady progress of assuming such national control." Specifically, Roosevelt suggests that Congress adopt a law giving an executive agency like the ICC the power to supervise and regulate those corporations that are engaged in interstate commerce, especially the railroads. The power must exist, he says, and it must rest with the representatives of the people. The ICC, in other words, should be used to give voice to the needs and the will of the American people. Roosevelt admits that the potential for abuse exists but stresses that this possibility cannot be used as an argument against placing power where it is likely to be employed fairly.[30]

TR's campaign for the rate reform culminated in his December 1905 annual message to Congress, in which he argues that, while the power to regulate rates must be exercised with moderation, caution, and self-restraint, it must exist nonetheless. Of course, he says, the government should not interfere with private business any more than is necessary. "I do not believe in the Government undertaking any work which can with propriety be left in private hands." At the same time, Roosevelt adds, "neither do I believe in the Government flinching from overseeing any work when it becomes evident that abuses are sure to obtain therein unless there is governmental supervision." Without suggesting the exact terms of the proposed law, Roosevelt calls attention to the need for a provision that would confer upon the ICC the power to decide whether a particular rate is both reasonable and just. If the rate in question is found to be unreasonable and unjust, then the ICC should be empowered, after full investigation of the complaint, to set the maximum reasonable rate. This decision, he continues, would go into effect within a reasonable period of time and would, of course, be subject to review by the courts. If, on the other hand, it is found that a favored shipper has been given an extremely low rate, then the Commission would have the right to fix this minimum rate as the maximum for all shippers. Roosevelt stresses that his intention is not to give the ICC, or any other agency, the power to initiate rates. The government will simply have the power to regulate a rate that has already been originated, and only after a complaint has been filed and investigated.[31]

Roosevelt stresses that his recommendations are not made in a spirit of hostility to the railroads, as it is both illegal and unethical to discriminate against individuals merely because they are wealthy. For the most part, he notes, the nation's railroads have done well. But those railroad men who wish to do well should not have to compete with those who have ill intentions, and the only way to guarantee this end is to give the national government the power to assure that "justice is done by the unwilling exactly as it is gladly done by the willing."[32] In other words, regulation assures that the ethical and public-minded corporation is not forced to engage in improper practices simply to compete with unscrupulous rivals. Roosevelt desires nothing more than to establish a moral standard. "Business success," he explains, "whether for the individual or for the Nation, is a good thing only so far as it is accompanied by and develops a high standard of conduct—honor, integrity, civic courage."[33] Echoing the sentiments found in *The Strenuous Life*, he reminds his fellow-citizens how dangerous it is for a society to sacrifice good character for the sake of material prosperity. In the end, Roosevelt's rhetoric stimulated public pressure that, in turn, overcame Senate resistance to the railway rate bill.[34]

Because he was widely seen as the representative of the people, Roosevelt was able to rally public support on behalf of his effort to increase the regulatory authority of the national government. People were more willing to support an activist government when TR pointed to a direct and immediate threat to the public interest, such as the impurity of food and drugs.[35] As Michael McGerr observes, Americans had worried for years about the purity of their food and drugs, about the safety of the dyes and preservatives used in food and the misrepresentation of food and drugs. Many of these concerns were substantiated by Harvey W. Wiley, the chief of the Bureau of Chemistry in the U.S. Department of Agriculture. The successful regulation of food and drugs, McGerr writes, required "a powerful sense of urgency" across "a broad, cross-class coalition." Aided by other Progressives, Roosevelt was able to persuade all classes of Americans to unite in their common identity as consumers. TR was able to do this and even attract the support of some businesses, "or at least force their acquiescence to regulation."[36] Roosevelt's efforts were aided by the reports of middle class journalists that exposed fraudulent advertising, the deception behind patent medicines, and sickening conditions in the meatpacking industry. The most famous of these exposés was Upton Sinclair's *The Jungle*, which reveals how meat was produced by Swift & Company, Armour & Company, and other meatpacking corporations. The novel sought to dramatize the plight of poor workers, but the most indelible impression it made was its disclosures about the meatpacking plants. After reading the book, people were disgusted, outraged, and concerned about their safety. One of these individuals was Roosevelt, who met with Sinclair and then sent his own investigators to inspect the conditions of Chicago's big meatpacking corporations.[37] They reported that "the stockyards and packing houses are not kept even reasonably clean, and that the method of handling and preparing food products is uncleanly and dangerous to health." Senator Albert J. Beveridge worked with the inspectors to draft meat-inspection legislation that was offered to the Senate on May 21, 1906. The bill called for the inspection of all meat that was purchased in interstate commerce, required that meat products be dated, and gave the Department of Agriculture the power to oversee conditions in the packing houses, with the cost of inspection to be paid by the packers themselves. Roosevelt threw his support behind the bill and, by threatening to publicize his packinghouse report, won its passage in Congress.[38]

THE CONSERVATION CRUSADE

Unlike the crusade for pure food and drugs, the conservation battle never managed to invoke a shared sense of identity among diverse groups of Americans. "Instead," McGerr writes, "there was a battle of different groups who acted on their interest as producers. In these circumstances, progressives could easily find themselves on the defensive, their cause described as socialist usurpation and their enemies trumpeting the virtues of individualism."[39] On the other hand, a great many Americans did fear the uncontrolled exploitation of the environment, and Roosevelt was more than willing to appeal to this mindset on behalf of reform.

Prior to his presidency, Roosevelt used the governorship of New York to establish himself as a man of action regarding conservation. Foreshadowing things to come, he worked to protect the Palisades Parkway and proposed conserving land in the Adirondack and Catskill mountains. When forest fires broke out in the Adirondacks, and local authorities refused to spend money to extinguish them, Roosevelt sent emergency firefighters to save the forests. Similarly, he ordered the State Board of Health to investigate complaints that property owners on Saratoga Lake were discharging sewage, domestic waste, and manufacturing refuse that endangered public health. Roosevelt received a report that described Kayaderosseras Creek, the inlet to Saratoga Lake, as "an open sewer." In response, Roosevelt issued an executive order that required the sanitary collection and disposal of this waste. Failure to comply with the order resulted in a fine, as well as a possible jail sentence. It was one of the first and toughest anti-pollution statutes in the country.[40]

Roosevelt supported the conservation movement for reasons both principled and pragmatic. It was clear in his earlier writings that he saw the western frontier as a place of "rugged and stalwart democracy," where every man stood for what he really was and could prove himself to be.[41] It was, in short, a place of freedom, new beginnings, and equal opportunity to remake oneself. But, unfortunately, the frontier was closing, and for this reason, Roosevelt used his writings to convey a sense of the pioneer spirit to Americans of all regions, classes, and ethnicities. It was important, he insisted, that the American people save their frontier and preserve a way of life that offered all individuals the chance to cultivate the frontier spirit that promoted good character. Along these lines, he advocated a rigid system of game laws and the establishment of great national forest reserves. These institutional reforms, coupled with personal example, would teach the American people how to balance those individualistic values that are healthy and vital to a society with positive collectivistic values.

The pragmatic side of Roosevelt's conservation efforts was simple: conservation assured economic development and served individual self-interest. In his speech to the Society of American Foresters, Roosevelt stresses that the object of his forest policy is not to preserve forests because they are beautiful, nor simply to preserve refuges for various birds and animals for their own sake. While these are desirable goals in themselves, TR's primary concern is continued *prosperity*. He understands that support for his environmental policies cannot be imposed on the people, but rather will come only from a conviction in the minds of the people that it is wise, useful, and necessary. In other words, people must be convinced that the ultimate prosperity of the nation depends, in no small part, on the intelligent and efficient management of natural resources. "You must remember," he tells the meeting of foresters, "that the forest which contributes nothing to the wealth, progress, or safety of the country is of no interest to the government, and it should be of little to the forester. Your attention should be directed not to the preservation of the forests as an end in itself, but as the means for preserving and increasing the prosperity of the Nation." For TR, the success of environmental reform depends, not upon preventing the use of resources, but upon making settlers, ranchers, and miners understand that conservation pays.[42]

"The forest problem is in many ways the most vital internal problem of the United States," TR declares. "The more closely this statement is examined the more evident its truth becomes." He argues that, in arid regions of the West, forest protection can maintain the stream flow that is necessary for irrigation. In the East, it can prevent floods, which are destructive to both agriculture and manufacturing. Similarly, there is an intimate relation between forests and the mineral industry, for mines cannot be developed without nearby timber. In many parts of the West, Roosevelt explains, use of the mine is limited to the man who has timber available close at hand. In addition, because forests provide wood for construction, forest protection is beneficial to manufacturing as well as to the railroads. In TR's opinion, even the grazing industry, which might at first glance appear to have little relation to forestry, depends upon the conservation of the forests: great areas of winter range would be entirely useless without the summer range in the mountains, where the forest reserves lie.[43]

No doubt, Roosevelt's experience in the West had led him to see the interdependence of nature and commerce, and he sought, in the interest of opportunity, to secure both in public policy. But exhaustion of the nation's forest supplies was not the only problem. There was, for one, the question of irrigation. To enlarge the area available for farming, Roosevelt maintained that the national government had to build up a system of irrigation for agriculture in the Rocky Mountains and plain states. In addition, overgrazing had to be stopped so that future generations would be able to feed their cattle. Roosevelt explains in his address to the residents of Salt Lake City that the region's ranges must be treated as "a great invested capital." TR stresses that, by destroying acres and acres of grassland, with no regard for the future, the old system of grazing undermined the development of the West and cannot be permitted to endure. "The wise man, the wise industry, the wise nation," he continues, "maintains such capital unimpaired and tries to increase it. . . . Our aim must be steadily to help develop the settler, the man who lives on the land and in growing up with it and raising his children to own it after him." Likewise, Roosevelt adds, the mountain forests must be protected from overgrazing. "Let all the grazing be done in them that can be done without injury to them, but do not let the mountain forests be despoiled by the man who will overgraze them and destroy them for the sake of three year's use, and then go somewhere else, and leave by so much diminished the heritage of those who remain permanently on the land." Roosevelt reminds his audience that he was once a stockman. Understanding their business like few others, he knows whereof he speaks and can testify to the fact that individual self-interest and collective good are not mutually exclusive.[44]

TR argued repeatedly that only collective action could serve individual interest, but it was an argument rarely embraced by Progressive reformers, many of whom thought individualism a problem. "What we want is the best for the people, not the individual," one reformer declared unapologetically. After all, most Progressives reasoned, it was individual self-interest that had destroyed the beauty of the landscape and endangered the nation's natural resources in the first place. The big businessmen, one Colorado newspaper declared, cared nothing "for the forest or the general good . . . And their business subverts the general good." It was this identification with the public interest that led conservationists—and Progressive reformers in general—to favor the kind of state activism that would restrain the individual and his so-called "rights."[45] In this, they had more in common with Socialism than with Roosevelt's brand of Progressivism. For his part, Roosevelt refused to abandon completely the long-cherished American principle of individual freedom, arguing instead that the collective good and self-interest complemented one another in the area of conservation.

As both Michael McGerr and Lewis Gould observe, Americans supported Roosevelt's conservation goals in principle, but because these proposals involved the management of natural resources under the supervision of the federal government, many were uncomfortable with the specifics. Federal regulation, after all, meant a reduced role for state and local governments. It also threatened individual property rights. Because of the controversial nature of conservation, Roosevelt's first term conservation reforms were achieved almost exclusively through executive action under existing law or the implied powers of the presidency. It illustrated well TR's broad conception of presidential power and his view of the presidential role as that of trustee of the public interest. By executive order, he created the Pelican Island wildlife refuge in Florida, the Crater Lake National Park in Oregon, and over fifty bird refuges in twenty states and territories. In 1902, Congress did pass the Newlands Act, which provided that many of the proceeds from the sale of public lands in sixteen western states should go into a fund to finance irrigation projects that were too large for either private or state development. Under this program, the national government built many dams and canals, but Congress was unwilling to enact other environmental reforms during Roosevelt's first term.[46] While many large cattle and lumber companies were willing to accept, and even welcome, orderly conservation reforms, smaller enterprises maintained that federal regulations threatened their very survival.[47]

After Roosevelt's 1904 reelection, Congress gave authority over the forest reserves to Gifford Pinchot's Bureau of Forestry, and Roosevelt continued the use of executive orders to increase the acreage of the nation's forest reserves. Throughout 1905 and 1906, the total of reserve forests increased from nearly 86 million acres to approximately 107 million acres. Eventually, the Forest Service won the authority to arrest those who broke laws and regulations relating to the forest reserves and national parks. As Gould writes, "In the hands of a vigorous and forceful executive such as Pinchot, these provisions represented a grant of discretion to implement his vision of how the nation should oversee its natural heritage." With Roosevelt's encouragement, Pinchot created new regulations that further centralized power in the hands of the federal government. Meanwhile, the President, who was worried about the corrupt disposal of federal lands, withdrew 66 million acres of possibly coal-rich government land in 1906. That same year, he was given the authority to establish national monuments, and by the end of his second term, he had established a total of eighteen.[48]

Throughout his second term, Roosevelt's conservation policy continued to encounter strong opposition, especially among westerners, who believed that conservation would undermine economic development. Critics also objected to Pinchot's ever-growing power. Specifically, they called him a "Russian Czar" or a "Turkish Sultan," a "rapacious venal, petty aristocrat maliciously bent on destroying everybody;" and they referred to antidemocratic practices as "Pinchotism." "[If] you had breathed the spirit of liberty for thirty years on Colorado mountain tops, you would understand and hate 'Pinchotism' as I do," said one resister.[49] Finally, in 1907, Republican Senator Charles Fulton of Oregon amended an agriculture appropriation bill to stipulate that "hereafter no forest reserve shall be created, nor shall any addition be made, to one heretofore created, within the limits of the states of Oregon, Washington, Montana, Colorado, or Wyoming, except by an act of Congress." Not to be outdone, Roosevelt, prior to signing the agriculture bill into law, established twenty-one more national forests in the West. One outraged western newspaper wrote, "Very few of the autocratic monarchs of the world would so dare to set aside the will of the people this way." To many, TR's approach to conservation—and to economic reform in general—meant greater centralization of power, which to the *Chicago Tribune* meant "a corresponding decrease in the old time sovereignty of the states or of the individual."[50] In the end, Roosevelt failed to persuade many westerners and conservatives, who were traditionally suspicious of centralized government, that individual self-interest and collective action were compatible.

ROOSEVELT'S RELATIONS WITH LABOR

To be sure, Roosevelt was willing to restrict individualism for the sake of the public good; however, it cannot be overemphasized that he regarded collective action as a means to serve and strengthen individual self-interest. As he argues in *The Strenuous Life*, most of society's problems stem from the inability of individuals to appreciate one another's point of view and work for the common good, although an individual must be permitted to exercise his own intelligence, thrift, energy, and self-mastery, or he will know nothing of self-respect. The demands of modern life called for a combination of individualism and collectivism, and Roosevelt did not just arrive at this conclusion in 1900, when *The Strenuous Life* was first published. Rather, this marriage of the individualism of America's founders to the collectivist ideal of emerging Progressivism had its roots in Roosevelt's experience as a rancher, as evinced in such early writings as *Ranch Life*. These combine celebrations of hardiness and self-reliance with explanations of what Roosevelt believes the western experience taught his fellow ranchers about mutual support. Specifically, it is in scheduling roundups, devising and enforcing new regulations, and uniting against cattle rustlers, as well as in forming collective organizations like the great Montana Stock Growers' Association and the Little Missouri Stockmen's Association, that individual self-interest and collective good are brought together. If they wished to prosper, individual ranchmen had to combine.

This lesson remained with Roosevelt throughout his presidency, especially when he was forced to address the conflict between capital and organized labor. Roosevelt had expressed some apprehension about organized labor. When "Big Bill" Haywood, the secretary-treasurer of the Western Federation of Miners, was accused of being linked to the assassination of the former governor of Idaho, Roosevelt had written in various letters that men like Haywood were just as "undesirable" as the selfish financiers. Regardless of whether Haywood was responsible for the murder of the governor, Roosevelt declared that he had "done as much to discredit the labor movement as the worst speculative financiers or most unscrupulous employers of labor and debauchers of legislatures have done to discredit honest capitalists and fair-dealing businessmen." With radical Socialists like Eugene Debs, Haywood stood in Roosevelt's mind as the representative of "those men who by their public utterances and manifestos, by the utterance of the papers they control or inspire, and by the words and deeds of those associated with or subordinated to them, habitually appear as guilty of incitement to or apology for bloodshed and violence." "If this does not constitute undesirable citizenship," Roosevelt concluded, "then there can never be any undesirable citizens."[51]

But these statements simply indicate that Roosevelt feared *radicalism* in labor, just as he had concerns about the actions of radical businessmen.

"I believe emphatically in organized labor," TR declares in a speech to the Brotherhood of Locomotive Firemen. "I believe in organizations of wage-workers. Organization is one of the laws of our social and economic development at this time." "But," he is quick to add, "I feel that we must always keep before our minds the fact that there is nothing sacred in the name itself. To call an organization an organization does not make it a good one. The worth of an organization depends upon its being handled with the courage, the skill, the wisdom, the spirit of fair dealing as between man and man, and the wise self-restraint, which I am glad to be able to say, your Brotherhood has shown."[52] Success, in Roosevelt's view, depends upon the ability of our people to stand "shoulder to shoulder" and "work in association . . . each working for all." According to TR, this was the lesson of the Civil War, whose battlefields were littered with mighty men—of blue and gray—who gave their lives for the common good.[53] This was also the lesson that Roosevelt learned at Santiago, where his Rough Riders included Catholics, Protestants, and Jews; men whose forefathers were English, Irish, German, French, and Indian; northerners and southerners; easterners and westerners; college graduates, and wageworkers; "the man of means and the man who all his life had owed each day's bread to the day's toil." Despite these differences, Roosevelt observes, his men acted with an underlying spirit of brotherhood. He understands and believes in the value of organized labor because he has experienced the benefits of association himself.[54] Thus, Roosevelt drew a sharp line between the preachers of violence and recklessness, on the one hand, and "the law-abiding and upright representatives of labor," on the other, and he gave his firm support to the latter. Moreover, he was willing to back his words of support with real action.

In 1902, when the United Mine Workers (UMW) in the anthracite coal region of northeastern Pennsylvania voted to suspend work, Roosevelt threw his support behind them. The dispute between the miners and coal operators revolved primarily around the issue of wages, but the UMW also wanted recognition as a bargaining agent. When efforts to reach a negotiated settlement broke down, approximately 125,000 miners went on strike. As the Northeast faced the prospect of a winter without coal, TR invited both the miners and the mine operators to a conference in Washington. On October 3, the miners and operators assembled in Washington, and Roosevelt immediately informed the group that, while he had no "right or duty to intervene in this way upon legal grounds or upon any official relation that I bear to the situation," he believed that "the urgency and the terrible nature of the catastrophe impending" demanded that he exert "whatever influence I personally can" to end the strike.[55]

Nothing much resulted from the October meeting. The mine owners accused the union of embracing violence and asked Roosevelt to dissolve the

UMW as a trust. They also urged him to use federal troops to "at once squelch the anarchistic conditions of affairs existing in the anthracite coal regions by the strong arm of the military at your command." For their part, the miners expressed their willingness to have Roosevelt "name a tribunal which shall determine the issues that have resulted in the strike." If the owners would accept the decision of the tribunal, so too would the union. The whole experience left Roosevelt angry with the mine owners, whose "wooden-headed obstinacy and stupidity" blinded them to the impending storm. On the other hand, he was greatly impressed by the attitude of John Mitchell, the leader of the UMW. The dignity and moderation with which Mitchell articulated his case left Roosevelt with "a very uncomfortable feeling that" the operators "might be far more to blame relatively to the miners than I had supposed."

After the failure of the October meeting, Roosevelt argued more and more that he was the representative of the public interest, which the mine owners refused to recognize. "The operators forget that they have duties toward the public, as well as rights to be guarded by the public through its governmental agents," he declared. "Do they not realize," he asked a friend, "that they are putting a very heavy burden on us who stand against socialism; against anarchic disorder?"[56] Ready for action, Roosevelt assembled a commission to investigate the causes of the strike and decided that, if a negotiated solution did not emerge, he would use the army to open the mines for all who wanted to work and "dispossess the operators and run the mines as a receiver" until the commission reported to him. He understood that this action "would form an evil precedent" but believed that it was the only approach "which would be effective in such an emergency."[57] As TR explains in his autobiography, he saw the crisis as great and was prepared to act as Jackson and Lincoln had during the crises of their own times.[58] After hearing from more than five hundred witnesses, Roosevelt's commission recommended a binding solution. The UMW did not win official recognition, but the miners received a ten percent increase in wages as well as a reduced workday.[59] The outcome was especially positive for Roosevelt. Not only did his intervention enhance the power of the presidency, but it gave him an historic opportunity to clarify his belief that the federal government was the true representative of the public interest and had both the right and the responsibility to oversee business-labor relations.[60]

A SQUARE DEAL FOR ALL AMERICANS

Roosevelt's support for economic regulation was rooted in a simple belief that remained rather consistent throughout his adult life: precisely because the principles of self-reliance and personal freedom were important, it was sometimes the responsibility of the entire community to use its collective power—and, if necessary, the institutions of the government—to help individuals do what they could not do for themselves. It has already been shown that Roosevelt's frontier and war experiences taught him how mutual support can strengthen individual well-being. In addition, it will be recalled that his 1895 review of Benjamin Kidd's *Social Evolution* argues that a widespread concern for the public good enables individuals to compete in the economic marketplace and thereby remain self-sufficient.[61] Finally, *The Strenuous Life* advocates combination and state action on behalf of the public interest but concedes that one cannot help the man who is unwilling to help himself. "The greatest possible good can be done by the extension of a helping hand at the right moment, but the attempt to carry anyone permanently can end in nothing but harm." From Roosevelt's standpoint, the best that government can do is "provide against injustice, and then let the individual rise and fall on his own merits." In other words, the gross misconduct of corporations and other individuals should be countered by the regulatory powers of the state. But once the individual has been saved from the tyranny and exploitations of other men, his own qualities of body and mind must determine success or failure in life.[62]

This was what Roosevelt meant when he declared that he believed in "a square deal" for all Americans. He did not mean that it was possible to guarantee every man success in the game of life. Time and again, Roosevelt stressed that it was not in the power of any human being to devise legislation by which everyone would achieve success and have happiness, and any man who claimed that he had the power to do so was to be dismissed as a charlatan. Individuals, Roosevelt declared, had a right to *pursue* happiness; they did not have an inherent right to happiness itself. According to TR, the only thing that anyone could do was to secure through governmental agencies and regulations an equal opportunity for each and every man, regardless of class, to show his "stuff." Roosevelt's Square Deal was not intended to discriminate against the rich; it was not intended to discriminate against the poor. Rather, its intent was simply to safeguard the right of every man to compete on a reasonably level economic playing field and do all that his powers and abilities permitted him to do.[63] "Let each stand on his merits, receive what is due him, and be judged according to his deserts. To more he is not entitled, and less he shall not have."[64]

Roosevelt discusses the principles at the heart of his Square Deal in his Address at the Jamestown Exposition, echoing the sentiments expressed in books like *Hunting Trips*, *Ranch Life*, *The Rough Riders*, and *The Strenuous Life*. "Decade by decade," he explains, "it becomes more and more necessary that, without sacrificing their individual independence, the people of this country shall recognize in more effective form their mutual interdependence, and the duty of safeguarding the interest of each in the ultimate interest of all." The United States, Roosevelt observes, was founded upon a principle of self-reliant individualism that should never be exchanged for "a deadening socialism." He concedes that it is possible for governmental action to destroy the individual's power of self-help. Nevertheless, he continues, "as the conditions of life grow more complex, it is not possible to trust our welfare only to the unbridled individual initiative of each unit of our population working as that unit wills." For this reason, he concludes, there must be laws to protect children, which were not needed when this country was still young. "We need laws for the control of vast corporations such as were not needed when the individual fortunes were far smaller than at present, and when these fortunes were not combined for business use. In the same way we need to change our attitude toward labor problems from what that attitude was in the days when the great bulk of our people lived in the country with no more complex labor relations than is implied in the connection between the farmer and the hired help."[65]

Likewise, in his address to the citizens of York, Pennsylvania, TR explains that great problems have accompanied the kind of industrial success that has made towns like York so prosperous. As a result, he continues, the national government must exercise "a constantly increasing supervision over and control of the great fortunes used in business." According to Roosevelt, this is the only way to assure that great corporations and great fortunes are used for, and not against, the interests of ordinary people, the general public. He stresses that his movement for the supervision of great wealth is not driven by hatred and malice. "Hatred and malice are mighty ugly sentiments, and are just as bad if you hate and envy a rich man as if you hate and look down upon a poor man." Roosevelt intends only "to give each man fair play." He wishes only to assure that the rights of the people are not trampled by the great corporations and men of wealth. "This Government will succeed because it shall never fall into such a pit as the republics of old fell into." It will be neither "a Government by a plutocracy" nor "a Government by a mob." Rather, it will be "a Government of the plain people, where each man zealously guards his own rights and no less scrupulously remembers his duty and pays due regard to the rights of others."[66]

HISTORY AND THE
IMPORTANCE OF INDIVIDUAL CHARACTER

Roosevelt stresses to his York audience that economic regulation must be accompanied by one other factor: *individual character*. "There is urgent need," he explains, "for betterment in a great many of our conditions; there is urgent need that we should each of us resolutely do his part in helping to solve the great problems of the day—the problems that need governmental action. But we never can afford to forget that the most important factor in the success of this country is the factor of individual citizenship." The most perfect laws can be devised "by the wit of man or the wit of angels," but they mean nothing, Roosevelt argues, if the average man is lazy, wasteful, and selfish. "Nothing can take the place of the individual factor, of the average man's quality and character, his industry, his energy, his thrift, his decency, his determination to be a good man in his home, a good neighbor, and a good citizen in his relations to the state." Roosevelt wants his fellow citizens to remain true to the principles of honesty, hard work, lawfulness, duty, and service. Moreover, he wants all Americans to demand the same of their neighbors. "The first factor in winning out in our national life must always remain the individual character. . . . Each one of us stumbles at times, and shame on any one of us who will not reach out a helping hand to his brother who stumbles. Help him in the only way that any real help can ever come; help him to help himself."[67]

It is necessary to have good laws and good institutions, Roosevelt notes in his Speech at the Pilgrim Memorial, but much more depends on "a high quality of individual citizenship." The American people, in his view, cannot permit themselves to be misled by the pleas of those who see unrestricted individualism as a cure to all social evil. At the same time, he acknowledges that it would be equally disastrous to adopt Socialism and thereby destroy the individualism that is "the fiber of our whole citizenship." For Roosevelt, extremism is not an option. "The rich man who with hard arrogance declines to consider the rights and the needs of those who are less well off, and the poor man who excites or indulges in envy and hatred of those who are better off, are alike alien to the spirit of our national life." Roosevelt is definite that wherever it is found, by practice and experimentation, or by the failure of individualistic methods, that collectivism and state interference are both wise and necessary, then this course of action must be pursued. "But while we can accomplish something by legislation," Roosevelt stresses, "legislation can never be more than a part, and often no more than a small part, in the general scheme of moral progress; and crude or vindictive legislation may at any time bring such progress to a halt." Socialism, Roosevelt explains, proposes to redistribute property according to need, but he contends that this plan is certain to sap individuals of their thrift, energy, and industry. According to TR, we must work for the real and permanent betterment of our political, economic, and social order, but we must also remember that such betterment will come "only by the slow, steady growth of the spirit which metes a generous, but not a sentimental, justice to each man on his merits as a man, and which recognizes the fact that the highest and deepest happiness for the individual lies not in selfishness but in service."[68]

Throughout his presidency, Roosevelt continued his efforts to nurture the spirit of individual responsibility through inspirational rhetoric and positive example. The office provided a unique, high profile, and influential public stage—a "bully pulpit"—from which to preach his gospel of good character to the entire nation. As in *Hero Tales* and *Men of Action*, Roosevelt used some of the nation's historic figures and lessons to inspire Americans to embrace those moral qualities (independence and communal concern) that he believed were indispensable to the good health and survival of a nation. The intent was to persuade the American people to embrace the qualities of "forethought, shrewdness, self-restraint, the courage which refuses to abandon one's own rights, and the disinterested and kindly good sense which enables one to do justice to the rights of others." By themselves, individualism and collectivism were incomplete. Americans, Roosevelt said, needed to embrace both. "Lack of strength and lack of courage unfit men for self-government on the one hand; and on the other, brutal arrogance, envy, in short, any manifestation of the spirit of selfish disregard, whether of one's own duties or of the rights of others, are equally fatal."

When Roosevelt used the lessons of history to support his thought and actions, he often celebrated the accomplishments and legacies of his two favorite Presidents, Washington and Lincoln. To TR, as set forth in his Remarks at the Washington Chapel, Lincoln teaches many lessons which all Americans should learn, among the most important of which is that, for good or bad, the American people "are indissolubly bound together, in whatever part of the country we live, whatever our social standing, whatever our wealth or our poverty, whatever form of mental or physical activity our lifework may assume." If Lincoln had failed in his great struggle for national unity, "it would have meant that the work done by Washington and his associates might almost or quite as well have been left undone." For this reason, TR cannot think of either Washington or Lincoln individually without thinking of the other as well, for each was devoted to the same effort on behalf of freedom. Americans are fortunate indeed that they "should have as their ideals two men, not conquerors, not men who have glory by wrongdoing; not men whose lives were spent in their own advancement, but men who lived, one of whom died, that the nation might grow steadily greater and better." "I think you will find," Roosevelt adds, "that the fundamental difference between our two great national heroes and almost any other men of equal note in the world's history, is that when you think of our two men you think inevitably not of glory, but of duty, not of what the man did for himself in achieving name, or fame, or position, but of what he did for his fellows." This principle of self-sacrifice is what Roosevelt wants Americans of his time to apply to their own social and economic problems.[69]

Duty and self-sacrifice, Roosevelt adds, were also evident in the men who fought during the two great crises in our national history, the Revolutionary War and the Civil War. "Only men with a touch of the heroic in them could have lasted out that three days at Gettysburg. Only men fit to rank with the great men of all time could have beaten back the mighty onslaught of that gallant and wonderful army of northern Virginia, whose final supreme effort faded at the stone wall on Cemetery Ridge on that July day forty-one years ago." But, Roosevelt argues, as hard as it must have been to rise to this "supreme height of self-sacrifice," it was harder yet for Washington's men at Valley Forge. Faced with months of gloom and hardship, they "warred not against the foreign soldiery, but against themselves, against all the appeals of our nature that are most difficult to resist—against discouragement, discontent, the mean envies and jealousies, and heart-burnings sure to arise at any time in large bodies of men, but especially sure to arise when defeat and disaster have come to large bodies of men." To Roosevelt, the lessons of Gettysburg and Valley Forge are both indispensable, and it seems hardly worthwhile to dwell more on one than on the other. Still, he concludes that modern Americans must learn the lesson of Valley Forge even more than that of Gettysburg. "I have not the slightest anxiety," TR explains, "but that this people, if the need should come in the future, will be able to show the heroism, the supreme effort that was shown at Gettysburg. . . . But the vital thing for this nation to do is steadily to cultivate the quality which Washington and those under him so preeminently showed during the winter at Valley Forge." Roosevelt sees the soldiers at Valley Forge as steadfast, brave, and devoted to a higher ideal—even when faced with difficulty, discouragement, and disaster. For this reason, he concludes, their triumph should be remembered and commemorated. But, Roosevelt adds, "if we treat their great deeds as matters merely for idle boasting, not as spurring us on to effort, but as excusing us from effort, then we show that we are not worthy of our sires, of the people who went before us in the history of our land."[70]

There have been many struggles for individual freedom, Roosevelt says in his Speech at Antietam, but none compares to the War for Independence and the great Civil War. According to the Rough Rider, the men who fought these wars demonstrated the true meaning of patriotism, courage, endurance, duty, and brotherhood. In each case, the most important reason for victory was character. "Leaders," TR explains, "will be developed in military and civil life alike; and weapons and tactics change from generation to generation, as methods of achieving good government change in civic affairs; but the fundamental qualities which make for good citizenship do not change any more than the fundamental qualities which make good soldiers." The spirit that led to the victories of 1781 and 1865 "has remained forever unchanged," and it is as vital to civil life as to military life. In short, Roosevelt suggests that those citizens who want good government and economic reform must exhibit a willingness to endure fatigue, hardship, and even danger. They must also learn to hate cowardice, laziness, and selfishness. "We need the same type of character now that was needed by the men who with Washington first inaugurated the system of free popular government, the system of combined liberty and order here on this continent; that was needed by the men who under Lincoln perpetuated the government which had thus been inaugurated in the days of Washington." The qualities needed to solve current political, economic, and social problems are, according to Roosevelt, "exactly the same as in the days when the first Congresses met to provide for the establishment of the Union; as in days seventy years later, when the Congresses met which had to provide for its salvation."[71]

Along with Washington, Lincoln, and the soldiers of both the American Revolution and the Civil War, Roosevelt believes that the Puritans stand as a great example to modern Americans. Specifically, in his Speech at the Pilgrim Memorial, TR concedes that the Puritans had their share of faults, but adds quickly that it is easy to belittle the great figures of the past by focusing "only on the points where they come short of the universally recognized standards of the present." Instead, men must be judged according to the standards of the age in which they lived. The Puritans, Roosevelt says, despite their less attractive characteristics, tamed a continent, tilled the land, established an economic and social system, and laid the foundations for "our whole American system of civil, political, and religious liberty achieved through the orderly process of law." To TR, their extraordinary success in subduing this continent and making it the foundation for a social life of ordered liberty was due primarily to the fact that they could combine individual initiative and self-reliance with communal concern and the ability to act in combination.[72]

The Puritan, Roosevelt continues, was stubborn and hardheaded. "He had lofty purposes, but he had practical good sense, too. He could hold his own in the rough workaday world without clamorous insistence upon being helped by others, and yet he could combine with others whenever it became necessary to do a job which could not be as well done by any one man individually." These were the qualities that enabled the Puritan settler to do his work, and they are the same qualities we must show in dealing with the problems of today. "The problems shift from generation to generation," he observes, "but the spirit in which they must be approached, if they are to be successfully solved, remains ever the same." In other words, as we face new social and industrial conditions, we must adopt both the independent and the community-oriented ways of the Puritans settlers. These men and women were not strict adherents to the principle of *laissez-faire*, Roosevelt contends. When they encountered behavior that violated both the rights of man and the commands of God, they did not hesitate to *regulate* against such conduct "with instant, unquestioning promptness and effectiveness." In sum, he finds that the Puritan spirit "never shrank from regulation of conduct if such regulation was necessary for the public weal." This is the spirit that he wants twentieth-century Americans to embrace.[73]

Some two hundred years after the Puritans settled New England, Roosevelt explains in his Address at Colorado Springs, hardy and venturesome backwoodsmen spread westward across the American continent. Like their forebears, the men and women of the frontier cleared dense forests, constructed houses, and tilled the land. Most important, Roosevelt adds, they spread American institutions and the spirit of individual freedom. Indeed, no other civilization in the history of the world has managed to spread the principle of liberty across so vast a continent as ours; not even the Greeks and the Romans were able to colonize and, at the same time, preserve both national unity and local and individual freedom. "When a Hellenic or Latin city sent off a colony, one of two things happened. Either the colony was kept in political subjection to the city or state of which it was an offshoot, or else it became a wholly independent and alien, and often a hostile, nation. Both systems were fraught with disaster." In the case of the Greeks, Roosevelt observes that local independence came at the expense of national unity. In the case of the Romans, national unity was preserved, but it came by means of "a crushing centralized despotism." The American pioneers, on the other hand, were "at once the strongest and the most liberty-loving among all the people who had been thrust out into new continents." Our constitutional system, Roosevelt asserts, has enabled us to do what the Greeks and Romans could never do; it has allowed us to preserve "the complete unity of an expanding race without impairing in the slightest degree the liberty of the individual." When, in a given territory, the number of settlers became sufficiently numerous, it was admitted in the Union and thereby permitted to share all the rights and all the duties of the citizens of the older states.[74]

With the exception of preserving the Union during the Civil War, Roosevelt concludes, there has been nothing so important as the American conquest and settlement of the West. "In all the history of mankind there is nothing that quite parallels the way in which our people have filled a vacant continent with self-governing commonwealths, knit into one nation." This feat, Roosevelt adds, was the result of a decades-long struggle that demanded qualities of daring, hardihood, and endurance. These traits, he asserts, are not merely indispensable to pioneers; they are also the qualities that determine success for all people. For this reason, it is altogether fitting and proper that the thought and action of the United States should be guided by the spirit of the West. For Roosevelt, the coward and the weakling had no place among the pioneer settlers, and they have no place among liberty-loving Americans today. In his view, the history of western development is a record of which all Americans should be proud, for it is a record of great daring and ceaseless strife against both man and nature. Yet, when we pay respect to the grim, hardy, and determined men who worked hard and risked much to lay deep the foundations of our civilization, Roosevelt wants everyone to remember that the only homage that counts is the homage of deeds. In other words, it is fine to gather in order to commemorate what has been done in the past, but "lip-loyalty" means nothing unless it is backed by real action. "It would be a sad and evil thing for this country if ever the day came when we considered the great deeds of our forefathers as an excuse for our resting slothfully satisfied with what has been already done."[75]

To TR, we must apply the courage and strength of the pioneers to the problems of the modern age. "We need the positive virtues of resolution, of courage, of indomitable will, of power to do without shirking the rough work that must always be done, and to persevere through the long days of slow progress or of seeming failure which always come before any final triumph, no matter how brilliant." At the same time, he maintains that these qualities must be accompanied by even higher ones. Stated simply, courage, strength, and intelligence must be accompanied by moral purpose. Without a firm moral sense, Roosevelt explains, the strong and wise man is nothing but a curse to himself and to his neighbors, and this truth applies to both private and public life. If Washington and Lincoln had been unintelligent, weak, and vacillating, the American nation might not have survived. But these great men would have posed an even greater threat to their countrymen, if they had been motivated entirely by self-seeking ambition and had cared nothing for either the rights of others or the dictates of moral law. A good citizen, Roosevelt proclaims, is a good spouse, a good parent, a good neighbor, and a good worker. "But," he concludes, "we cannot stop even with this. Each of us has not only his duty to himself, his family, and his neighbors, but his duty to the State and to the nation." Every American has an obligation—in both private and public life—to serve the principles of patriotism, freedom, responsibility, honesty, and justice.[76]

THE IMPORTANCE OF NATIONAL CHARACTER

Roosevelt not only encouraged Americans to embrace hard work, honesty, consideration, and justice but also called upon them to apply this standard to *the conduct of nations.* In other words, his demand for virtue applied as much to the nation as to the individual. As he explains in his 1907 Jamestown Address, "The nation, which is but the aggregate of the individuals comprising it, will rise or fail to rise in any great crisis according to the ideals and standards that it has kept in mind in ordinary days, and according to the way in which it has practically trained itself to realize these ideals and come up to these standards." Roosevelt wants the United States to treat other nations the same way that each and every American is to treat his family, friends, and neighbors. It must, therefore, work hard; insist upon the principles of honesty, justice, and fair dealing; exhibit kindness and consideration; and, if necessary, stand firm and fight for righteousness.[77]

Often, as in speeches like his address to the men and women of Waukesha, Wisconsin, Roosevelt alternates in speaking about individual and national responsibilities. He begins this address by stating his belief that, while the United States is destined to play a great part on the world stage, the American people have the power to decide whether their nation will play its part "well or ill." "We must hold our own," Roosevelt declares. "If we show ourselves weaklings we will earn the contempt of mankind . . . but . . . strength should go hand in hand with courtesy, with scrupulous regard in word and deed, not only for the rights, but for the feelings, of other nations." Then, in the very next sentence, he speaks of the *individual's* duty to follow this standard as well. "I want to see a man able to hold his own. I have no respect for the man who will put up with injustice. If a man will not take his part, the part is not worth taking. . . . On the other hand, I have a hearty contempt for the man who is always walking about to pick a quarrel, and above all, wanting to say something unpleasant to someone else."[78] Let each and every American tend to his or her individual responsibilities, Roosevelt declares. "Do not shirk any duty; do not shirk any difficulty that is forced upon us, but do not invite it by foolish language." He acknowledges that this is all common sense advice, "the kind of common sense that we apply in our own lives, man to man, neighbor to neighbor." But the purpose of the speech is to stress that what is true among individuals is also true, on a larger scale, among nations. Roosevelt believes that weak and cowardly nations ought to be despised as much as weak and cowardly men. At the same time, he emphasizes that both individuals and nations should be careful not to talk ill of others and give needless offense. This, Roosevelt concludes, is his theory of what America's foreign policy should be.[79] It is what he meant previously by quoting the old proverb: "Speak softly and carry a big stick."[80]

Guided by this theory of *national character*, Roosevelt pursued a foreign policy that was both conciliatory and aggressive. He supported America's conflict with the Philippines, which had been freed of Spanish rule during the

Spanish-American War only to become a possession of the United States. But, after years of guerilla warfare against the United States, which resulted in barbaric acts on both sides, Roosevelt came to understand his country's discomfort with imperial expansion. He ended the war and promised to prepare the islands for eventual self-government. This is not meant to suggest that he was reluctant to assert American power in the Western Hemisphere, where TR relied on the Monroe Doctrine to argue that the United States would not allow European nations to acquire territory in Central or South America. Foreign powers were not permitted to send troops to enforce their rights against bankrupt Latin American nations, although Roosevelt was prepared to use American forces to guarantee these rights. This application of the Monroe Doctrine to the area of economic imperialism was termed the "Roosevelt Corollary," and it was enforced when both Venezuela and Santo Domingo disputed their foreign debts. In both cases, Roosevelt pushed for arbitration and managed to avoid armed conflict. Building on these successes, he also played the role of mediator in a dispute between France and Germany over Morocco, and even won the Nobel Peace Prize for mediating the negotiations to end the Russo-Japanese War.

On the other hand, when it came to disputes that involved the United States, Roosevelt was reluctant to rely exclusively on diplomacy. When, for example, the United States and Canada were unable to agree on the southern boundary of Alaska, he made preparations for war and sent additional troops to southern Alaska. Ultimately, he accepted an arbitration panel of six impartial jurists, three chosen by each side, but ordered that his representatives not compromise the principle involved. TR was even more heavy-handed in his dealings with Cuba, demanding that the new Cuban constitution contain provisions that guaranteed to the United States the right to intervene to protect order, and that prohibited Cuba from making treaties that granted special privileges to nations other than the United States. But perhaps his most aggressive foreign policy initiative was his support of a Panamanian revolt against Colombia, which allowed him to acquire the Isthmus of Panama and build the Panama Canal. Roosevelt was determined to build a canal that would serve America's economic and military interests by making it easier for its ships to circle the world. Initially, he signed a treaty with Colombia. But, when it was rejected by the Colombian Congress, Roosevelt was informed of a planned revolt against Colombia and ordered Secretary of War Elihu Root to send additional troops and ships to the coast of South America. Invoking a treaty signed in 1846, which gave the United States the right of way in the Isthmus of Panama, American ships were employed to "maintain free and uninterrupted transit" during the confusion. The Panamanian revolution succeeded, and the new government agreed to sign a treaty that allowed the United States to build its canal.[81]

While some of the above examples demonstrate that Roosevelt often acted on the belief that foreign policy is governed by national self-interest, they should not be taken to suggest that he rejected such abstract moral principles as justice and human rights. In 1897, Roosevelt condemned timid European rulers for ignoring the massacre of hundreds of thousands of Armenians by the Turks so as to preserve peace in their own lands. War was averted, he argued, but it came at the cost of great bloodshed and "infinitely more suffering and degradation to wretched women and children than have occurred in any European struggle since the days of Waterloo."[82] Such moral condemnation is consistent with the remarks that TR makes in his Sixth Annual Message to Congress: "It is a mistake, and it betrays a spirit of foolish cynicism, to maintain that all international governmental action is, and must ever be, based upon mere selfishness, and that to advance ethical reason for such action is always a sign of hypocrisy. This is no more necessarily true of the action of governments than of the action of individuals." According to Roosevelt, to ascribe purely base motives to either an individual or a nation is a sure sign of a base nature. He adds that a nation cannot often afford to disregard its own interests, any more than a private individual can do so, but it is also true that the really great nation, like the average person, often acts with concern for a genuine public spirit and the rights of others. In other words, Roosevelt believes that ethical concerns do and should guide international action and decision-making. "It is neither wise nor right for a nation to disregard its own needs," Roosevelt concludes, "and it is foolish—and may be wicked—to think that other nations will disregard theirs. But it is wicked for a nation only to regard its own interest, and foolish to believe that such is the sole motive that actuates any other nation." In Roosevelt's opinion, our aim should be "to raise the ethical standard of national action just as we strive to raise the ethical standard of individual action."[83] But TR's emphasis on good character is also apparent in the statements that he made regarding the social/moral issues of his time.

NOTES

1. Michael McGerr, *A Fierce Discontent: The Rise and Fall of the Progressive Movement in America (1870–1920)* (New York: Free Press, 2003), 150–51.

2. McGerr, *Fierce Discontent*, 152.

3. Eric Foner, *The Story of American Freedom* (New York: W. W. Norton and Company, 1999), 117–18.

4. McGerr, *Fierce Discontent*, 152, 154. See also Foner, *Story of American Freedom*, 120–21; Richard Hofstadter, *Social Darwinism in American Thought* (Boston:

Beacon Press, 1992); Sidney Fine, *Laissez Faire and the General-Welfare State* (Ann Arbor: The University of Michigan Press, 1964).

5. McGerr, *Fierce Discontent*, 153, 154.

6. McGerr, *Fierce Discontent*, 153–54.

7. Michael McGerr, "Theodore Roosevelt," in *The American Presidency*, eds. Alan Brinkley and Davis Dyer (Boston: Houghton Mifflin Company, 2004), 275.

8. Theodore Roosevelt, "Fifth Annual Message," in *Presidential Addresses and State Papers*, vol. 4 (New York: Review of Reviews, 1910), 563.

9. Roosevelt, "Fifth Annual Message," 563–64.

10. Theodore Roosevelt, "Address to the Harvard Union," in *Presidential Addresses and State Papers*, vol. 6 (New York: Review of Reviews, 1910), 1176–77.

11. Roosevelt, "Fifth Annual Message," 564.

12. Theodore Roosevelt, "Fourth Annual Message," in *Presidential Addresses and State Papers*, vol. 3 (New York: Review of Reviews, 1910), 128.

13. Roosevelt, "Fifth Annual Message," 565–66.

14. Theodore Roosevelt, "Christian Citizenship," in *The Strenuous Life*, vol. 13 of *The Works of Theodore Roosevelt*, National Edition (New York: Charles Scribner's Sons, 1926), 494.

15. G. Wallace Chessman, *Theodore Roosevelt and the Politics of Power* (Prospect Heights: Waveland Press, 1994), 70, 73.

16. Kathleen Dalton, *Theodore Roosevelt: A Strenuous Life* (New York: Vintage Books, 2002), 182.

17. See, for example, Theodore Roosevelt to Edward O. Wolcott, September 15, 1900, in *Campaigns and Controversies*, vol. 14 of *The Works of Theodore Roosevelt*, National Edition (New York: Charles Scribner's Sons, 1926), 363–64.

18. See Theodore Roosevelt, "Address at the Independent Club," in *Campaigns and Controversies*, vol. 14 of *The Works of Theodore Roosevelt*, National Edition (New York: Charles Scribner's Sons, 1926).

19. See Theodore Roosevelt, "Social Evolution," in *American Ideals*, vol. 13 of *The Works of Theodore Roosevelt*, National Edition (New York: Charles Scribner's Sons, 1926).

20. Roosevelt, "Social Evolution."

21. See Theodore Roosevelt, "Address at Indianapolis," in *Presidential Addresses and State Papers*, vol. 6 (New York: Review of Reviews, 1910); Theodore Roosevelt, "Remarks at the Washington Memorial Chapel," in *Presidential Addresses and State Papers*, vol. 3 (New York: Review of Reviews, 1910); Theodore Roosevelt, "The Heirs of Abraham Lincoln," in *Social Justice and Popular Rule*, vol. 17 of *The Works of Theodore Roosevelt*, National Edition (New York: Charles Scribner's Sons, 1926); Theodore Roosevelt, "Lincoln," in *Hero Tales from American History*, vol. 10 of *The Works of Theodore Roosevelt*, National Edition (New York: Charles Scribner's Sons, 1926); Theodore Roosevelt, *The Square Deal: 1903–1905*, vol. 4 of *The Letters of Theodore Roosevelt*, ed. Elting Morison (Cambridge: Harvard University Press, 1951), 1049–50; Nicholas Roosevelt, *Theodore Roosevelt: The Man as I Knew Him* (New York: Dodd, Mead, 1967), 43; Joseph Bucklin Bishop, *Theodore Roosevelt and His Time Shown in His Own Letters*

(New York: Charles Scribner's Sons, 1920), 352; Charles T. White, *Lincoln and Prohibition* (New York: The Abingdon Press, 1921), 111.

22. McGerr, *Fierce Discontent*, 155–57; McGerr, "Theodore Roosevelt," 274. See also Lewis Gould, *The Presidency of Theodore Roosevelt* (Lawrence: University Press of Kansas, 1991), 49–53; Forrest McDonald, *The United States in the 20th Century: 1900–1920* (Reading: Addison–Wesley Publishing, 1970), 96–97; George E. Mowry, *The Era of Theodore Roosevelt and the Birth of Modern America, 1900–1912* (New York: Harper and Row, 1962), 130–31.

23. Theodore Roosevelt, *Autobiography*, vol. 20 of *The Works of Theodore Roosevelt*, National Edition (New York: Charles Scribner's Sons, 1926), 417–18.

24. McGerr, *Fierce Discontent*, 157–59; Gould, *Presidency of Theodore Roosevelt*, 212–18.

25. Theodore Roosevelt, "Second Annual Message," in *Presidential Addresses and State Papers*, vol. 2 (New York: Review of Reviews, 1910), 610, 620.

26. Gould, *Presidency of Theodore Roosevelt*, 106–8; McDonald, *United States in the 20th Century*, 94.

27. Theodore Roosevelt, "Third Annual Message," in *Presidential Addresses and State Papers*, vol. 2 (New York: Review of Reviews, 1910), 650–52.

28. Roosevelt, "Fourth Annual Message," 134–35.

29. Gould, *Presidency of Theodore Roosevelt*, 150.

30. Theodore Roosevelt, "Speech at the Iroquois Club," in *Presidential Addresses and State Papers*, vol. 4 (New York: Review of Reviews, 1910), 370–71.

31. Roosevelt, "Fifth Annual Message," 568–69.

32. Roosevelt, "Fifth Annual Message," 572–73.

33. Roosevelt, "Fifth Annual Message," 574–75.

34. For a description of the passage of the railway rate bill, see Gould, *Presidency of Theodore Roosevelt*, 159–65; Mowry, *Era of Theodore Roosevelt*, 203–06; John M. Blum, *The Republican Roosevelt* (Cambridge: Harvard University Press, 1981), 87–105; Jeffrey Tulis, *The Rhetorical Presidency* (Princeton: Princeton University Press, 1987), 97–116.

35. McGerr, "Theodore Roosevelt," 275.

36. McGerr, *Fierce Discontent*, 160.

37. McGerr, *Fierce Discontent*, 160–61. See also Upton Sinclair, *The Jungle*, ed. James R. Barrett (Urbana: University of Illinois Press, 1988), 73, 94–96, 130.

38. Gould, *Presidency of Theodore Roosevelt*, 167–69; McGerr, *Fierce Discontent*, 162–63.

39. McGerr, *Fierce Discontent*, 160.

40. Paul Grondahl, *I Rose Like a Rocket: The Political Education of Theodore Roosevelt* (New York: Free Press, 2004), 322–23.

41. Theodore Roosevelt, *The Wilderness Hunter*, vol. 2 of *The Works of Theodore Roosevelt*, National Edition (New York: Charles Scribner's Sons, 1926), xxix.

42. Theodore Roosevelt, "Address to the Society of American Foresters," in *Presidential Addresses and State Papers*, vol. 1 (New York: Review of Reviews, 1910), 250–51.

43. Roosevelt, "Address to the Society of American Foresters," 251–52. See also McGerr, *Fierce Discontent*, 165–66; McGerr, "Theodore Roosevelt," 276. McGerr correctly observes that Roosevelt was a brand of conservationist who "wanted conservation to promote efficient economic development." But he sees Roosevelt's support for conservation as contradictory: "Characteristically, Roosevelt embodied all the contradictions of the conservation movement. The naturalist who loved birds and the former rancher who loved the West wanted to preserve nature. . . . The hunter who had stalked animals and had lived off the land wanted to preserve natural resources for economic development." Moreover, McGerr stresses how Roosevelt's conservation policies limited individual freedom for the sake of the collective good. On the contrary, I am attempting to show that Roosevelt's conservation policies were but one more example of his belief that collective action could serve individual self-interest.

44. Theodore Roosevelt, "Speech at Salt Lake City," in *Presidential Addresses and State Papers*, vol. 2 (New York: Review of Reviews, 1910), 438–40.

45. McGerr, *Fierce Discontent*, 165.

46. Gould, *Presidency of Theodore Roosevelt*, 111, 62; McGerr, *Fierce Discontent*, 166–67; Mowry, *Era of Theodore Roosevelt*, 124–25; Dalton, *A Strenuous Life*, 245–46.

47. McGerr, *Fierce Discontent*, 166–67; Gould, *Presidency of Theodore Roosevelt*, 199–202.

48. Gould, *Presidency of Theodore Roosevelt*, 199–202; Dalton, *Strenuous Life*, 247–48.

49. McGerr, *Fierce Discontent*, 168; Gould, *Presidency of Theodore Roosevelt*, 201–02.

50. McGerr, *Fierce Discontent*, 168; Gould, *Presidency of Theodore Roosevelt*, 169, 203–07.

51. McGerr, *Fierce Discontent*, 140–41; Gould, *Presidency of Theodore Roosevelt*, 234–35. See also Theodore Roosevelt to Honore Jaxon, 22 April 1907, *The Big Stick: 1905–1907*, vol. 5 of *The Letters of Theodore Roosevelt*, ed. Elting Morison (Cambridge: Harvard University Press, 1952), 653–54.

52. Theodore Roosevelt, "Address to the Locomotive Firemen," in *Presidential Addresses and State Papers*, vol. 1 (New York: Review of Reviews, 1910), 159.

53. Roosevelt, "Address to the Locomotive Firemen," 164–65.

54. Roosevelt, "Address to the Locomotive Firemen," 166–67.

55. McGerr, *Fierce Discontent*, 122–23; Gould, *Presidency of Theodore Roosevelt*, 68; Mowry, *Era of Theodore Roosevelt*, 134–36.

56. McGerr, *Fierce Discontent*, 123–24.

57. Gould, *Presidency of Theodore Roosevelt*, 69. See also Theodore Roosevelt to Winthrop Murray Crane, October 22, 1902, vol. 3, *The Letters of Theodore Roosevelt, The Square Deal: 1901–1903*, ed. Elting Morison (Cambridge: Harvard University Press, 1951), 362.

58. Gould, *Presidency of Theodore Roosevelt*, 69–70. See also Roosevelt, *Autobiography*, 455.

59. McGerr, *Fierce Discontent*, 124–25; McGerr, "Theodore Roosevelt," 276–77; Gould, *Presidency of Theodore Roosevelt*, 71; Mowry, *Era of Theodore Roosevelt*, 137–39.

60. McGerr, "Theodore Roosevelt," 277.

61. Roosevelt, "Social Evolution," 239–40.

62. Theodore Roosevelt, "Civic Helpfulness," in *The Strenuous Life*, vol. 13 of *The Works of Theodore Roosevelt*, National Edition (New York: Charles Scribner's Sons, 1926), 380; Theodore Roosevelt, "Promise and Performance," in *The Strenuous Life*, vol. 13 of *The Works of Theodore Roosevelt*, National Edition (New York: Charles Scribner's Sons, 1926), 398.

63. Theodore Roosevelt, "Address at Dallas," in *Presidential Addresses and State Papers*, vol. 3 (New York: Review of Reviews, 1910), 321–22.

64. Theodore Roosevelt, "Address at Raleigh," in *Presidential Addresses and State Papers*, vol. 4 (New York: Review of Reviews, 1910), 476.

65. Theodore Roosevelt, "Address at the Jamestown Exposition," in *Presidential Addresses and State Papers*, vol. 6 (New York: Review of Reviews, 1910), 1301–2.

66. Theodore Roosevelt, "Speech at York," in *Presidential Addresses and State Papers*, vol. 5 (New York: Review of Reviews, 1910), 844–45.

67. Roosevelt, "Speech at York," 843–44.

68. Theodore Roosevelt, "Speech at the Pilgrim Memorial," in *Presidential Addresses and State Papers*, vol. 6 (New York: Review of Reviews, 1910), 362–64.

69. Roosevelt, "Remarks at the Washington Memorial Chapel," 31, 34–35.

70. Roosevelt, "Remarks at the Washington Memorial Chapel," 32–34.

71. Theodore Roosevelt, "Speech at Antietam," in *Presidential Addresses and State Papers*, vol. 2 (New York: Review of Reviews, 1910), 487–88.

72. Roosevelt, "Speech at the Pilgrim Memorial Monument," 1346–47.

73. Roosevelt, "Speech at the Pilgrim Memorial Monument," 1349–51.

74. Theodore Roosevelt, "Address at Colorado Springs," in *American Ideals*, vol. 13 of *The Works of Theodore Roosevelt*, National Edition (New York: Charles Scribner's Sons, 1926), 453–54.

75. Roosevelt, "Address at Colorado Springs," 454–56.

76. Roosevelt, "Address at Colorado Springs," 456–58.

77. Roosevelt, "Address at the Jamestown Exposition," 1307–8.

78. Theodore Roosevelt, "Speech at Waukesha," in *Presidential Addresses and State Papers*, vol. 1 (New York: Review of Reviews, 1910), 268–69.

79. Roosevelt, "Speech at Waukesha," 271–72.

80. See also Theodore Roosevelt's "Address at the Minnesota State Fair," in *American Ideals*, vol. 13 of *The Works of Theodore Roosevelt*, National Edition (New York: Charles Scribner's Sons, 1926), 474.

81. McGerr, "Theodore Roosevelt," 280–82; Michael P. Riccards, *The Ferocious Engine of Democracy: From Teddy Roosevelt Through George W. Bush* (New York: Cooper Square Press, 2003), 10–15, 17–20.

82. Theodore Roosevelt, "Washington's Forgotten Maxim," in *American Ideals*, vol. 13 of *The Works of Theodore Roosevelt*, National Edition (New York: Charles Scribner's Sons, 1926), 184–85.

83. Theodore Roosevelt, "Sixth Annual Message," in *Presidential Addresses and State Papers*, vol. 5 (New York: Review of Reviews, 1910), 955–56.

Chapter Six

The Preacher President

Theodore Roosevelt saw economic regulation as a way to level the economic playing field so that individuals might realize their potential. But he also employed inspirational rhetoric and personal example to promote his particular conception of the ideal American character, one that was devoted to both self-reliance and service. This was how Roosevelt intended to reconcile individualism and collectivism through a strategy that is at once institutional and personal. There can be no doubt that Roosevelt saw society as interdependent and, as he argued the advantages of certain institutional restraints on economic activity, he also preached whole-heartedly a "gospel" of character and individual responsibility. Regulation alone was insufficient. Roosevelt's skepticism about its ability to correct all the injustices of society was rooted in his early personal transformations, both physical and mental, achieved through sheer will and iron self-discipline; in his deep-seated respect for Abraham Lincoln's notion of promoting civic friendship and social responsibility through the use of rhetoric and persuasion; and in his appreciation for America's individualistic cultural identity, which he had explored at length in his western writings.

But, as Michael McGerr observes, Roosevelt's individualistic convictions are easily seen in his approach to *social* reform. Studies of Roosevelt's place in the Progressive movement generally ignore these crusades, even though they constitute a strand of Progressivism that is as important as the regulation of business interests. As McGerr suggests, the Progressives were like a jazz band, "in which each instrumentalist improvised a unique melody on top of a shared set of chords."[1] Wealth, for example, allegedly made the upper class behave in a selfish and indulgent manner, so some Progressives advocated taxes on inheritance and income.[2] At the same time, others maintained that the problems of the poor and working classes were the product of preventable social conditions related to poor sanitation and safety at home and at work, no access to recreational facilities, lack of education, limited competition in the marketplace, and/or no public regulation of working hours, wages, and standards in business.[3] Finally, fearing the extent to which Social Darwinism had perverted the principle of individualism, and believing that the public's appetite for pleasure promoted individualism, some Progressives even attempted to regulate private adult behavior.[4] In short, the enemies of Progressivism were real, and they included not just large business conglomerates and corrupt wealth but also prostitution, divorce, and alcohol. Roosevelt spoke to these latter matters as well, and his words are an essential dimension of his political thought.

OLIVER CROMWELL AND TR'S VIEWS ON RESPONSIBLE MORAL LEADERSHIP

Like his father, Roosevelt was no moral relativist. Armed with a clear, definite, and demanding moral code, he honored marriage and motherhood, expressed concern over falling birthrates and rising divorce rates, lectured the American people on how the increasing use of birth control devices both reduced the population and encouraged prostitution, and agreed that certain materials corrupted youth and denigrated American culture. In short, he had no difficulty in distinguishing between right and wrong and believed it was his public duty to warn the American people that a permissive moral attitude would lead to national ruin. Yet, while he supported the spirit behind the various Progressive crusades against indecency, prostitution, divorce, and alcohol, TR was reluctant to use the powers of the federal government to enforce private morality. No doubt, this stemmed from individualistic conceptions that made him unlike most reformers.

A revealing expression of Roosevelt's views regarding the proper relationship between leadership and moral reform can be found in his biography of Oliver Cromwell. As he explained to publisher Charles Scribner, "I have tried to show Cromwell, not only as one of the great generals of all time, but as a great statesman who on the whole did a marvelous work, and who, where he failed, failed because he lacked the power of self-repression possessed by Washington and Lincoln." Roosevelt was "thoroughly interested" in his subject. In fact, he admired this Puritan opponent to absolutist royal authority. At the same time, he could not help but conclude that, by making himself a dictator, Cromwell acted unnecessarily and destroyed the possibility of making permanent the effects of his revolution.[5]

Cromwell was the leader of the Roundheads, the group of predominantly Puritan landholders, tradesmen, and manufacturers who opposed the royal power and religious policies of Charles I. As king, Charles took England into wars with Spain and France, both of which were unsuccessful and increased the king's desperation for money. Charles raised the needed revenue by forcing loans from his subjects, punishing those who failed to comply by quartering soldiers in their homes or throwing them into prison without a trial. He also resolved to rule without Parliament and did so for eleven years. But, after provoking an uprising by attempting to introduce Episcopalian church government in Presbyterian Scotland, he summoned Parliament to obtain the funds needed to punish the Scots. The Puritan leaders of the House of Commons, determined to take control of the government, executed the king's first minister and passed a law that not only forbade the crown to dissolve Parliament but also required the convening of sessions at least once every three years. In 1642, Charles marched with his armed guard into the House chamber and attempted to arrest five of the Puritan leaders. All of them escaped, but this sparked the English Civil War. The pro-Parliament forces eventually won the English Civil War, and in January 1649, Charles I was beheaded. For a brief period, Parliament continued to act as England's legislative body, but the real power rested with Cromwell, the head of the army, who soon grew frustrated by the attempts of legislators to perpetuate their power and profit by confiscating the wealth of their opponents. In 1653, Cromwell marched a detachment of troops into the Parliament and ordered the members to disperse. From this point on, the Commonwealth ceased to exist, and a dictatorship was established under a constitution that was drafted by officers of the army. This so-called Instrument of Government made Cromwell the ruler for life and allowed him to use the police powers of the state to enforce strict Calvinistic doctrines, such as the prohibition of any public recreation on Sundays, the only holiday for workers. After Cromwell's death, elections were held, and the new Parliament proclaimed as king Charles II, the son of Charles I.[6]

Roosevelt concludes that Cromwell lived at a time when the word of God was quoted by nearly all people and on every occasion, no matter how trivial. "It is very possible," he acknowledges, "that quite as large a proportion of people nowadays strive to shape their internal lives in accordance with the Ten Commandments and the Golden Rule; indeed, it is probable that the proportion is far greater; but professors of religion then carried their religion into all the externals of their lives." Roosevelt observes that this was certainly true of Cromwell, who "belonged among those earnest souls who indulged in the very honorable dream of a world where civil government and social life alike should be based upon the Commandments set forth in the Bible." But,

Roosevelt suggests, this dream, while noble, has "a very dangerous side: so dangerous indeed that in practice the effort is apt to result in harm, unless it is undertaken in a spirit of the broadest charity and toleration; for the more sincere the men who make it, the more certain they are to treat, not only their own principles, but their own passions, prejudices, vanities, and jealousies as representing the will, not of themselves, but of Heaven." In short, Roosevelt believes that, while it is noble—in theory—to work for the achievement of God's will on earth, this effort—in practice—tends to lead to the "merciless persecution" of so-called heretics as well as the end of free thinking and free action. For Roosevelt, this does not mean that men and women should not come together to search for the truth. Nor does it imply that moral considerations have no place in government. Rather, Roosevelt stresses, it means simply that "each body of seekers must be permitted to work out its own beliefs without molestation, so long as it does not strive to interfere with the beliefs of others."[7]

According to Roosevelt, the problem with Cromwell was that he possessed no real appreciation of "the vital importance of the reign of law to the proper development of orderly liberty." While Roosevelt acknowledges that Cromwell deserves praise for his spirituality as well as his fervent opposition to corruption, he concludes that the British ruler desired only to remedy specific and immediate evils. Cromwell was, in other words, too impatient to found the kind of legal and constitutional system that would be able to prevent the recurrence of wrongdoing and evil. It is this tendency, Roosevelt believes, that caused Cromwell to deviate from the path later trod by George Washington. Unlike America's preeminent founding father, Cromwell proved unable to help establish a system of free government and the rule of law. His government was, instead, merely personal and based essentially on the principle that might makes right. Impatient with the delays and shortcomings of ordinary constitutional and legal proceedings, Cromwell overturned constitutions and disregarded statutes whenever it served his purposes to do so. But such a remedy is *always* dangerous, Roosevelt stresses, even when absolutely necessary. When the strong man is both able and permitted to set himself above the law, there can be no result other than social decay.[8]

It is certainly true, Roosevelt says, that Cromwell partially perceived and understood the principles of liberty and toleration, but "the ideal after which he strove was not reached in his time." Perhaps, TR suggests, it was too soon to be realized. Roosevelt believes that Cromwell should be honored for his aspirations toward the ideal, yet he encourages the readers of his biography to remain mindful of "how far short of reaching it he [Cromwell] fell."[9] Again, Roosevelt observes, it helps to compare the leader of the Roundheads to the leader of the American Revolution. Unlike Cromwell, Washington fully appreciated the meaning of liberty. Roosevelt notes that Washington would not allow his officers to make him a dictator, nor did he allow his army to march against the Continental Congress that failed to provide for it. "Unlike Cromwell," Roosevelt explains, "he [Washington] saw that the safety of the people lay in working out their own salvation, even though they showed much wrong-headedness and blindness, not merely to morality, but to their own interests; and, in the long run, the people justified this trust." In short, Roosevelt asserts that it is the mark of a true leader to permit the people to decide important moral matters for themselves.[10] Of course, Roosevelt acknowledges, 17th century Englishmen had a more difficult time with the concept of liberty than modern Americans, who, Roosevelt believes, understand and cherish the principle of individual freedom. After all, he adds, the United States was conceived in liberty, and its founders recognized from the beginning that differences of opinion, if tolerated, would only add to the greatness and strength of the nation. Roosevelt concludes, "The truth is, that a strong nation can only be saved by itself, and not by a strong man, though it can be greatly aided and guided by a strong man." Roosevelt's message is clear: moral suasion, as opposed to prohibitory law, is the way to improve the character of a nation that is truly capable of freedom. True statesmen appreciate the difference between *leading* the people and *mastering* them.[11]

ADDRESSING ISSUES OF MORAL BEHAVIOR

There were, to be sure, a few occasions on which Roosevelt sought legal and/or institutional means to fight private immorality. He worked, for example, to suppress coverage of Harry Thaw's sensational murder trial. On June 25, 1906, Thaw shot and killed the famed architect Stanford White. When Thaw's trial began, newspapers began to print the sordid details that had led up to the murder: Thaw had competed with White for the affections of the actress Evelyn Nesbit, whom White had drugged and raped when she was sixteen. Thaw's lawyers attempted to portray him as a wronged husband whose innocent wife had been ruined by White. They argued that their client had "struck for the purity of the home, for the purity of American womanhood, for the purity of American wives and daughters," but Roosevelt agreed with those who feared that scandalous details about White's sexual promiscuity and Thaw's violence and drug use would "excite prurient imaginations" and corrupt the nation's youth. The President urged his postmaster general to learn whether the government had the power to stop mailing privileges for any newspaper that featured the Thaw trial transcripts. The postmaster informed him that no such power existed.[12]

Roosevelt made a handful of other efforts to achieve social reform through coercive means. He urged the banning of a movie that showed the black versus white Jack Johnson-James Jeffries fight, because whites had rioted in thirty cities after Johnson won. In addition, he decided to bar an alien's reentry into the United States after he took a woman who was not his wife to Canada, and he ordered the Justice Department to fine the *New York Herald* $3,000 for publishing personal ads that advertised the services of prostitutes. Along these lines, Roosevelt, who believed the newspaper accounts of 60,000 girls drugged, kidnapped, and forced into prostitution, even agreed, by proclamation, to join European countries in a cooperative effort to abolish the transnational trafficking of women for the purposes of prostitution. He also recommended harsh punishment for the "flagrant man swine" who forced girls into prostitution.[13] With the exception of these individual and isolated examples, however, TR made few attempts to legislate his personal moral beliefs. This does not mean that Roosevelt was unwilling to act as a crusader for moral reform; he simply chose to rely more on rhetorical persuasion than on prohibitory legislation. The presidency, after all, offered him the most high-profile platform—"the bully pulpit"—from which to preach his message of proper living, and he did not confine his sermons to once a week.[14]

One of Roosevelt's favorite sermon topics was family life. In his address to the National Congress of Mothers, he declares that "the Nation is in a bad way if there is no real home, if the family is not of the right kind; if the man is not a good husband and father, if he is brutal or cowardly or selfish, if the woman has lost her sense of duty, if she is sunk in vapid self-indulgence or has let her nature be twisted so that she prefers a sterile pseudointellectuality to that great and beautiful development of character which comes only to those whose lives know the fullness of duty done, of effort made and self-sacrifice undergone." In short, Roosevelt maintains that the welfare of the nation depends upon whether the average father, mother, and child exercise good character. According to TR, wealth, intelligence, and artistic talent are no substitutes for a healthy home life, and this, in turn, depends upon family members possessing the qualities of hard work, honesty, decency, common sense, duty, and sacrifice.[15] "There are certain old truths," Roosevelt argues, "which will be true as long as this world endures, and which no amount of progress can alter. One of these is the truth that the primary duty of the husband is to be the homemaker, the breadwinner for his wife and children, and that the primary duty of the woman is to be the helpmeet, the housewife, and mother." Roosevelt stresses that he admires educated women and believes that women are just as capable as men. Nevertheless, he expects women to do their duty, and this duty, in his view, entails marriage and motherhood.[16]

According to Roosevelt, the duty of women is more difficult, more important, and more honorable than that of men. "No ordinary work done by a man is either as hard or as responsible as the work of a woman who is bringing up a family of small children; for upon her time and strength demands are made not only every hour of the day but often every hour of the night," and "if the family means are scant she must usually enjoy even her rare holidays taking her whole brood of children with her." To Roosevelt, the lives of most women "are often led on the lonely heights of quiet, self-sacrificing heroism." For this reason, a good mother is the perfect personification of Roosevelt's American ideal; she lives a life of constant effort and self-sacrifice. He stresses that this is not to imply that exceptional women cannot lead great careers outside the home. But the careers of both men and women must always be regarded as additions to, not substitutes for, their homework. Roosevelt is not speaking about exceptions but is focused instead on the primary duties of husbands and wives, fathers and mothers. He is speaking of the average men and women who comprise the American nation.[17]

Hard work and self-sacrifice are Roosevelt's expectations for both women and men, and he does not expect any woman to submit to a man's "gross and long-continued ill-treatment." "No wrongdoing is so abhorrent as wrongdoing by a man toward the wife and the children who should arouse every tender feeling in his nature. Selfishness toward them, lack of tenderness toward them, lack of consideration for them, above all, brutality in any form toward them, should arouse the heartiest scorn and indignation in every upright soul." A woman is as entitled to her self-respect as is a man and should have all the rights a man does. Roosevelt regards marriage as "a partnership in which each partner is in honor bound to think of the rights of the other as well as of his or her own." For Roosevelt, duties are as important as rights, and it is certainly not a bad thing for an individual to be more habitual in performing duties than in insisting upon rights.[18] TR views parenthood as hard work and a great responsibility, for mothers and fathers shape the destinies of all the generations to follow, and in bringing up their children, they must remember that firmness and wisdom are as essential as love and tenderness. Children, he says, must grow up to possess "the softer and milder virtues" as well as "those stern and hardy qualities." Nonetheless, he concedes, some children "will go wrong in spite of the best training," while others "will go right even when their surroundings are most unfortunate." But exceptions such as these do not permit the conclusion that a secure, loving, and disciplined upbringing is inconsequential.

Roosevelt believes that "an immense amount depends upon the family training," for it is in childhood that the virtues TR believes essential to the future health of the nation must be learned. Mothers cannot permit their sons to be selfish and think only of themselves; otherwise, they are responsible for the sadness and despair of the women who will be their future wives. Likewise, mothers cannot permit their daughters to grow up idle, lazy, and knowing only enjoyment. Boys and girls alike are to be taught "not to look forward to lives spent in avoiding difficulties but to lives spent in overcoming difficulties." Roosevelt wants them to be taught that work is a blessing, not a curse, and that life, while enjoyable, demands responsibility and steadfast resolution. He concludes by acknowledging that many good people, through no fault of their own, are denied the blessing of children. For these individuals, he has nothing but respect and sympathy. But he has no similar feeling for "the man or woman who deliberately foregoes these blessings, whether from viciousness, coldness, shallow-heartedness, self-indulgence, or mere failure to appreciate aright the difference between the all-important and the important." To Roosevelt, these people deserve the same contempt as the soldier who runs away during battle, or the able-bodied man who is content to eat in idleness the bread that others provide for the support of his family.[19]

Roosevelt leaves his audience with a reference to statistics that indicate a falling birthrate as well as a rising divorce rate. Even more shocking, in his opinion, is the fact that these negative developments are defended in various books and articles. He notes one article that appeared in the *Independent* in which a clergyman declares that the ambition of most Americans should be to raise just two children in order to give them an opportunity "to taste a few of the good things in life." "This man," Roosevelt laments, who is supposed to be a moral teacher, "actually set before others the ideal, not of training children to do their duty, not of sending them forth with stout hearts and ready minds to win triumphs for themselves and their country, not of allowing them the opportunity and giving them the privilege of making their own place in the world, but, forsooth, of keeping the number of children so limited that they might 'taste a few good things!'" For TR, luxury is not the way to give a child a fair chance in life; rather, true happiness belongs to those who are both self-reliant and selfless.[20] Roosevelt believes that the people of the United States should be appalled by the falling population rates that threaten the survival of the American race. Any race that permits its population to decrease to the point of extinction proves conclusively that it is unfit to exist. From his perspective, neither an individual nor a nation should prefer the life of ease and self-indulgence to the greater pleasures that come to those who work hard and know all about toil, weariness, endurance, and duty. "Save in exceptional cases the prizes worth having in life must be paid for, and the life worth living must be a life of work for a worthy end, and ordinarily of work more for others than for one's self."[21]

Roosevelt's concern about America's declining population is also a major part of his Sixth Annual Message to Congress in which he notes that there are parts of the United States where the birth rate is lower than the death rate. "Surely it should need no demonstration to show that willful sterility is, from the standpoint of the Nation, from the standpoint of the human race, the one sin for which the penalty is National death, race death; a sin for which there is no atonement." Roosevelt will excuse no man or woman from performing the primary duties of life, which is why he opposes divorce. "When home ties are loosened," he explains, "when men and women cease to regard a worthy family life, with all its duties fully performed, and all its responsibilities lived up to, as the life best worth living; then evil days for the commonwealth are at hand." He warns against the lax and arbitrary state divorce laws and urges Congress to collect further statistics on marriage and divorce in America. While aware of how difficult it is to pass a constitutional amendment regarding divorce, Roosevelt insists that the question of marriage and divorce is a matter of congressional concern. In his opinion, the divorce laws of the various states are too prone to abuse and scandal.[22] Many Progressives agreed. Upset with the lax laws of some states, which attracted outsiders seeking quick and easy divorces, these reformers advocated uniform state laws or a national statute. But it was impossible to persuade the state legislatures to accept a uniform code, and a national divorce law, as Roosevelt himself admitted, seemed unconstitutional. Still, Roosevelt insisted that families were a cornerstone of national life and therefore a legitimate public concern. The antidivorce movement, however, failed to attract the support of most Americans.[23]

Along with the fight against divorce, the Progressives waged a major campaign against alcohol. Progressive reformers possessed an optimistic belief that behavior was influenced by environment, not heredity, and saw in vice "the loss of self-control and the celebration of selfishness." As with divorce (which, in the words of Anna B. Rogers, represented "the latter-day cult of individualism; the worship of the brazen calf of Self"), Progressives lamented the consequences of individualism for the drunkard and were especially concerned with its impact on innocent people. "The drunkard," one reformer observed, "and the drunkard's interests are not the chief consideration, though these are not lost sight of. It is the drinker as a husband, a father, a voter, a worker, and a citizen—the man as a social factor, who is being considered."[24] Driven by a supreme concern for this "social factor," organizations like the Women's Christian Temperance Union (WCTU) lobbied state legislatures for stricter liquor laws and temperance instruction in the public schools, while the Anti-Saloon League focused attention on the saloon and argued on behalf of the local option, or the right of individual communities to decide whether to close their saloons. Regardless of its slight differences in focus and strategy, the movement as a whole was well-organized, middle-class, and firmly rooted in evangelical Protestantism. It was precisely because the Republican Party had many evangelical Protestants in their ranks that party leaders like Roosevelt felt enormous pressure to support Prohibition.[25]

For reasons both practical and principled, however, Roosevelt refrained from preaching publicly about Prohibition. It was one of the most controversial issues of its time, and TR, like other astute politicos, did not want to alienate a large segment of the electorate. At the same time, he saw any kind of nationwide restriction on alcohol as unenforceable and sure to result in nothing but "contempt of the law." "My experience with prohibitionists," he wrote William Howard Taft, "is that the best way to deal with them is to ignore them. I would not get drawn into any discussion with them under any circumstances." He agreed that "there are plenty of country districts where prohibition has worked well," and he indicated his support for the local option, which permitted localities, where popular sentiment demanded it, to prohibit the sale of liquor. "But to pass prohibitory laws to govern localities where the sentiment does not sustain them is simply equivalent to allowing free liquor, plus lawlessness, and is the very worst possible way of solving the problem."[26]

The views in TR's letter to Taft were not written hastily, nor taken simply for reasons of political expediency. Rather, they were the result of personal experience, specifically his attempt as New York City's police commissioner to enforce the city's Sunday closing law. In the mid-1890s, Roosevelt was forced to explain repeatedly that, while he would not have voted for this unpopular law as a legislator, he was an executive officer and therefore had the responsibility to enforce it. For him, the question was whether public officials were to be true to their oaths of office. "Our opponents of every grade and of every shade of political belief," he wrote in 1895, "take the position that government officials, who have sworn to enforce the law, shall violate their oaths whenever they think it will please a sufficient number of the public to make the violation worthwhile."[27] By enforcing the Sunday closing law honestly and impartially, Roosevelt was working to stop corruption in the Police Department. Not only was it more difficult for men with political influence to bribe officers and high officials in city government, but it was also less likely that police captains and patrolmen would bully those who had no pull whatsoever. Unfortunately, Roosevelt claimed, his critics refused to recognize this and, by choosing to place popular opinion ahead of the law, encouraged lawlessness.[28] In the end, he refused to buckle to the pressure, but the experience taught him that good citizenship was undermined by the willingness of legislators to pass laws that they did not wish to see enforced.

Despite his reluctance to speak out against liquor, Roosevelt embraced the spirit behind the temperance movement, for it was consistent with his belief that good citizenship depended upon good morals, central to which was the belief that individuals needed to think of others and not just themselves. As he tells the Holy Name Society, individuals must show by their words and actions that they are capable of thinking outside themselves. From TR's standpoint, every man and woman should be hard working, spirited, and unselfish in dealing with friends and strangers alike. They should be able to hold their own with the strong yet be ashamed to oppress the weak. Perhaps most important, TR wants all adults to be mindful of the example they offer to young people. They must remember that preaching alone is insufficient; action must support words. "There is no good in your preaching to your boys to be brave, if you run away. There is no good in your preaching to them to tell the truth if you do not. There is no good in your preaching to them to be unselfish if they see you selfish with your wife, disregardful of others." Children, Roosevelt explains, admire those who face life with an unshakable sense of duty, responsibility, and optimism. He recognizes that there is a tendency among some adolescent boys to think that wrongdoing proves their manhood. But this, Roosevelt asserts, is a false view of life, and the only way to prevent young boys from getting this impression is for adults to set an example of proper living. "Example is the most potent of all things," Roosevelt declares. If adults lie, shirk responsibility, act maliciously, use coarse and blasphemous language, and engage in selfish behavior in the presence of the young, then it is almost guaranteed that these younger people will do the same.[29]

THE SPECIAL PROBLEM OF RACE

For all of Progressivism's effort to overcome class divisions and bring different groups together to achieve economic, social, and moral change, the movement did not challenge one prevalent social/moral problem: racial segregation. The reason, McGerr argues, is that Progressive reformers believed segregation was the only realistic way to protect blacks from fierce brutality and even annihilation. Unlike other Americans, most Progressives did not support segregation because of anger, hatred, or even a desire to unify whites but did so because it permitted their reform efforts to continue under conditions of stability and peace. Only under the protective "shield of segregation" could both whites and blacks continue to be transformed.[30] The anomaly and the negative consequences of excusing racial segregation are all too obvious. As the Supreme Court would eventually rule in *Brown v. Board of Education* (1954), the separation of the races is inherently unequal, for the policy is usually interpreted as denoting the inferiority of one group, which in turn leads to the loss of respect, opportunity, power, and rights.[31] Nonetheless, most Progressive reformers were not bothered by the inequitable effects of segregation, for many of them, including Roosevelt, believed in the inferiority of blacks. TR's position sparks some important questions about how he saw this inferiority, whether he believed in the possibility of an interracial, egalitarian society, and if so, what, if anything, he did to promote it.

In a 1906 letter to the southern author, Owen Wister, Roosevelt declares that "as a race and in the mass they [Negroes] are altogether inferior to the whites." Similarly, to another southerner, Henry Smith Pritchett, Roosevelt's asserts that the passage of the Fifteenth Amendment, granting voting rights to blacks, had been a mistake and that, in nine cases out of ten, disenfranchisement was justified.[32] Not surprisingly, these statements exposed Roosevelt to criticism that he was not, after all, really dedicated to the principles of Lincoln, who he claimed to admire for both preserving the Union and emancipating the slaves. Like most other Progressives, he saw the Civil War as an apocalyptic battle against the evil of slavery in which, through the loss of life, the sins of the nation were purged. The war—and Lincoln's handling of it— had saved the soul of the nation.

It is understandable that a reader might conclude that the sentiments expressed in Roosevelt's letters to Wister and Pritchett represent a full articulation of his views. Then again, Roosevelt was a professional politician, and to achieve his public goals required that he get votes and maintain public support. In public statements as well as private correspondences, skilled politicians tend to emphasize the points that they have in common with the audience in question. "A Statesman," Winston Churchill declared, "in contact with the moving current of events and anxious to keep the ship on an even keel and steer a steady course may lean all his weight now on one side and now on the other. His arguments in each case when contrasted can be shown to be not only very different in character, but contradictory in spirit and opposite in direction: yet his object will throughout have remained the same."[33] Thus, when faced with changing circumstances, a political leader may alter his language and/or methods in order to remain consistent. This does not mean that he abandons his wishes or motivating purpose.

Perhaps Roosevelt really believed the words he wrote, although it may be noted that the very same letter to Wister mentions the latest scientific theory, "which is that the Negro and the white man as shown by their skulls, are closely akin." In other words, the white man and the Negro do not appear to be biologically different. Roosevelt concedes that, while some of the criticisms that have been levied against the black man are true, "a great deal that is untrue is said against him," and "much more is untruthfully said in favor of the white man who lives beside and upon him." It is noteworthy that Roosevelt refers to these negative remarks about African-Americans as "*your* views of the Negro" (emphasis added), suggesting that they are not *his* views. Roosevelt begins by stating that blacks are "altogether inferior" to whites but then proceeds not only to discuss biological theory, which points to similarity between the races, but also to criticize some southern assumptions about the differences between blacks and whites. Taken together, these sentences appear to be an equivocation, wherein Roosevelt could be indicating that he does not agree fully with the notion that the white man is *naturally* superior to the black man.

But, if Roosevelt does not believe in the black man's natural inferiority, to what inferiority is he referring? The next few sentences point to a possible answer, for TR adds to his criticism of the prevailing southern mindset that "these white men of the South who say that the Negro is unfit to cast a vote, and who by fraud or force prevent his voting, are equally clamorous in insisting that his votes must be counted as cast when it comes to comparing their own representation with the representation of the white men of the North." In short, Roosevelt criticizes those southerners who declare blacks unfit to vote but nonetheless insist that the black population be counted when it comes to determining the apportionment of congressional representatives. In the district of one southern representative, for example, "three out of every four men are Negroes; the fourth man, a white man, does not allow any of these Negroes to vote, but insists upon counting their votes, so that his one vote offsets the votes of four white men in New York, Massachusetts, or Pennsylvania." Roosevelt stresses that his remarks are not meant to suggest that he supports the right of each and every Negro to vote; however, he does maintain that the North cannot continue to tolerate southern hypocrisy on the matter of black suffrage. He acknowledges that the condition of many southern blacks has improved despite disenfranchisement. Booker T. Washington is a good example of this; Roosevelt claims not to know a single southern white who is as decent a man as Washington. It is precisely for this reason, he concludes, that all similarly intelligent, hard-working, refined, and respectable individuals should be rewarded with the right to equal democratic participation.

TR asks, "not that the average Negro be allowed to vote, not that ninety-five per cent of the Negroes be allowed to vote, not that there be Negro domination in any shape or form, but that these occasionally good, well-educated, intelligent and honest colored men and women be given the pitiful chance to have a little reward, a little respect, a little regard, if they can by earnest useful work succeed in winning it."[34] Note that Roosevelt's focus on moral and intellectual qualities/distinctions implies that Negro inferiority is more a matter of nurture than of nature. If this is the case, then he is simply echoing the opinion of Jefferson, Lincoln, and various others from the Enlightenment, all of whom maintained that both barbaric conditions in Africa and racial oppression in the United States afforded little opportunity for blacks to realize their potential. According to this view, such inferiority can be overcome if social conditions are changed; it is merely a question of time and effort.

It is reasonable to ask why, if TR is willing to recommend suffrage for some blacks (the honest, decent, and intelligent ones), he does not insist on suffrage for all blacks. After all, white suffrage is not reserved exclusively for the honest, decent, and intelligent members of that race. The answer, stated crudely, is that politics is the art of the possible. Roosevelt's remarks seem to indicate that he believes in the need to work toward greater respect for equal rights. But, while he knows what is good and right for society, he also knows how much of that good is attainable in the here-and-now. He appears also to understand that the achievement of greater good is often jeopardized by those reformers who grasp for too much too soon. The best, in other words, can be an enemy of the good. Thus, in contrast to both the reformers and the reactionaries, he will concentrate his efforts on the possible and proceed one step at a time.

In sum, Roosevelt's view that blacks were "altogether inferior to the whites" implied a qualitative, not a biological, inferiority; and he always maintained that this condition of inequality was temporary, at least on an individual basis. As he wrote William Henry Lewis, a Virginia-born African-American and an 1895 graduate of Harvard Law School, the American people needed to be encouraged to judge their fellow citizens, both white and black, according to merit alone. In this letter to Lewis, TR explains that he followed his own advice as governor, appointing to various boards and commissions those black men who impressed him as decent, upright, and accomplished. "The path of the race upward," he concludes, "will necessarily be painful (and a great deal of all life is necessarily painful as far as it goes); and we are not only bound to help the race in every way on the upward path but to work for them."[35] Equality, then, would come slowly and painfully, but it would come so long as black Americans, like their white counterparts, agreed to embrace those qualities of good character that Roosevelt discussed in his many speeches, articles, and books.

This is why, in his 1905 address to Florida Baptist College, Roosevelt gives his black audience the same advice that can be found in nearly all of his public writings. "What I say to this body of my colored fellow-citizens is just exactly what I would say to any body of my white fellow-citizens. . . . We need education, morality, industry; we need intelligence, clean living, and the power to work hard and effectively." For this reason, he continues, every community, black and white alike, must support educational institutes like Florida Baptist College. While it is certainly true that an education alone will not guarantee good citizenship, it is also true that good citizenship depends on a good education. All races of Americans must be educated, Roosevelt declares. Moreover, it must be stressed to white and black citizens alike that "the truly religious man is the man who is decent and clean in his private life; who is orderly and law-abiding; the man who hunts down the criminal and does all he can to stop crime and wrong-doing; the man who treats his neighbor well; who is a good man in his own family and therefore a good man in the state."[36]

For Roosevelt, it is not only the white man's duty, but it is to his interest to see that the African-American's rights to life, liberty, and property are protected. In a 1905 speech at the Tuskegee Institute, he emphasizes that the denial of legal protection to the Negro man is a breach of the law, and every time a law is broken "every individual in the community has the moral tone of his life lowered." Roosevelt adds that any government that permits lawbreaking breeds contempt for law; it invites every man to become a law unto himself; it invites anarchy. Moreover, such lawlessness is not confined to any one section of the United States. Lynching, for instance, still occurs in both the North and the South. Roosevelt wants brave men and women in each and every American community to stand up against these wrongs and, in doing so, serve as models of good citizenship for all others to follow.[37] But, while Roosevelt believes that white Americans have obligations to their Negro brothers and sisters, he stresses that the latter are also expected to help themselves. They must lead lives of sobriety, industriousness, and lawfulness. If they work hard, save money, secure homes, pay their taxes, and lead clean, decent, and modest lives, Roosevelt insists that black Americans will eventually win the respect of their white neighbors. Of course, he admits, this will take a great deal of time. But, Roosevelt concludes, the black race "cannot expect to get everything at once." It must learn patience and "prove itself worthy by showing its possession of perseverance, of thrift, of self-control."[38]

Institutionally speaking, Roosevelt believed that the federal government could do little to improve the plight of African-Americans. Rather, the principal hope of the African-American lay in the justice and good will of the American people; and Roosevelt, like Lincoln, hoped to promote this higher morality by relying on inspirational rhetoric and personal example. Recall that Lincoln, despite his support for emancipation (first, by proclamation and, later, via constitutional amendment), saw rhetorical appeals to the spirit of friendship as the only way to *convince* his fellow countrymen to put aside their differences and recommit themselves to the ideal that had been at the heart of America's founding: respect for the equal freedom of all. It was in this same spirit of civic friendship that Roosevelt preached his message of equal rights. By quoting liberally from Lincoln's speeches and explaining how the sixteenth President promoted the idea of friendship as an alternative to moral denunciation, Roosevelt attempted to convince his fellow countrymen, especially other Republicans, to use their collective power to protect the rights of all individuals, regardless of race.

In an address to the Republican Club of the City of New York, Roosevelt reminds his audience that Lincoln fought for both the preservation of the Union and the freedom of slaves; and although he warred fiercely, he never lost a feeling of tenderness for his fellow countrymen, northerner and southerner alike. As modern Americans attempt to deal with the continuing discord between blacks and whites, Roosevelt urges his audience to show the qualities of Lincoln: "steadfastness in striving after the right, and his infinite patience and forbearance with those who saw that right less clearly than he did; his earnest endeavor to do what was best, and yet his readiness to accept the best that was practicable when the ideal best was unattainable; his unceasing effort to cure what was evil, coupled with his refusal to make a bad situation worse by any ill-judged or ill-timed effort to make it better."[39] More specifically, Roosevelt advises his fellow-northerners to appreciate the difficulty and perplexity of the South's racial problems. Guided by the spirit of true friendship as well as an honest wish to help, he suggests that they join their southern brothers in the fight to secure equal rights and better treatment for both whites and blacks. At the same time, he adds, the men and women of the North must remember that their own attitude toward the Negro is, generally speaking, far from ideal. Northerners, like their southern counterparts, must learn to act "in good faith upon the principle of giving to each man what is justly due him, of treating him on his worth as a man, granting him no special favors, but denying him no proper opportunity for labor and the reward of labor."[40]

"Our effort," Roosevelt declares unequivocally, "should be to secure to each man, whatever his color, equality of opportunity, equality of treatment before the law." To meet the expectations that Lincoln had for his country, as well as the dictates of righteousness, the American people cannot be indifferent to the oppression or maltreatment of a great portion of their fellow citizens. Roosevelt maintains that those men and women who exhibit the qualities of energy, industriousness, perseverance, and kindness must be helped, not hindered, in their struggle for self-improvement. According to the Rough Rider, this is essential to the continued prosperity and exceptionality of the United States. Roosevelt concedes that achieving the ideal of a color-blind society will take time and will not be possible unless both whites and blacks exercise patience, thoughtfulness, and charity.[41] "The ideal of elemental justice meted out to every man," Roosevelt continues, "is the ideal we should keep ever before us. It will be many a long day before we attain to it, and unless we show not only devotion to it, but also wisdom and self-restraint in the exhibition of that devotion, we shall defer the time for its realization still further."

In striving to live according the dictates of a higher moral law, Roosevelt concludes, we must remember two things. Ultimately, he says, the fate of America's black population, like that of its whites, is more dependent upon individual effort than upon the outside efforts of the community. Despite equal opportunity and protection under the law, vicious, venal, and ignorant blacks will still fail, but it is a fate they will bring upon themselves. "Laziness and shiftlessness, these, and above all, vice and criminality of every kind, are evils more potent for harm to the black race than all acts of oppression of white men put together." Still, TR stresses, each and every white man, northerner and southerner, must be willing to act as his black brother's keeper. In communities and neighborhoods across America, those whites who consider themselves to be true friends of the Negro must support their kind thoughts with real action. In particular, Roosevelt begs his fellow citizens to support the many ministers, judges, editors, and law enforcement officers who have led the crusade against lynching in the South.[42] To him, the best way to honor the memory of Lincoln is to rededicate the nation to the cause of uplifting the lowly and protecting the humble. Let us triumph over prejudice and come to regard all of our fellow countrymen as brothers and sisters. This, Roosevelt declares, is the spirit to which both Washington and Lincoln dedicated themselves, and it proceeds not from weakness but from the greatest strength of character. "For weal or for woe we are knit together, and we shall go up or go down together; and I believe that we shall go up and not down, that we shall go forward instead of halting and falling back, because I have an abiding faith in the generosity, the courage, the resolution, and the common sense of all my countrymen."[43]

To lead by *personal example*, Roosevelt became the first President to entertain a black man in the White House. On October 16, 1901, Booker T. Washington, the founder of the Tuskegee Normal and Industrial Institute of Alabama, was invited to dinner. Washington's life demonstrated what Roosevelt preached throughout his presidency: that any American, through hard work, perseverance, and decency, could climb the social ladder. By all accounts, the dinner was most enjoyable. According to Roosevelt, it felt "so natural and so proper" to have Washington at his table.[44] The Roosevelt-Washington dinner was significant for many reasons. For one, anthropologists say that eating is more than a physiological act that alleviates hunger; rather, the dinner table and the "rules" of eating are miniature models of a society's rules about interpersonal relationships. "In all societies, both simple and complex," Peter Farb and George Armelagos explain, "eating is the primary way of initiating and maintaining human relationships. . . . Once the anthropologist finds out where, when, and with whom the food is eaten, just about everything else can be inferred about the relations among the society's members. . . . To know what, where, how, when, and with whom people eat is to know the character of their society."[45] Similarly, theologian John Dominic Crossan concludes, "What we do at the dinner table serves as a map of economic, social, and political differences." This is what was so radical about the lunch counter sit-ins of the 1960s. The segregated lunch counter was a miniature model, a symbol, of what the majority of citizens believed were acceptable and unacceptable forms of association. Therefore, when blacks and whites sat down to eat at the same tables, they were declaring the coming of a new order. While the segregated table had symbolized society's acceptance of human separation and discrimination, the "open table" symbolized human community and equality.

Consider, for example, Jesus' willingness to eat with sinners, tax collectors, and women. By doing so, he was acting out the parable of the great banquet. In the story, a man prepared a great dinner and invited many guests. He instructed his servant to tell those who had been invited, "Come, for everything is now ready." But all of the invited guests began to make excuses for being unable to come. The servant returned and reported this to his master. At that point, the owner of the house became angry and ordered his servant, "Go out quickly into the streets and alleys of the town and bring in the poor, the crippled, the blind and the lame." In his determination to crowd an empty table, the master allowed an assortment of characters, mostly society's outcasts, to enter his home. He permitted a mixing of different sexes, classes, and persuasions that totally undermined the conventions of first century life. Jesus was maligned because his table likewise made none of the distinctions and discriminations that society deemed appropriate. By preparing a nondiscriminatory table, Jesus was making a radical demand for a nondiscriminatory society.[46]

Perhaps Roosevelt did not have the lessons of either anthropology or the New Testament in mind when he invited Washington to dinner. By his own admission, TR hesitated at the last minute. Almost immediately, however, this hesitancy made him ashamed and more determined than ever to break with precedent.[47] Moreover, although he later conceded that his dinner with Washington may have been a *political* mistake, he never doubted the righteousness of his action.[48] At any rate, the reaction of the country to the dinner illustrates the point that eating is a reflection of society's basic values. Many of Roosevelt's countrymen thus understood the social significance of the dinner. One African-American man telegraphed, "Greatest step for the race in a generation." "The hour is at hand," another rejoiced, "to make the beginning of a new order." A third man recalled how young TR seconded the nomination of an African-American to chair the 1884 Republican convention, writing, "Your act in honoring [Washington] was a masterly stroke of statesmanship— worthy of the best minds this country has produced." At the same time, the reaction from most southerners was one of pure outrage. The *Memphis Scimitar* observed, "The most damnable outrage which has ever been perpetrated by any citizen of the United States was committed yesterday by the President, when he invited a nigger to dine with him at the White House. It would not be worth more than a passing notice if Theodore Roosevelt had sat down to dinner in his own home with a Pullman car porter, but Roosevelt the individual and Roosevelt the President are not to be viewed in the same light." Other papers expressed disgust at the idea that Mrs. Roosevelt and Washington might have been touching thighs under the table. Roosevelt was also accused of promoting a "mingling and mongrelization" of the Anglo-Saxon race. In Charleston, South Carolina, United States Senator Benjamin Tillman declared, "The action of President Roosevelt in entertaining that nigger will necessitate our killing a thousand niggers in the South before they will learn their place again."[49] Roosevelt never again invited Washington to dinner, but it is significant that he never apologized to his critics.

Though Roosevelt was doubtful of the federal government's institutional ability to combat the South's unfair treatment of blacks, he was willing to lead the charge by rewarding a handful of accomplished African-Americans with appointments to various federal offices. When the collector of customs in Charleston, South Carolina died, Roosevelt appointed a black Republican, Dr. William D. Crum, to the position. Not surprisingly, this action sparked heated protest throughout South Carolina. In response, Roosevelt denied that he had promised not to appoint a black to any federal office and noted that he had made a number of such appointments in Georgia, Mississippi, Alabama, Louisiana, Pennsylvania, and the District of Columbia. He would not make a special exception for South Carolina, especially when he appointed only men of "high character and good capacity," adding, "I do not intend to appoint any unfit man to office. So far as I legitimately can I shall always endeavor to pay regard to the wishes and feelings of the people of each locality; but I cannot consent to take the position that the door of hope—the door of opportunity—is to be shut upon any man, no matter how worthy, purely upon the grounds of race or color." If the people of Charleston, Roosevelt continued, believed that the "great bulk of their colored people" were not fit to hold any public office, then perhaps it was worth while to put "a premium upon the effort among them to achieve the character and standing which will fit them." To do so,

Roosevelt suggested, it was necessary to let black Americans know that if they displayed "the qualities of good citizenship—the qualities which in a white man we feel are entitled to reward," then they would not be denied the hope of similar reward.[50] After a long battle in the Senate, Crum was finally approved. Nevertheless, Roosevelt was forced to make the same essential argument again and again to justify similar appointments. "So far from feeling that they [the appointments] need the slightest apology or justification," he stated, "my position is that on the strength of what I have done I have the right to claim the support of all good citizens who wish not only a high standard of Federal service but fair and equitable dealing to the South as well as to the North, and a policy of consistent justice and good-will toward all men."[51]

In fighting against racial discrimination, Roosevelt was defending the idea that individual character and merit should determine success in the race of life. Roosevelt understood that a society that refused to reward deserving individuals hurt not only those individuals but also the public-at-large. After all, hard work, energy, diligence, self-restraint, and sacrifice contribute to the wealth and progress of a nation. But, if certain individuals are discouraged, and even punished, when striving to get ahead, why should they bother cultivating these qualities? Thus, in the area of civil rights, TR saw additional evidence that individual self-interest and the collective good complement one another. At the same time, Roosevelt was extremely uncomfortable with the idea that the law could regulate interpersonal relationships in an effort to abolish all distinctions based on color. Social prejudice, in other words, could not be overcome by legislation or executive fiat. If the two races were to develop and strengthen feelings of trust and mutual appreciation, it would have to be the result of voluntary consent. In TR's view, then, racial discrimination, like other social/moral problems, could be fought most effectively by moral suasion. That is, public officials like TR could *lead* people to listen to the better angels of their nature and overcome their racial prejudices, but in doing so, these leaders had to respect individual freedom.

NOTES

1. Michael McGerr, "Theodore Roosevelt," in *The American Presidency*, eds. Alan Brinkley and Davis Dyer (Boston: Houghton Mifflin Company, 2004), 279; Michael McGerr, *A Fierce Discontent: The Rise and Fall of the Progressive Movement in America (1870–1920)* (New York: Free Press, 2003), 73.

2. McGerr, *Fierce Discontent*, 98.

3. McGerr, *Fierce Discontent*, 99.

4. McGerr, *Fierce Discontent*, 84.

5. Theodore Roosevelt to Charles Scribner, 10 August 1899, *The Years of Preparation: 1898–1900*, vol. 2 of *The Letters of Theodore Roosevelt*, ed. Elting Morison (Cambridge: Harvard University Press, 1951), 1047.

6. Theodore Roosevelt, *Oliver Cromwell*, vol. 10 of *The Works of Theodore Roosevelt*, National Edition (New York: Charles Scribner's Sons, 1926), 187–273, 297–337.

7. Roosevelt, *Oliver Cromwell*, 215–16.

8. Roosevelt, *Oliver Cromwell*, 219–20.

9. Roosevelt, *Oliver Cromwell*, 234.

10. Roosevelt, *Oliver Cromwell*, 249–50.

11. Roosevelt, *Oliver Cromwell*, 334–35.

12. Kathleen Dalton, *Theodore Roosevelt: A Strenuous Life* (New York: Vintage Books, 2002), 307–8.

13. Dalton, *Strenuous Life*, 308–9.

14. McGerr, "Theodore Roosevelt," 279.

15. Theodore Roosevelt, "Address to the National Congress of Mothers," in *Presidential Addresses and State Papers*, vol. 3 (New York: Review of Reviews, 1910), 282–83.

16. Roosevelt, "Address to the National Congress of Mothers," 283–84.

17. Roosevelt, "Address to the National Congress of Mothers," 284–85.

18. Roosevelt, "Address to the National Congress of Mothers," 286–87.

19. Roosevelt, "Address to the National Congress of Mothers," 287–88.

20. Roosevelt, "Address to the National Congress of Mothers," 289–90.

21. Roosevelt, "Address to the National Congress of Mothers," 291.

22. Theodore Roosevelt, "Sixth Annual Message," in *Presidential Addresses and State Papers*, vol. 5 (New York: Review of Reviews, 1910), 946–47. See also McGerr, *Fierce Discontent*, 97.

23. McGerr, *Fierce Discontent*, 91.

24. McGerr, *Fierce Discontent*, 85–86.

25. McGerr, *Fierce Discontent*, 87–88.

26. Quoted in McGerr, *Fierce Discontent*, 88. See also Theodore Roosevelt to William Howard Taft, 16 July 1908, *The Big Stick: 1907–1909*, vol. 6 of *The Letters of Theodore Roosevelt*, ed. Elting Morison (Cambridge: Harvard University Press, 1952), 1131.

27. Theodore Roosevelt, "The Enforcement of the Law," in *Campaigns and Controversies*, vol. 14 of *The Works of Theodore Roosevelt*, National Edition (New York: Charles Scribner's Sons, 1926), 183–84.

28. Roosevelt, "The Enforcement of the Law," 187, 189–90.

29. Theodore Roosevelt, "Address to the Holy Name Society," in *Presidential Addresses and State Papers*, vol. 2 (New York: Review of Reviews, 1910), 460–62.

30. McGerr, *Fierce Discontent*, 183, 194–95; McGerr, "Theodore Roosevelt," 279. According to McGerr, Roosevelt believed in the inferiority of African-Americans and "did little to change white Americans' attitude and behavior toward blacks." My analysis of Roosevelt's public letters and speeches leads me to take a somewhat different interpretation of his view regarding African-Americans.

31. 347 U.S. 483 (1954).

32. Theodore Roosevelt to Owen Wister, 27 April 1906, *The Big Stick: 1905–1907*, vol. 5 of *The Letters of Theodore Roosevelt*, ed. Elting Morison (Cambridge: Harvard University Press, 1952), 226; Theodore Roosevelt to Henry Smith Pritchett, 14 December 1904, *The Square Deal: 1903–1905*, vol. 4 of *The Letters of Theodore Roosevelt*, ed. Elting Morison (Cambridge: Harvard University Press, 1951), 1066.

33. Quoted in Harry V. Jaffa, *Crisis of the House Divided: An Interpretation of the Issues in the Lincoln–Douglas Debates* (Chicago: University of Chicago Press, 1982), 46. See also Winston S. Churchill, *Thoughts and Adventures* (London: Thornton Butterworth, 1932), 39.

34. Roosevelt to Wister, 226.

35. Theodore Roosevelt to William Henry Lewis, July 26, 1900, *The Years of Preparation: 1898–1900*, vol. 2 of *The Letters of Theodore Roosevelt*, ed. Elting Morison (Cambridge: Harvard University Press, 1951), 1364–65.

36. Theodore Roosevelt, "Speech at Florida Baptist College," in *Presidential Addresses and State Papers*, vol. 4 (New York: Review of Reviews, 1910), 511–12.

37. Theodore Roosevelt, "Speech at the Tuskegee Institute," in *Presidential Addresses and State Papers*, vol. 4 (New York: Review of Reviews, 1910), 524.

38. Roosevelt, "Speech at the Tuskegee Institute," 525–26.

39. Theodore Roosevelt, "Address to the Republican Club of New York City," in *Presidential Addresses and State Papers*, vol. 3 (New York: Review of Reviews, 1910), 226.

40. Roosevelt, "Address to the Republican Club," 227–28.

41. Roosevelt, "Address to the Republican Club," 228–29.

42. Roosevelt, "Address to the Republican Club," 230–32.

43. Roosevelt, "Address to the Republican Club," 234–35.

44. TR to Carl Schurz, quoted by Edmund Morris, *Theodore Rex* (New York: The Modern Library, 2001), 52.

45. Quoted in John Dominic Crossan and Richard G. Watts, *Who is Jesus?* (Louisville: Westminster John Knox Press, 1996), 54. See also Peter Farb and George Armelagos, *Consuming Passions: The Anthropology of Eating* (Boston: Houghton Mifflin, 1980), 4, 211.

46. Crossan and Watts, *Who is Jesus?*, 54–56.

47. Morris, *Theodore Rex*, 52.

48. See, for example, Louis J. Harlan, *Booker T. Washington: The Wizard of Tuskegee, 1901–1915* (New York: Oxford University Press, 1983), 321; Owen Wister, *Roosevelt: The Story of a Friendship* (New York: MacMillan, 1930), 254.

49. Quoted in Morris, *Theodore Rex*, 54–55. See also Lewis Gould, *The Presidency of Theodore Roosevelt* (Lawrence: University Press of Kansas, 1991), 23; Harlan, *Booker T. Washington*, 313; *Washington Post*, October 18, 1901; *Atlanta Constitution*, October 17, 1901; *Memphis Scimitar*, October 17, 1901; *New York Tribune*, October 17, 1901; *Richmond Dispatch*, October 18, 1901; *Atlanta Constitution*, October 18, 1901; *Washington Post*, 19 October 1901; *St. Louis Mirror*, 31 October 1901; *Richmond News*, October 18, 1901.

50. Theodore Roosevelt to James Adger Smyth, November 26, 1902, *The Square Deal: 1901–1903*, vol. 3 of *The Letters of Theodore Roosevelt*, ed. Elting Morison (Cambridge: Harvard University Press, 1951), 383–85. See also Gould, *Presidency of Theodore Roosevelt*, 121.

51. Theodore Roosevelt to Clark Howell, 24 February 1903, *The Square Deal: 1901–1903*, vol. 3 of *The Letters of Theodore Roosevelt*, ed. Elting Morison (Cambridge: Harvard University Press, 1951), 431.

Chapter Seven

The New Nationalism

As Roosevelt neared the end of his second term as President, he focused on selecting a successor who shared his political outlook and would continue the policies he had initiated. By 1908, he believed that man to be William Howard Taft, his close friend and secretary of war. With Roosevelt's help, Taft received the Republican presidential nomination and won the general election. But Taft soon found himself in trouble with the Progressive wing of his party. For one, he supported a tariff reform bill that fell far short of Progressive expectations and added insult to injury by referring to it as "the best tariff bill the Republican party has ever passed, and therefore the best tariff bill that has been passed at all."[1] In addition, Taft named Richard Ballinger, a corporate lawyer, to replace Roosevelt's secretary of the interior, James R. Garfield, a staunch conservationist. When Ballinger invalidated TR's removal of a million acres of forests and mineral reserves from public land, thereby making it available for development, many Progressives, including Gifford Pinchot, Roosevelt's friend and the head of the National Forest Service, charged the new interior secretary as an enemy of conservation. Soon thereafter, Pinchot publicly criticized Taft's decision to defend Ballinger from charges that he transferred public lands to business interests with whom he had once been associated, and the forest chief was fired for insubordination. Pinchot then traveled to Africa, where Roosevelt was completing a hunting expedition. He presented his side of the story, including several anti-Taft messages from other Progressives.[2] In early May, TR wrote Senator Henry Cabot Lodge, "For a year after Taft took office, for a year and a quarter after he had been elected, I would not let myself think ill of anything he did. I finally had to admit that he had gone wrong on certain points; and I then also had to admit to myself that deep down underneath I had all along known he was

wrong, on points as to which I had tried to deceive myself, by loudly pro-
claiming to myself, that he was right."[3] By January 1912, Roosevelt was determined to prevent Taft from receiving the Republican nomination for President, and he believed that the only way to do this was to become a candidate
himself. But the Republican Party's refusal to support TR despite his popular
support led him to accept the nomination of the Progressive Party.

In the spring of 1910, however, Roosevelt still hoped to avoid splitting the
Republican Party. He may have sympathized with the Progressives, but he
understood political reality, telling Pinchot that it would probably be "necessary to renominate Taft, and eminently desirable to re-elect him over anyone
whom there is the least likelihood of the Democrats naming." Roosevelt
added that Taft might yet prove to be "a perfectly respectable President."
Hence, he promised Taft that, upon his return from Africa, he would remain
silent about political matters for at least sixty days. On August 17, TR complained to Henry Cabot Lodge that Taft was associated with the conservative
leaders of Congress but admitted that the anti-Taft wing of the Republican
Party had "tended to fall exclusively into the hands of narrow fanatics, wild
visionaries and self-seeking demagogues." Rather than choosing sides in the
intra-party war, he would tour the country in an attempt to heal party wounds,
although he acknowledged that his effort might fail and invite the wrath of
both factions.[4]

It was only a matter of time before the Republican Party was torn beyond
repair. In the spring of 1910, Taft decided to launch a campaign to purge Progressives from the Republican Party. Despite his efforts, the Progressives
won major victories in the various Republican primaries held through the
spring and summer, especially in the Upper Midwest—Michigan, Wisconsin,
and Iowa. But it was Kansas that proved to be the center of the political storm.
Told that the election was a referendum on the policies of President Taft, voters turned out four of the state's six conservative Republican congressmen.
Taft and the conservatives also lost California to Hiram Johnson, who toured
the Golden State in his "red devil" automobile, shouting "Bully!" and waving
his hands like TR.[5] The message was clear to Taft, who predicted that the Republicans would lose the midterm elections of 1910. The American people
were not convinced that the tariff legislation was "the best bill that the Republican party ever passed," and Roosevelt's supporters were now out for
blood. By late August, the Rough Rider was touring the Midwest to assure
Progressive Republicans that he was not responsible for the actions of the
man he had backed in 1908. "Remember," he wrote Lodge, "that there are a
great multitude of men inclined to forgive me on the ground that I was de-
ceived, as they were, but who would not forgive me if I now went ahead, as
they would regard it, to continue the deception."[6]

Roosevelt was determined to redeem himself in the eyes of Progressives. In Denver, at the start of his cross-country tour, he criticized the courts as the greatest enemy of Progressivism. Roosevelt alleged that the courts had created a borderland where neither the federal government nor the states could exercise proper control over powerful corporations. Conservative judges, he charged, had handed down decisions "arbitrarily and irresponsibly limiting the power of the people." After the Denver speech, and before the local newspapers even had time to report what he had said, Roosevelt pushed onward to Kansas. It was after midnight and raining hard, but large crowds gathered at the various depots that lined the track, hoping just to catch a glimpse of Roosevelt's train.[7] Finally, TR arrived at Osawatomie, Kansas, where he delivered one of the most famous speeches of his public career.

At Osawatomie, Roosevelt articulated a New Nationalism, which reiterated the principles upon which his life and political career rested. In the strictest sense, the New Nationalism is a collection of speeches that Roosevelt gave on his journey of nearly 5,500 miles between August 23 and September 11, 1910. More generally, it is a program of reform that Roosevelt advocated from 1910 up to the election of 1912, the specific components of which are consistent with Roosevelt's previous speeches and writings. First, the New Nationalism sought to expand the role of the national government in matters related to corporate regulation and the conservation of the natural heritage. The program also preferred balance between competing interests, such as labor and capital, measuring the behavior of each in terms of the public interest. Most important, it was at once individualist and collectivist. Roosevelt continued to argue that the collectivist responses of the entire community could assure greater opportunity for all to realize their fullest potential. As he had said so often, the public had no responsibility to carry the man who preferred to give up, but it could help those who were disciplined, hard working, and responsible.

THE PURPOSE OF GOVERNMENT

The occasion for Roosevelt's Osawatomie Address was the dedication of a battlefield where John Brown had fought fifty-four years before, but the focus of Roosevelt's speech is Abraham Lincoln, not John Brown. The Progressives, and certainly TR, embraced Lincoln as representing the ideal in popular government, nationalism, and unity. In the speech, Roosevelt asserts that the major problems facing the country stem from the absence of a sense of national unity. The nation is too parochial and narrow-minded in its outlook. Far too many people pursue wealth and personal advantage at the expense of the national interest. In Roosevelt's view, both capital and labor are threatening to tear the country apart; they are also dividing the Republican Party of Lincoln. Fortunately, Roosevelt declares, the Great Emancipator, who faced and solved the greatest problems of the nineteenth century, taught lessons that are applicable to the problems of the twentieth century. Indeed, TR claims, Lincoln forecast the present struggle between labor and capital and offered a viable solution. "Labor," Lincoln declared, "is prior to, and independent of, capital. Capital is only the fruit of labor, and could never have existed if labor had not first existed. Labor is the superior of capital, and deserves much the higher consideration." On the other hand, Roosevelt reminds his fellow Americans, it cannot be forgotten that Lincoln promoted the rights of capital as well. The rights of capital, he quotes Lincoln as saying, are "as worthy of protection as any other rights." According to TR, Lincoln believed that there should be no war upon the owners of property, for property is "the fruit of labor . . . property is desirable; is a positive good in the world." Lincoln, Roosevelt adds, concluded that no man who is "houseless" should attempt to "pull down the house of another," but rather a man should work diligently to build a house for himself and, through his own positive example, help to assure that his own property will be protected from the violence of others. These words, Roosevelt concludes, represent the attitude that all fair-minded Americans should embrace today.[8]

For Roosevelt, the essence of the current struggle is "to equalize opportunity, destroy privilege, and give to the life and citizenship of every individual the highest possible value both to himself and to the commonwealth." But TR sees this as nothing new; it is what the Union army fought for in the Civil War. Perfect justice, Roosevelt concedes, will never be attained, but practical equality of opportunity for all citizens can be and will have two great results. First of all, "every man will have a fair chance to make of himself all that in him lies; to reach the highest point to which his capacities, unassisted by special privilege of his own and unhampered by the special privilege of others, can carry him, and to get for himself and his family substantially what he has earned." Second, "equality of opportunity means that that commonwealth will get from every citizen the highest service of which he is capable." As he did throughout his presidency, Roosevelt is calling for a "square deal" for all Americans. By this, he does not mean that every man is guaranteed success in the game of life, but he does mean to assure a chance for every man, regardless of class, to compete on a level economic playing field. "When I say I want a square deal for the poor man," Roosevelt explains, "I do not mean that I want a square deal for the man who remains poor because he has not the energy to work for himself. If a man who has had a chance will not make good, then he has got to quit."[9] The community owes him nothing.

Roosevelt's "square deal" depends upon the citizens of the United States being able to use the powers of their national government to control the activities of powerful corporations. It is clear, he asserts, that there must be governmental supervision of all businesses that are engaged in interstate commerce, especially the railways. TR is quick to add that he does not want to see the national government assume ownership of the railways, which leaves the only alternative of a "thoroughgoing and effective regulation." He adds that governmental supervision and control should extend especially to those economic combinations that control the necessities of life—meat, oil, and coal, for example. Combination in industry is a natural development, TR claims, and the effort to prevent all combination in business has failed miserably. In Roosevelt's view, the solution lies, not in attempting to prevent combinations, but in controlling them to serve the public interest. This entails not only holding corporate officers personally responsible when corporations break the law but also increasing the powers of the Interstate Commerce Commission, the Bureau of Corporations, and the Hepburn Act.[10] As was the case during his presidency, Roosevelt's discussion of regulation is a practical application in the public arena of his belief in both individual and communal responsibility.

The Osawatomie Address parallels various presidential messages of TR to Congress. In his Fourth Annual Address, for instance, Roosevelt acknowledges, "Great corporations are necessary, and only men of great and singular mental power can manage such corporations successfully, and such men must have great rewards." "But these corporations," he adds, "should be managed with due regard to the interests of the public as a whole. Where this can be done under the present laws it must be done. Where these laws come short, others should be enacted to supplement them."[11] Again, in his Fifth Annual Message, he declares, "I am in no sense hostile to corporations. This is an age of combination, and any effort to prevent all combination will be not only useless, but in the end vicious, because of the contempt for law which the failure to enforce law inevitably produces." The corporation is here to stay. The only question is how to assure that it acts with due regard for the public interest. TR's answer is thoroughly pragmatic: the corporation should be favored when it does good and should be checked when and where it acts illegally and unjustly.[12] In the same message, Roosevelt argues that the national government, as the only true representative of the people, has both the right and the responsibility to supervise the activities of the great trusts and, when necessary, to prevent and punish them for acting in ways that undermine the health of social and industrial life. Most of the trusts, he observes, do not operate within the jurisdiction of the states; rather, they engage in interstate commerce, and interstate commerce is the peculiar field of the national government.[13]

Roosevelt concludes his Osawatomie Address by pointing to the proper division of responsibility between the states and the nation: a state should be concerned with matters that affect only the people of that state, while the national government should be concerned with matters that affect all of the people. For Roosevelt, there can be no legal/institutional limbo, or "neutral ground," to serve as a safe-haven for criminals, especially men of great wealth who have access to "the vulpine legal cunning" that teaches them how to avoid the regulations of both the national government and the states. Roosevelt does not want an overcentralization of governmental power, but he believes that Congress is not doing enough to protect the people from the dangers of ever-growing economic power. He demands that the representatives of the people in Congress work for those matters that concern the American people as a whole. Roosevelt believes that the national government belongs to all Americans, and where the interests of the whole people are affected, the national government has an obligation to guard those interests effectively. "The American people," he concludes, "are right in demanding that New Nationalism, without which we cannot hope to deal with new problems."[14]

This New Nationalism, Roosevelt says, puts national interests before sectional or personal ones. It has no patience with the confusion that results from local governments, which attempt to treat national issues as local issues, and is even more impatient with the impotence that results from too much separation of governmental powers, which Roosevelt sees as allowing local selfishness to bring the efforts of the national government to a deadlock. Rather than checks and balances, the New Nationalism holds that the President is the "steward of the public welfare." The President is the representative of all the people rather than any one class or section. In short, Roosevelt's New Nationalism calls for the protection of private property but places people over property whenever the choice must be made.[15] The primary object of government is "the welfare of the people," Roosevelt maintains, adding that the material progress and prosperity of a nation are desirable only insofar as they lead to the moral and material development of all good citizens. But social and economic reform must be coupled with personal morality. It is important that individuals have the right organization and the right leadership, but Roosevelt insists that good laws and good administration must be *additions to*, and not substitutes for, the qualities of good citizenship.[16]

For TR, the most crucial factor in any man's success is his character. If an individual does not possess good character, "then no law that the wit of man can devise, no administration of the law by the boldest and strongest executive, will avail to help him. We must have the right kind of character—character that makes a man, first of all, a good man in the home, a good father, a good husband—that makes a man a good neighbor. You must have that, and then, in addition, you must have the kind of law and the kind of administration of the law which will give those qualities in the private citizen the best possible chance for development."[17] These sentiments clearly mirror the lessons of Roosevelt's western writings.

Similarly, the Osawatomie Address is an echo of TR's earlier presidential speeches, as for example, one to the citizens of York, Pennsylvania, in which he declares that the most perfect laws can be devised "by the wit of man or the wit of angels," but they mean nothing if the average man is lazy, wasteful, and selfish. As Roosevelt reminds his York audience, "Nothing can take the place of the individual factor, of the average man's quality and character, his industry, his energy, his thrift, his decency, his determination to be a good man in his home, a good neighbor, and a good citizen in his relations to the state." Roosevelt's political thought rests on his foundational belief that we must remain true to the principles of honesty, hard work, lawfulness, duty, and service, and that we must demand the same of our neighbors. "The first factor in winning out in our national life must always remain the individual character. . . . Each one of us stumbles at times, and shame on any one of us who will not reach out a helping hand to his brother who stumbles. Help him in the only way that any real help can ever come; help him to help himself."[18] It is necessary to have good laws and good institutions, Roosevelt likewise asserts in his 1907 Address at the Pilgrim Memorial, but much more depends on "a high quality of individual citizenship." Wherever it is found, by practice and experimentation, or by the failure of individualistic methods, that collectivism and state interference are both wise and necessary, then this course of action must be pursued. "But," he continues, "while we can accomplish something by legislation, legislation can never be more than a part, and often no more than a small part, in the general scheme of moral progress; and crude or vindictive legislation may at any time bring such progress to a halt."[19]

A few days before his Osawatomie Address, Roosevelt delivered a speech to the Colorado Legislature, in which he discusses the relationship between the national government and the states. Again, Roosevelt argues that those matters that concern all Americans should be handled by the national government, "while the affairs which concern us only in each of our several localities are treated by our state legislatures." It is to be regretted that the development of governmental power, especially at the national level, has not kept pace with the complex industrial development of the past forty years. The United States, Roosevelt notes, has changed from a predominantly agricultural economic system into "a complex industrial community with a great development of corporations, and with conditions such that by steam and electricity the business of the nation has become completely nationalized." As a result, he believes that the needs of the American people have changed dramatically. To illustrate his point, Roosevelt observes that there once was no need for laws that addressed the rights of the farm laborer; if mistreated, he could travel either westward to the frontier or eastward to the growing cities. But, Roosevelt adds, the majority of today's employees face great corporations rather than individual employers. This is why the government must begin to recognize the right of collective bargaining. Roosevelt likewise notes that a hundred years ago, "when the sailboat and the canal boat and the wagon and the pack train represented the only means of communication," individual state governments could control what was, in essence, purely *intrastate* commerce. But now, he concludes, with the growth of national railroads and *interstate* commerce, the laws must be adapted.[20] Roosevelt says this does not mean that each locality does not have its own special problems to address. Nevertheless, he concludes, "there are certain things to which all of us in every state should pay heed, we in New York and you in Colorado, the people of every state and the people of the national capital."[21]

According to the Rough Rider, the conservation of natural resources is a perfect example of a matter that involves federalism (that is, a combination of state and federal control). Roosevelt acknowledges that there are instances when the protection of vital natural resources is best handled by the states. In these instances, the rights of states help to secure popular rights. As he had in various presidential addresses, Roosevelt says that, when the doctrine of states' rights is employed on behalf of the people's rights, he is a believer in states' rights. Still, he wants all Americans to remember that there are a number of cases where only the power of the national government will secure the rights of the American people. When and where this is the case, Roosevelt is a devout nationalist. He reminds his audience that big business has become nationalized, "and the only effective way of controlling and directing it and preventing the abuses in connection with it is by having the people nationalize the governmental control in order to meet the nationalization of big business itself." Within its own sphere of authority, the state has every right to regulate against the destruction of the environment, which TR notes was his own attitude as governor of New York. But Roosevelt does not believe that most states have worked to protect their forests, coal lands, ranges, and/or water supplies, thereby proving that the protection of natural resources is really the common concern of all.[22]

Inherent in Roosevelt's discussion of conservation is a belief that the government has the responsibility to do for individuals when they are unable to do for themselves. TR maintains that natural resources must be used to benefit all of the people, not monopolized and exploited for the benefit of a few. Early in the nineteenth century, TR tells his audience at Osawatomie, there were good men who believed that the nation should sell great quantities of public lands for large sums of money, thereby enabling wealthy men to cultivate these lands for their own uses. Fortunately, this plan was not adopted. Instead, the leaders of the people "took the proper democratic ground that the land should be granted in small sections to the men who were actually to till it and live on it." This, Roosevelt declares, is what Americans must do today, for there is no other matter (except for survival in war) that compares in importance with the obligation of making this land even better for our descendents than it is for us. For Roosevelt, conservation is a moral issue that involves the duty of all citizens to ensure the safety and future continuance of the nation.[23]

But the obligation of the national government is greater than just conserving forests, waters, lands, and minerals; it is responsible as well for conserving the health and vitality of the American people. "The man who wrongly holds that every human right is secondary to his profit must now give way to the advocate of human welfare." Roosevelt associates himself with those believers in human welfare, who maintain that men hold their wealth "subject to the general right of the community to regulate its use to whatever degree the public welfare may require it." But he believes that it may go even further—that the government has the right to regulate the use of any property that is in the public interest. This includes the right to regulate the terms and conditions of labor, "which is the chief element of wealth." Roosevelt reiterates his conviction that every man should have a chance to "reach a place in which he will make the greatest possible contribution to the public welfare." He is careful to add his usual disclaimer that there is no public obligation to carry the man who would rather lie down but insists that society has an obligation to see that the worthy man gets a fair chance to show his worth. No man can be a good citizen unless he is given a living wage and "hours of labor short enough so that after his day's work is done he will have time and energy to bear his share in the management of the community." Roosevelt concludes that many individuals are prevented from being good citizens by the conditions in which they are forced to live. To correct this, the people, acting in their collective capacity, must enact comprehensive workman's compensation laws, regulate against child labor, and enforce better conditions in the workplace.[24]

In his Fargo Address, Roosevelt returns to his theme that the progress of wage workers, like that of all other citizens, depends on individual initiative and effort, but here he details *three* different factors involved in individual progress. First, and most important, there is individual initiative. Yet Roosevelt believes that the other two factors are important, specifically what can be done by laborers in cooperation with each other and what can be done by the government as the instrument through which the people work collectively. Roosevelt declares that leaving all matters of contract between employers and employees to individual action sounds nice in theory, but it could, in reality, mean the destruction of individualism, for where the individual is so weak that he must accept whatever big business chooses to give him, his liberty becomes a mere sham. Roosevelt reasons that, to promote true individualism, the government must support effective and organized collective action on the part of American workers. The right of wage earners to act jointly through the process of collective bargaining should be assured. "Only thus," Roosevelt stresses, "can they be put upon a plane of economic equality with their corporate employers. Only thus is freedom of contract made a real thing and not a mere legal fiction."[25]

Roosevelt does not mean to suggest that he supports any and all practices of organized labor. "Labor organizations," he concedes, "have the weaknesses and defects common to all forms of human organizations." Roosevelt says that the man who declares unions never do any wrong is obviously incorrect and should be mistrusted accordingly. Sometimes labor is right, and sometimes it is wrong. As with corporations, Roosevelt stands with labor when it acts well, and he stands opposed to labor organizations when they act improperly. But Roosevelt *always* stands with the public. While a strike may be a necessary means of helping workers to stand up for their rights, it should be viewed as a last resort. Moreover, violence is never an appropriate way of airing grievances. TR suggests that the public is likely to favor those strikes that are undertaken for important reasons (and as a last resort) but is unlikely to support any organization that resorts to lawless violence. It is therefore essential for the labor movement to combine discipline with self-control.[26] The American government, Roosevelt maintains, is founded upon the theory that artificial weights should be lifted from all shoulders, and that those men and women who exhibit the qualities of energy, industriousness, perseverance, and kindness must be helped, not hindered, in their struggle for self-improvement. This, according to Roosevelt, is the essence of what makes the United States so exceptional, and the ideal must apply to all people. The Rough Rider finds that it is not only the duty of the laborer, but it is also the duty of the American people, to do all that can be done to improve the ability of the average individual to move up the economic ladder.

THE NEW NATIONALISM: A COMPARATIVE PERSPECTIVE

As mentioned, the New Nationalism was not greatly different from the Square Deal that Roosevelt advocated and pursued during his presidency. Indeed, he acknowledges as much in his September 1910 Syracuse Speech: "In my western speeches, I said chiefly what I again and again said in messages to Congress when I was President. I very slightly developed the doctrines contained in these presidential addresses in order to meet the development of new conditions."[27] The purpose of both programs was to guarantee greater equality of opportunity for individuals to "show their stuff" and realize their dreams. Roosevelt justified state action on the grounds that it eliminated artificial economic obstacles that mitigated, and even discouraged, hard work, self-restraint, and personal responsibility. Those individuals who exhibited the qualities of energy, industriousness, perseverance, and kindness were to be helped in their struggle for personal accomplishment and economic security. At the same time, Roosevelt recognized the importance of communal concern, arguing that economic regulations helped every individual reach a place in which he would make the greatest possible contribution to the public welfare. Many were prevented from being good citizens by the conditions in which they lived.

In addition, both the New Nationalism and the Square Deal were indebted to Alexander Hamilton's broad view of national power, especially his belief in an energetic President. Throughout his public career, Roosevelt did not mask his deep reverence for the principles and practices of Hamilton. TR believed that Hamilton was "the most brilliant American statesman who ever lived, possessing the loftiest and keenest intellect of his time." He was a man of "singularly noble and lofty character" with "brilliant audacity and genius," which equipped him for the "giant tasks of constructive statesmanship with which he successfully grappled." In debates with those who invoked the name of Thomas Jefferson to defend their positions, Roosevelt would remind them that, while Jefferson sought to restrict the powers of the central government "to the point of impotence," Hamilton acted on the principle that there were inherent powers in the federal government that existed outside of the enumerated powers granted to it by the Constitution. This, Roosevelt believed, was the principle that modern Americans had to embrace, for a narrow interpretation of the Constitution placed the government "at a great disadvantage in the battle for industrial order."[28]

Roosevelt was not alone in his embrace of Hamiltonianism. At the beginning of the twentieth century, many reformers celebrated the legacy of the famous Federalist. Herbert Croly, for example, was described as "neo-Hamiltonian" by contemporaries like Judge Learned Hand, though in fact Croly argued that neither Jeffersonian beliefs nor Hamiltonian beliefs were entirely adequate to contemporary national problems. Nevertheless, Croly acknowledged his admiration for Hamilton over Jefferson: "I shall not disguise the fact that, on the whole, my own preferences are on the side of Hamilton rather than Jefferson."[29] The existence of the American union, Croly argues in *The Promise of American Life*, is due primarily to the efforts of Hamilton, who understood that the central government had to be used to promote the national interest. Moreover, Croly says, Hamilton knew that good government could not be secured without good leadership. National leaders should have the self-confidence to disregard popular opinions that opposed the exercise of political power for the good of the whole nation. But, Croly adds, while Hamilton deserves praise for emphasizing the benefits of centralized power and elite leadership, he did not see the need to establish a broad base of popular support for the realization of his nationally minded programs. Hamilton was too fearful of the people and thus ignored the other half of the overarching national purpose that Croly advocates: democracy.[30] Croly concedes that Jefferson is the personification of American democracy, but the problem with Jefferson is that his version of equality was an "intellectual and moral conformity" that undermined the possibility of intelligent and experienced leadership. Croly believes that true democracy means popular deliberation guided by the able, and that the key to reconciling the tension between democracy and elitism is to strengthen the national government and thereby make it attractive to those accomplished people who wish to serve the public interest.

To Croly, Roosevelt is the contemporary figure who best illustrates his conception of democratic leadership; however, he criticizes Roosevelt's frequent use of Jeffersonian language, as when the Rough Rider defends his Square Deal on the grounds that it guarantees equal rights. To be sure, Croly differs from Roosevelt in that the former, like most Progressives, does not place great emphasis on the concept of individual rights. For him, the traditional American conception of rights as freedoms from governmental intrusion translates too easily into a defense of private property rights that justifies survival of the fittest and thereby intensifies the plight of the have-nots. In short, while Croly sees a rights-based system as encouraging selfishness rather than sacrifice on behalf of the common good, Roosevelt accepts that individuals will act in their own interests and rejects only a radical brand of individualism that ignores human suffering. In addition, Croly's long-term solution to the problems of American capitalism is more radical and potentially more destructive of individualism than anything ever advanced by Roosevelt. Like Roosevelt, Croly recognizes that industrial organization is part of a process of economic and social advance, that federal regulation of the marketplace is needed, and that regulation should not undermine the efficiency of big business.[31] But Croly insists that regulation is less desirable in the long run. He reasons that continued profits will render the interests of businessmen different from those of the community. Moreover, as the country grows, regulated monopolies, through no effort of their own, will acquire new markets and thereby assume the character of natural monopolies. Thus, Croly suggests that dominant trusts should be taken over gradually by the government.[32] In all of his speeches, however, Roosevelt rejects any desires to nationalize corporations. In fact, he justifies both the Square Deal and the New Nationalism as the best ways to halt "the very undesirable move" toward Socialism.[33]

Differences aside, Roosevelt was Croly's modern-day ideal of dynamic presidential leadership. Not only was he thinking of Roosevelt as he developed his views on regulation and administrative reform, but he likewise sought to reconcile the tension between the needs of the individual and those of the community by invoking inspirational imagery and the concept of brotherhood. "It has been admitted throughout [*The Promise*]," Croly writes, "that the task of individual and social regeneration must remain incomplete and impoverished, until the conviction and the feeling of human brotherhood enters into possession of the human spirit."[34] "The common citizen," Croly adds, "can become something of a saint and something of a hero, not by growing to heroic proportions in his own person, but by the sincere and enthusiastic imitation of heroes and saints, and whether or not he will ever come to such imitation will depend upon the ability of his exceptional fellow-countrymen to offer him acceptable examples of heroism and saintliness."[35] Croly is perhaps referring to Roosevelt's own effort to reconcile individualism and collectivism by relying on inspirational stories of various people, including himself, who learned how to balance those individualistic and collectivistic values that are healthy and vital to a society.

The possibility that TR was Croly's heroic model led many of Roosevelt's contemporaries to view Croly as responsible for the New Nationalism.[36] As Edward Stettner shows in his book, *Shaping Modern Liberalism: Herbert Croly and Progressive Thought*, some historians have since argued that Croly converted Roosevelt from the conservatism of his presidency to the progressivism of his 1912 presidential campaign, while others have taken the opposite position.[37] But, William Leuchtenburg observes, the former view assumes that Roosevelt as President was a fraud, "a conservative masquerading as a reformer."[38] Croly's book did appeal to Roosevelt, who wrote the author, "I do not know when I have read a book which I felt profited me as much as your book on American life. There are a few points on which I do not entirely agree with you, yet even as to these my disagreement is on minor matters . . . I shall use your ideas freely in speeches I intend to make." Nevertheless, Croly himself acknowledged that "[Roosevelt] is the original and supreme Hamiltonian revivalist."[39] Even the familiar cliché, normally attributed to Croly, that Hamiltonian means could be used to achieve Jeffersonian ends is suggested in TR's *Gouverneur Morris*, a book written in 1888.[40] It is not clear that Croly, prior to writing *The Promise of American Life*, read this or some of Roosevelt's other writings on early American development, but it seems reasonable to conclude that Croly's impact on Roosevelt was much less important than some suggest, and possibly a great deal less than Roosevelt's impact on Croly.[41]

Roosevelt repeatedly stressed that the New Nationalism promoted economic regulation as an addition to, not a substitute for, the qualities of good citizenship.[42] According to him, the most crucial factor in any man's success was his character. If a man, as a husband, father, neighbor, worker, and citizen, was not honest, hard-working, devoted, and caring, then no amount of regulation or administrative reform would be sufficient to improve his lot in life. Legal and institutional reforms were meant only to give an individual the best possible chance to develop his talents and advance in the race of life.[43]

Woodrow Wilson, TR's Democratic opponent in the election of 1912, also sought to affirm American individualism, although he offered a different plan for achieving this principal goal: the New Freedom. Wilson distinguished between big business, which resulted from natural growth, and a monopolistic trust, which was an artificial product. The great trusts had not grown; they had been created by state-granted privileges. The high protective tariff, for example, was a policy of favoritism, and the favorites flourished at the expense of the rest. Perhaps, Wilson admitted, there was a time when the tariff did not increase prices, but that time was past. Instead of simply keeping American industries alive and therefore keeping American workers employed, the favors of protection had become so permanent that businessmen, seeing they had no need to fear foreign competition, decided to join together in great combinations that undermined competition and raised the cost of living. Wilson charged that Roosevelt's approach to the problem of trusts meant the denial of individual freedom, for the great corporate trusts were not interested in equality of opportunity; they would just as soon squeeze out the beginner, cripple his credit, and discriminate against those who supplied or purchased from rivals. Wilson was unwilling to accept the concentration of industry as inevitable, and he did not believe that the regulation of monopoly was the only course open to the people of the United States. Wilson concluded that any attempt by the government to supervise the affairs of the great trusts would strengthen, not weaken, the dangerous alliance between government and business. The big businessmen would continue their efforts to capture the government in order not to be restrained by it. Wilson added that Roosevelt's plan to supervise the great monopolistic combinations that had formed under the protection of the tariff was nothing more than the proposition that the people should be controlled by two masters: the great corporations and the government.[44]

But Roosevelt insisted that free competition among individuals would follow from the regulation of monopoly: "I am not for monopoly. We intend to restore competition."[45] Wilson's position, he asserted, was simply inadequate to the conditions of modern life. This is the theme of TR's Address at San Francisco's Coliseum, in which he repeats and criticizes Wilson's declaration that "the history of liberty is a history of the limitation of governmental power, not the increase of it." This belief, Roosevelt declares, "is a bit of out-worn academic doctrine which was kept in the schoolroom and the professo-rial study for a generation after it had been abandoned by all who had expe-rience of actual life. It is simply the *laissez-faire* doctrine of the English political economists, three-quarters of a century ago. It can be applied with profit, if anywhere at all, only in a primitive community under primitive con-ditions. . . . To apply it now in the United States at the beginning of the twen-tieth century, with its highly organized industries, with its railways, telegraphs, and telephones, means literally and absolutely to refuse to make a single effort to better any one of our social or industrial conditions." More-over, TR continues, Wilson is wrong from an historical standpoint. Certainly, if Wilson is referring to the absolute rule of kings, then the history of liberty is a history of the limitation of governmental power. But, if he is referring to the modern American system, in which power rests in the people, and the kings who enjoy privilege are the kings of finance and industry, then liberty does not necessarily require the limitation of governmental power.[46]

If Wilson's statement means anything, Roosevelt declares, it means that every law intended to promote social and industrial justice ought to be repealed, and every law proposed should be abandoned. TR asks whether Wilson really wishes to repeal the laws that regulate against unsafe and unsanitary working condi-tions. Does Wilson mean to repeal the Interstate Commerce Commission? Does Wilson oppose those who wish to limit the hours of working men and women to eight hours a day? Does he oppose either the six-day workweek or the elimina-tion of occupational disease? If not, then his statement means nothing whatso-ever. "In other words," Roosevelt concludes, "Mr. Wilson's promise is either a promise that is not to be kept or else it means the undoing of every particle of social and industrial advance we have made and the refusal to go forward along the lines of industrial and social progress." Roosevelt's Progressive Party pro-poses a workman's compensation act, TR reminds his audience. The Rough Rider then questions whether Wilson is against this proposition, given his re-marks about limiting governmental power for the sake of liberty. "Either he is against his own principle or he is against these reforms. He can choose either horn of the dilemma he wishes; but one or the other he must choose." Accord-ing to Roosevelt, Wilson's problem is that the history of which he speaks is the history of absolute monarchies. "He is thinking of government as embodied in an absolute king or in an oligarchy or aristocracy. He is not thinking of our gov-ernment, which is a government by the people themselves."[47]

The only chance that regular people have to protect themselves and their children from horrible working conditions, Roosevelt insists, is by extending, not limiting, the powers of the government. By acting collectively through government, the people will be able to check the irresponsible and exploitative actions of powerful financiers, big business executives, and big corporation lawyers. But to limit governmental power, as Wilson proposes to do, is to leave every great industrial concern free to do as it chooses with its employees and the public-at-large. Women and children would be forced to work as many hours a day as their bosses demand, and great corporations would be able to reduce wages to a starvation level, while increasing the price of their goods "as high as monopolistic control will permit."[48] The people, Roosevelt asserts, have one weapon that they can use against the colossal business combinations, and that weapon is the government of the United States. If Wilson is given the opportunity to limit the powers of the government, then he shall throw away the best instrument that the people have to limit and check the actions of the great corporations. Remember, TR adds, that the great corporations prefer a proposal like Wilson's; they do not want anything from the government except to be left alone. This is why, in every great suit involving a corporation, a corporate lawyer can be found protesting the extension of governmental power. This is why, the Rough Rider continues, every court decision that favors a corporation declares the unconstitutionality of extending governmental power. There once was a time when limiting governmental power meant increasing liberty for the people, Roosevelt concedes. At the start of the twentieth century, though, the limitation of governmental power means enslaving the people to the great corporations.[49]

Roosevelt emphasizes that he is for liberty, but that liberty does not mean the freedom of the powerful to exploit and oppress the weak. "We recognize no sacred right of oppression. We recognize no divine right to work injustice," he declares in his Speech at Madison Square Garden. Of course, he acknowledges, private property rights are essential to the preservation of free government, but Roosevelt argues, "We will not consent to make the Constitution a fetish for the protection of fossilized wrong." In short, the individual's right to justice, life, and liberty must be placed on an equal footing with the right to property.[50] Roosevelt admits that there are injustices in life that government is powerless to remedy, but he insists that it does not follow from this that no form of injustice can be remedied. Roosevelt will not attempt the impossible, and he recognizes that much depends on individual initiative and personal responsibility. Still, he concludes, there are many wrongs that it is possible to right. If elected, he promises to continue his efforts to strike down privilege and equalize individual opportunity.[51]

THE CALL FOR DIRECT DEMOCRACY

In 1912, when TR failed to win the Republican presidential nomination, he formed a third party, the Progressive Party, and attempted to win the presidency under that banner. In addition to an economic platform that called for stronger national regulation of interstate corporations—safety and sanitation standards, the abolition of child labor, an eight-hour day, a six-day workweek, a decent minimum wage, and compensation for industrial accidents and deaths—the Progressives advanced a direct democracy program that included women's suffrage, direct primaries, the direct election of U.S. senators, the initiative, the referendum, the recall of judges, and the recall of judicial decisions. The impetus behind the push for direct democracy was the expectation that these reforms would connect the people directly to their government, rather than to narrow, parochial, and often-corrupt party organizations, thereby freeing elected officials to act as dynamic moral leaders. They, and not their party, would embody and implement the public's desire for economic and social justice.[52]

Roosevelt insisted that the expansion of federal regulatory power and democratic reform were interrelated goals. Through direct popular rule, the evils of big business could be most effectively corrected, and a "square deal" thereby assured for all citizens. In "Nationalism and Popular Rule," he stresses that popular rule permits the wealthy to exercise as much influence over the government as ordinary people. Popular rule simply means that all citizens are guaranteed the same right to influence the decisions of government. Each and every individual will have "his full share as a citizen, and only just so much more as his abilities entitle him to by enabling him to render to his fellow citizens services more important than the average man can render." According to Roosevelt, the surest way to bring about mob rule is to base government on wealth and privilege, and mob rule is as reactionary as plutocracy. The Progressives, he writes, are doing all they can to protect the country from the instability that would result from the unhealthy oscillation between control by a plutocracy and control by a mob. Hence, genuine reformers support the following principles: laws to prevent the corrupt use of money in politics; election of United States senators by direct vote; direct primaries for the nomination of elected officials; direct election of delegates to presidential nominating conventions; and the introduction of the initiative, referendum, and recall.[53]

With respect to the initiative and referendum, Roosevelt emphasizes that they should be used, not to destroy republican government, but to correct it whenever it fails to represent the true will of the people. In the majority of instances, he admits, it is better to leave the decision-making to the professional legislators. Not only are they delegated the authority to decide important legislative matters, but most of them have an understanding of the law as well as a specific policy expertise. Most ordinary citizens also lack the time to follow all the minutiae of legislation. Nevertheless, he asserts that, when legislators fail to represent the interests and the will of their constituents, the people should have the power to take legislative action themselves.[54] The initiative and referendum should not become the normal mode of governmental operation, but Roosevelt argues that the power to take such action should be guaranteed so that, if the representatives fail to represent the people on an important policy matter, the people shall have the means to correct that failure. There is no need to place constitutional restraints on the legislature. Indeed, TR advises reformers to give the legislature a free hand and employ the initiative and referendum simply to supplement and occasionally reverse the work of the legislature.[55] He also suggests that opponents of the referendum and initiative would do well to remember that these measures are much less radical than the New England town meeting, at which all town matters are decided, without appeal, by a vote of the townspeople in attendance. The initiative and referendum simply represent the next step in democratic governance, building upon the practices of New England.[56]

In normal circumstances, Roosevelt concedes, a representative should be allowed to represent his constituents. If he should find that he differs with them on a specific issue, then he must follow his own conscience; however, a representative of the people should not try to achieve his objective by tricking his constituents or by attempting to thwart their wishes behind closed committee doors. Moreover, a representative should never place career considerations above the dictates of his conscience. If an issue is of sufficient importance, Roosevelt believes that an elected official should be prepared to face electoral defeat rather than surrender principle. At the same time, he insists that a good representative sees it as his duty to lead his constituents to accept his views. In sum, TR holds that the representative's job is neither to abandon his own belief nor to try to beat his constituents by deception. If a split on some matter of principle is irreconcilable, and he is unable to convert the people to his way of thinking, then he must fight fairly for his convictions and, as Roosevelt suggests, happily accept defeat.[57]

For Roosevelt, it is also important for reformers to remember that measures like the initiative and referendum are merely means and not ends: "their success or failure," he insists, "is to be determined not on *a priori* reasoning but by actually testing how they work under varying conditions." Moreover, "it is foolish to treat these or any other devices for obtaining good government and popular rule as justifying sweeping condemnation of all men and communities where other governmental methods are preferred." The initiative and referendum might, in certain states, give the best and most immediate effect to the will of the people, but they are not the beginning and end of good government for TR. If the people of various states should decide that they are not ready to adopt either device, then all Progressives must respect that decision. "Personally," Roosevelt declares, "I should like to see the initiative and referendum, with proper safeguards, adopted generally in the States of the Union, and personally I am sorry that the New England town meeting has not spread throughout the Union. But I certainly do not intend to part company from other Progressives who fail to sympathize with me in either view." It is enough that reformers agree the end is good government. For Roosevelt, good government safeguards the interests of all people by securing justice and equal opportunity in both economic and political matters. Any device that achieves this end is good, "and the value of each device must be tested purely by the answer to the question, Does it or does it not secure the end in view?"[58]

Roosevelt worried that the special interests were achieving their narrow ends by working through corrupt legislators, but he saved his harshest criticism for judges. Because the majority of judges, Roosevelt charged, defended private property rights at the expense of the popular will, the people should have the right to recall them. In his Address before the Ohio Constitutional Convention, he declares that an "upright" judiciary understands and sympathizes with popular needs. A judge is a public servant, and like the other public servants in the executive and legislative branches of government, TR wants the judge to follow his conscience. Yet the people also have the right to follow their consciences, and when they have decided on a policy matter, they must have public servants who will execute that policy.[59]

Roosevelt stresses that the judicial recall should not be used except as a last resort, when it has become obvious that nothing else will achieve the desired end. The desired end is to keep those judges off the bench who have grown completely and irreconcilably out of touch with social needs. Roosevelt regards impeachment as a theoretical solution to the problem of eliminating all bad judges. It is a slow process and tends to work best as a remedy for impropriety — dishonesty and corruption — not for a misguided interpretation of the law. TR's belief is that the recall offers a quicker and more effective remedy for the economic and social injustices of which the people rightly complain. This does not mean that the people should employ the remedy recklessly. After all, Roosevelt admits, even national heroes like George Washington and Abraham Lincoln made mistakes. TR agrees that we must be cautious about using the recall against a good judge who has rendered one unwise and improper decision. Nevertheless, he notes that many states have long been allowing the recall of judges via the processes of reappointment and reelection.[60]

But there is one kind of recall that Roosevelt hopes to see used quite regularly: the recall of *judicial decisions*. He warns that the people must be cautious about interfering with decisions that affect only the parties to a particular case, but when a judge incorrectly decides a constitutional question that will bind the other branches of government, the people should have the right to recall that decision. Roosevelt maintains that we should respect the place of the judiciary in our constitutional scheme; however, it is silly to deify judges or anyone else. To support his argument, Roosevelt repeats Lincoln's declaration from his First Inaugural Address: "If the policy of the government upon vital questions affecting the whole people is to be irrevocably fixed by decisions of the Supreme Court . . . the people will have ceased to be their own rulers, having to that extent practically resigned their government into the hands of that eminent tribunal."[61]

Throughout his Ohio Speech, TR invokes Lincoln's name on behalf of the public's right to override judicial decisions. "Lincoln actually applied in successful fashion the principle of the recall in the *Dred Scott* case. He denounced the Supreme Court for that iniquitous decision in language much stronger than I have ever used in criticizing any court, and appealed to the people to recall the decision—the word 'recall' in this connection was not then known, but the phrase exactly describes what he advocated."[62] TR's claim, however, is dubious. Lincoln agreed to abide by the particular decision regarding whether Scott was entitled to freedom, but he refused to accept the decision as an authoritative precedent for settling national policy on slavery, arguing that it was based on "assumed historical facts which were not really true."[63] He added, however, that the same court that made this erroneous decision had often overruled its own decisions. His intent was to do whatever he could to induce the court to overrule this decision.[64] Thus, Lincoln held out hope that the *Dred Scott* decision would eventually be overturned by the justices themselves. This would depend, in part, on the election of a President who would appoint different justices, particularly ones who would not twist the law to mean anything they wanted it to mean. In the meantime, Lincoln would devote his energy to teaching his fellow citizens about the true ideals that had been at the heart of the American founding.[65] Roosevelt declares that Lincoln was successful in persuading the people to recall the decision of the Court, concluding that it "became dead letter without the need of any constitutional amendment."[66] But this is not an accurate interpretation of history. In actuality, it took a long and bloody civil war, as well as the passage of the Thirteenth and Fourteenth Amendments, to overturn *Dred Scott*.

Roosevelt's conviction that the recall would make judges more sympathetic to the popular will excited the hostility of William Howard Taft, who maintained that, because judges decided questions involving personal rights, the recall (as well as other direct democracy reforms) subjected individual rights to the whims of popular opinion. The likely outcome of this was despotism. According to Taft, if any branch of government exceeded those powers to which it was limited by the Constitution, its actions should be declared null and void. But who was to determine whether a given act was unconstitutional? Taft asserted that it was the right and the responsibility of the judiciary to say what the law meant. This was the reasoning of *Marbury v. Madison*, in which Chief Justice John Marshall declared that "the Constitution is either the superior paramount law, or it is on a level with ordinary legislative acts, and like other acts, is alterable when the legislature shall please to alter it." Taft agreed wholeheartedly with Marshall's reasoning, adding that it had been accepted "as sound practice" for over 125 years. The opposing theory was that each branch of government should be faithful to its own best understanding of the Constitution. But Taft explained that the problem with this theory was that it allowed the majority in power to define which rights were worthy of protection and which were not.[67] In Taft's view, the maintenance of individual rights depended upon judges having the leeway to decide against the majority whenever justice and the law so required.[68] The recall of judges and judicial decisions, Taft concluded, "lays the ax at the foot of the tree of well-ordered freedom and subjects the guaranties of life, liberty, and property without remedy to the fitful impulse of a temporary majority of an electorate."[69]

But Roosevelt regarded Taft's criticisms as overblown. For one, the Rough Rider insisted that the recall should apply only to *state* courts: "What the Supreme Court of the nation decides to be law binds both the national and the state courts and all the people within the boundaries of the nation. But the decision of a state court on a constitutional question should be subject to revision by the people of the state." When a state supreme court declared a particular statute unconstitutional, Roosevelt believed that the people should have the right to bring before the voters at some subsequent election the question of whether the judges' interpretation of the Constitution should be sustained. If not sustained, then the popular verdict would be accepted as final, subject only to the decisions of the Supreme Court. Moreover, Roosevelt was the first to recognize that the people were fallible. He conceded that, while sufficiently intelligent and moral to govern themselves, the people would not always make the right decisions. It was possible, he admitted, that his proposed reforms could result in a tyranny of the majority. But the present problem was not the tyranny of the majority but rather "the tyranny of the bosses and of the special interests." Declaring that his opponents talked "as if the judges were somehow imposed on us by Heaven," TR asserted that judges were men with the same imperfections and frailties as other men. Some were brilliant, principled, and concerned with serving the public good, while others allowed themselves to be the puppets of political bosses and special interests.[70] By undermining the efforts of the people who were acting collectively through the government to achieve greater equality of opportunity, these puppet judges posed the greatest threat to freedom, specifically the right of every individual to compete on a reasonably level playing field. This, after all, was the promise of the New Nationalism.

NOTES

1. Paolo Coletta, *The Presidency of William Howard Taft* (Lawrence: University Press of Kansas, 1973), 45–75; Forrest McDonald, *The United States in the 20th Century: 1900–1920* (Reading: Addison-Wesley Publishing, 1970), 166–74.

2. Coletta, *Presidency of William Howard Taft*, 84–94; McDonald, *United States in the 20th Century*, 174–76; William E. Leuchtenburg, introduction to *The New Nationalism*, by Theodore Roosevelt (Gloucester: Peter Smith, 1971), 4.

3. Theodore Roosevelt to Henry Cabot Lodge, May 5, 1910, *Selections from the Correspondence of Theodore Roosevelt to Henry Cabot Lodge (1884–1918)*, vol. 1 (New York: Charles Scribner's Sons, 1925), 380.

4. Leuchtenburg, introduction, 5–6.

5. Leuchtenburg, introduction, 6–7; Coletta, *Presidency of William Howard Taft*, 113–17.

6. Roosevelt to Lodge, 380.

7. Leuchtenburg, introduction, 7.

8. Theodore Roosevelt, "Speech at Osawatomie," in *The New Nationalism* (Gloucester: Peter Smith, 1971), 24–25.

9. Roosevelt, "Speech at Osawatomie," 25–27.

10. Roosevelt, "Speech at Osawatomie," 27–29.

11. Theodore Roosevelt, "Fourth Annual Message," in *Presidential Addresses and State Papers*, vol. 3 (New York: Review of Reviews, 1910), 128.

12. Theodore Roosevelt, "Fifth Annual Message," in *Presidential Addresses and State Papers*, vol. 4 (New York: Review of Reviews, 1910), 563.

13. Roosevelt, "Fifth Annual Message," 563–64.

14. Roosevelt, "Speech at Osawatomie," 35–36.

15. Roosevelt, "Speech at Osawatomie," 36.

16. Roosevelt, "Speech at Osawatomie," 38–39.

17. Roosevelt, "Speech at Osawatomie," 39.

18. Theodore Roosevelt, "Speech at York," in *Presidential Addresses and State Papers*, vol. 5 (New York: Review of Reviews, 1910), 843–44.

19. Theodore Roosevelt, "Speech at the Pilgrim Memorial," in *Presidential Addresses and State Papers*, vol. 6 (New York: Review of Reviews, 1910), 362–64.

20. Theodore Roosevelt, "Speech before the Colorado Legislature," in *The New Nationalism* (Gloucester: Peter Smith, 1971), 41–42.

21. Roosevelt, "Speech before the Colorado Legislature," 46.

22. Theodore Roosevelt, "Speech at Denver," in *The New Nationalism* (Gloucester: Peter Smith, 1971), 53–55.

23. Roosevelt, "Speech at Osawatomie," 32.

24. Roosevelt, "Speech at Osawatomie," 33–34.

25. Theodore Roosevelt, "Speech at Fargo," in *The New Nationalism* (Gloucester: Peter Smith, 1971), 98–99.

26. Roosevelt, "Speech at Fargo," 99–102.

27. Theodore Roosevelt, "Speech at Syracuse," in *The New Nationalism* (Gloucester: Peter Smith, 1971), 165.

28. Stephen F. Knott, *Alexander Hamilton and the Persistence of Myth* (Lawrence: University Press of Kansas, 2002), 87–90.

29. Edward Stettner, *Shaping Modern Liberalism: Herbert Croly and Progressive Thought* (Lawrence: University Press of Kansas, 1993), 76, 38. See also Herbert Croly, *The Promise of American Life* (New York: The Macmillan Company, 1909), 29.

30. Stettner, *Shaping Modern Liberalism*, 38. See also Croly, *Promise of American Life*, 40–42.

31. Stettner, *Shaping Modern Liberalism*, 40–46, 49, 53–55, 65–68. See also Croly, *Promise of American Life*, 364–65.

32. Stettner, *Shaping Modern Liberalism*, 69–70. See also Croly, *Promise of American Life*, 372.

33. Theodore Roosevelt, "Sixth Annual Message," in *Presidential Addresses and State Papers*, vol. 5 (New York: Review of Reviews, 1910), 930.

34. Quoted in Stettner, *Shaping Modern Liberalism*, 55. See also Croly, *Promise of American Life*, 453.

35. Quoted in Stettner, *Shaping Modern Liberalism*, 55. See also Croly, *Promise of American Life*, 454.

36. *American Magazine*, for example, described Croly as "the man from whom Colonel Roosevelt got his 'New Nationalism.'" See also Leuchtenburg, introduction, 11.

37. See Stettner, *Shaping Modern Liberalism*, 82–83, 189–90. As Stettner reminds his readers, Richard Hofstadter (*The American Political Tradition and the Men Who Made It*, 482) writes that the political thought of "the new Roosevelt of 1910–1912" was influenced by two books: Charles R. Van Hise's *Concentration and Control* and Herbert Croly's *The Promise of American Life*. Similarly, David Levy (*Herbert Croly of the New Republic: The Life and Thought of an American Progressive*) argues that Croly actually worked on the Osawatomie Address. In making this assertion, he relies on a recollection by Walter Lippmann. But, as Stettner notes, Elting Morison's chronology of Roosevelt's appointments shows no meeting with Croly between August 1 and the Osawatomie Address, which was delivered on August 31, 1910. On the other hand, Stettner continues, John Milton Cooper (*The Warrior and the Priest*, 145) argues that, despite the term "New Nationalism," TR was delivering a familiar refrain in his Osawatomie Address. Cooper adds that "aside from a somewhat greater specificity about regulatory legislation, nothing in *The New Nationalism* was new to

Roosevelt except the phrase." Likewise, John Morton Blum (*The Republican Roosevelt*, 107) contends that Roosevelt's principles were evident "long before Herbert Croly wrote his *Promise of American Life*." Finally, Charles Forcey notes the "marked similarity" between *The New Nationalism* and *The Promise of American Life*. According to him, this was "a coincidence of reasoning." Forcey concludes, "When the measure of Croly's influence on Roosevelt is taken . . . the profound impact of Roosevelt's own career on the philosopher has to be counted. The relation of the two men was one of interaction, with Roosevelt's impress much stronger. Croly was quite consciously trying to formulate and carry further tendencies that had been manifest in Roosevelt's Presidency." See Charles Forcey, *The Crossroads of Liberalism: Croly, Weyl, Lippmann, and the Progressive Era, 1900–1925* (New York: Oxford University Press, 1961), 129–30.

38. Referenced in Stettner, *Shaping Modern Liberalism*, 189. See also Leuchtenburg, introduction, 11.

39. Quoted in Forcey, *Crossroads of Liberalism*, 129.

40. See Theodore Roosevelt, *Gouverneur Morris*, vol. 7 of *The Works of Theodore Roosevelt*, National Edition (New York: Charles Scribner's Sons, 1926), 323, 327.

41. Leuchtenburg, introduction, 12–13; Stettner, *Shaping Modern Liberalism*, 82.

42. Roosevelt, "Speech at Osawatomie," 38–39.

43. Roosevelt, "Speech at Osawatomie," 39.

44. Woodrow Wilson, *The New Freedom* (Englewood Cliffs, N.J.: Prentice-Hall, 1961), 91, 93, 97, 102–4, 109, 122. For a wonderful summary of Wilson's thought, see William Leuchtenburg, introduction to *The New Freedom*, by Woodrow Wilson (Englewood Cliffs: Prentice-Hall, 1961), 1–17.

45. Mowry, *Theodore Roosevelt and the Progressive Movement*, 280; John Allen Gable, *The Bull Moose Years: Theodore Roosevelt and the Progressive Party* (Port Washington, N.Y.: Kennikat Press, 1978), 125.

46. Theodore Roosevelt, "Address at the Coliseum," in *Social Justice and Popular Rule*, vol. 17 of *The Works of Theodore Roosevelt*, National Edition (New York: Charles Scribner's Sons, 1926), 306–7.

47. Roosevelt, "Address at the Coliseum," 308–9.

48. Roosevelt, "Address at the Coliseum," 309–10.

49. Roosevelt, "Address at the Coliseum," 312–13.

50. Theodore Roosevelt, "Speech at Madison Square Garden," in *Social Justice and Popular Rule*, vol. 17 of *The Works of Theodore Roosevelt*, National Edition (New York: Charles Scribner's Sons, 1926), 337.

51. Roosevelt, "Speech at Madison Square Garden," 338.

52. James W. Ceaser, *Presidential Selection: Theory and Development* (Princeton: Princeton University Press, 1979), 31, chap. iv; Jeffrey K. Tulis, *The Rhetorical Presidency* (Princeton: Princeton University Press, 1987), 18.

53. Theodore Roosevelt, "Nationalism and Popular Rule," in *Social Justice and Popular Rule*, vol. 17 of *The Works of Theodore Roosevelt*, National Edition (New York: Charles Scribner's Sons, 1926), 53–54.

54. Roosevelt, "Nationalism and Popular Rule," 56–57.

55. Theodore Roosevelt, "Address before the Ohio Constitutional Convention," in *Social Justice and Popular Rule*, vol. 17 of *The Works of Theodore Roosevelt*, National Edition (New York: Charles Scribner's Sons, 1926), 135.

56. Roosevelt, "Nationalism and Popular Rule," 60–61.

57. Roosevelt, "Nationalism and Popular Rule," 59.

58. Roosevelt, "Nationalism and Popular Rule," 62.

59. Roosevelt, "Address before the Ohio Constitutional Convention," 136–37.

60. Roosevelt, "Address before the Ohio Constitutional Convention," 138.

61. Roosevelt, "Address before the Ohio Constitutional Convention," 138–39.

62. Roosevelt, "Address before the Ohio Constitutional Convention," 139.

63. Abraham Lincoln, "Speech at Springfield," in *The Language of Liberty: The Political Writings and Speeches of Abraham Lincoln*, ed. Joseph R. Fornieri (Washington, D.C.: Regnery Publishing, 2003), 200.

64. Lincoln, "Speech at Springfield," 202; Abraham Lincoln, "Speech at Chicago," in *The Language of Liberty: The Political Writings and Speeches of Abraham Lincoln*, ed. Joseph R. Fornieri (Washington, D.C.: Regnery Publishing, 2003), 227.

65. Abraham Lincoln, "First Debate at Ottawa," in *The Language of Liberty: The Political Writings and Speeches of Abraham Lincoln*, ed. Joseph R. Fornieri (Washington, D.C.: Regnery Publishing, 2003), 271.

66. Roosevelt, "Address before the Ohio Constitutional Convention," 139.

67. William Howard Taft, *Popular Government*, vol. 5 of *The Collected Works of William Howard Taft* (Athens: Ohio University Press, 2003), 105–6.

68. William Howard Taft, "Veto Message," in *The Collected Works of William Howard Taft*, vol. 4, ed. David H. Burton (Athens: Ohio University Press, 2002), 152–53.

69. William Howard Taft, "Address at Toledo," Reel 569, Series 9A, 12, William Howard Taft Papers, Library of Congress.

70. Theodore Roosevelt, "Address at Philadelphia," in *Social Justice and Popular Rule*, vol. 17 of *The Works of Theodore Roosevelt*, National Edition (New York: Charles Scribner's Sons, 1926), 202–3.

Chapter Eight

TR, the New Freedom, and the World War

After Inauguration Day 1913, TR wasted no time before criticizing Woodrow Wilson, the first Democratic President since Grover Cleveland (1893–1897). In a letter to Henry Cabot Lodge, Roosevelt wrote, "I regard Wilson with contemptuous dislike. He has ability of a certain kind, and he has the nerve that his type so often shows in civil and domestic affairs where there is no danger of physical violence. He will jump up and down on cheap politicians, and bully and cajole men in public life who are anxious not to part company with their political chief. But he is a ridiculous creature in international matters. He is a narrow and bitter partisan, and he is intellectually thoroughly dishonest."[1] But Roosevelt did not confine his animosity to private correspondences. In various public writings, he characterized Wilson as dishonest, cowardly, and inept. This maligning of Wilson's words and actions, which lasted until TR's death in 1919, was based in part perhaps on simple envy. Still, even a cursory glance at his myriad speeches, editorials, and books written between 1913 and 1919 shows that Roosevelt had real ideological differences with Wilson.

THE CONTINUING CRUSADE AGAINST THE NEW FREEDOM

By the summer of 1913, Roosevelt was writing that Wilson's New Freedom meant nothing more than the freedom of the powerful to prey on the weak.[2] Wilson's program was based on a fear of economic combination. But some combinations, TR argued, existed for good purposes, just as some existed for bad purposes alien to the public good, and the government had a responsibility to suppress the trusts that worked evil, while favoring those that served well the interests of the public. "If a corporation or a combination makes for efficiency we favor it, providing the benefits are shared with reasonable equality among the employers and capitalists, the workers and the general public," Roosevelt declared. "If, however, the so-called efficiency represents merely profits for the employer obtained by exploiting the workmen or mistreating his rivals, or swindling the general public, then our desire is not merely to stop the practices but to punish those who take part in them."[3] Roosevelt thought the Wilson administration viewed such state interference as paternalistic. In doing so, it failed to recognize, in TR's opinion, that there was only one way to stop those who would make slaves of the feeble, and that was by employing the regulatory power of the government.[4] Roosevelt insisted that all honest, hard-working, and visionary businessmen should make money and prosper, for in the end, good wages and quality services depended on the success of business. His aim was to use government on behalf of the public interest, demanding justice as a right, not asking for it as a favor. He believed government could and should protect employers, employees, and the public from the schemes and exploitations of selfish individuals. Only thus, he argued, did regular folks have any hope of climbing the ladder to success.[5]

Increased governmental action, TR stressed time and again, did not mean any impairment or weakening of individualism. The combination of both collective action and individual initiative, he explained, was essential to the success of the modern state. In Roosevelt's opinion, this was as true in civil life as it was in military life. No amount of "personal prowess" would make soldiers a formidable foe, unless they also possessed the ability to act for the sake of the common good. On the other hand, TR believed that no amount of collective organization could compensate for lack of individual discipline, hardihood, and bravery. "We not merely recognize but insist upon the fact that in the life career of any man or any woman the prime factor as regards success or failure must be his or her possession of that bundle of qualities and attributes which in their aggregate we denominate as character; and yet that, in addition, there must be proper social conditions surrounding him or her. Recognition of and insistence upon either fact must never be permitted to mean failure to recognize the other and complementary fact. The character of the individual is vital, and yet, in order to give it fair expression, it must be supplemented by collective action through the agencies of government."[6]

In reply to the criticisms that Wilson levied against him, Roosevelt reasoned that the conditions of modern life demanded "the partial substitution of collectivism for individualism, not to destroy, but to save individualism." In simpler communities, he argued, there really was no need for collective action; every man or family looked after his or its interests in such matters as the prevention of fires, the construction of drainage systems, and the supply of water, light, and transportation. In a modern city, however, it was absurd to expect every man to continue to do this, or to conclude that an individual lacked initiative because he surrendered such tasks to those public officials whose job it was to engage in the collective activities of society. In other words, the amount and the nature of activities in a modern and complex community were such that an increase in collective activity was an addition to, not a substitute for, individual initiative and personal responsibility. The increase of collectivism for social and economic purposes did not entail the deadening of individual character and initiative such as would result from the implementation of Communistic or Socialistic doctrines. Roosevelt stressed that his goal was not Socialism. Instead, he claimed to be preaching "a sanely altruistic individualism," where hard work, discipline, and personal responsibility were *combined with* "a lively sense of consideration and duty toward others," and where society's recognition of the need for collective action went hand-in-hand with its devotion to individual action.[7]

According to TR, the many problems associated with industrialization, specifically those associated with trusts and child labor, could be solved only by positive national action. In this, Roosevelt declared that he, not Wilson, was the true disciple of Thomas Jefferson, Andrew Jackson, and Abraham Lincoln, all of whom believed that America had a government of the people, by the people, to be used for the people in order to improve the condition of the average man and woman. Roosevelt charged that no one was a Progressive who did not believe in employing Hamiltonian means to achieve Jeffersonian ends, which was the defense of all individual rights—and not just those of property.[8] Specifically, TR called for a living wage and disability insurance, opposition to child labor, the establishment of an eight-hour day and a six-day week, the fixing of minimum safety and health standards for various occupations, and the defense of organized labor.[9] According to Roosevelt, Wilson's only solution to the problems of industry was antitrust, but merely breaking up powerful combinations did nothing to improve the conditions of wageworkers. The latter required "thoroughgoing, efficient, and, if necessary, drastic" oversight of those corporations that engaged in interstate commerce.[10]

In truth, Wilson's reforms were more akin to Roosevelt's than either man cared to admit. For his part, Roosevelt simply ignored Wilson's role in enacting such measures as the Federal Trade Commission Act, which essentially endorsed TR's proposition that a regulatory agency be empowered to exercise continuous governmental supervision over big business; the Federal Reserve Act, which left ownership of the nation's banks in private hands but vested oversight in a regulatory board appointed by the President; the Keating-Owen bill, which excluded the products of child labor from interstate commerce; the Adamson Act, which established the eight-hour day for railroad workers; and workmen's compensation for those on jobs under government contract.[11] The domestic initiatives of the Wilson administration on which Roosevelt focused exclusively were tariff reform and antitrust. Not surprisingly, TR's remarks were harshly critical. Wilson won passage of a measure that sharply reduced rates on numerous imports, but Roosevelt scoffed that tariff reform was meant only to distract people from the more important issues of the day.[12] Contrary to the claims of the Democratic Party, Roosevelt explained, tariff reform did not reduce the cost of living or improve the conditions of farmers and wageworkers.[13] Similarly, he lambasted Wilson's attack on the trusts, arguing that those who behaved badly should be held liable, regardless of whether they were big or small.[14] It is, of course, no surprise that Roosevelt did not paint a complete picture of Wilson's record. After all, it had to be frustrating for him to watch Wilson approach (perhaps even surpass) his own Square Deal record of reform, especially considering that Wilson had originally opposed many of these initiatives. Indeed, Wilson's conversion to the Progressive cause seemed attributable more to presidential politics than to any change of heart and mind, for the bulk of his domestic achievements came in 1916, when he was running for reelection.[15] But Roosevelt did not harangue Wilson for this seeming opportunism, because by 1915, his attention was focused almost exclusively on the prospect of war, specifically on issues of neutrality and national preparedness.

ROOSEVELT'S CALL FOR PREPAREDNESS

Prior to 1917, the United States had never engaged in a war that took its troops to European soil, and initially, the majority of Americans, including President Wilson, had no wish to break that precedent. A war in Europe meant involvement in the ancient feuds of the Old World, which violated the advice given by generations of American statesman, including George Washington. Moreover, Germany seemed to pose no immediate danger to the United States. Its imperialistic behavior appeared little different from that of Great Britain and France, and political leaders like Wilson understood that American entry into the war as an ally of Great Britain and a foe of Germany was likely to anger two large and politically important immigrant groups: Irish-Americans and German-Americans. In short, the majority of Americans cherished their long-standing isolation from European affairs and opposed entry into the war. Wilson responded by issuing a neutrality proclamation and by repeatedly stating his belief that the United States was obligated to remain impartial in both thought and deed.[16]

Roosevelt was outraged, declaring that the United States was obligated to protest German aggression against sovereign nations like Belgium and Luxembourg. The fate of these devastated nations, he writes in *America and the World War*, offers an instructive example of how foolish it is to believe that mere treaties will protect well-meaning and neutral nations from the tyrannical designs of others.[17] Both Belgium and Luxembourg mistakenly believed that peaceful measures and treaties would secure them against harm. But most nations, like most individuals, often act according to the dictates of self-interest, and any treaty that prevents a nation from achieving either real or imagined needs will be treated as garbage, unless it is backed by force.[18] The attack on Belgium, Roosevelt continues, was no doubt consistent with what Germany sincerely believed was needed in its struggle for existence. But Germany's struggle for life does not make it right that the Belgian people must endure mass destruction and death. Belgium is not responsible for its own destruction; it was a peaceful and neutral power that had been guilty of no offense whatsoever. The Germans, TR charges, are to blame for what is occurring in Belgium; they deemed that their national interests depended on violating Belgium's rights.[19] Roosevelt urges that the American people, acting through their government, offer their sympathy and support to the people of Belgium, but at the same time learn the lesson taught by Belgium's fall.[20] In short, America must be prepared to defend its life and its liberty through the use of force, and the successful use of force depends on military preparedness. If the American people are wise and farsighted, they will insist upon preparedness and pay any price to achieve this end.[21]

Peace is worthless, Roosevelt declares, unless it serves the cause of justice. Roosevelt sees peace as an agent for achieving righteousness, but if he must choose between righteousness and peace, he will choose righteousness every time. For the Rough Rider, there is no nobler international goal than to protect the existence and independence of industrious, orderly, and peaceful states.[22] Any peace, therefore, that fails to redress the wrongs committed against Belgium and also fails to protect against the recurrence of such wrongs is neither a real nor a worthy peace. Similarly, for Roosevelt, there is no value in the so-called peace that was obtained when a concert of European powers refused to interfere with Turkey's decision to butcher hundreds of thousands of Armenian men, women, and children.[23] He notes that President Wilson has been applauded for announcing that America's peace and security depend on strict neutrality that forbids even a whisper of protest against the wrongdoing of other nations. Yet Roosevelt finds it shameful that America's desire to preserve peace for itself means abandoning the effort to secure peace for other unoffending nations. Once again, TR laments, self-interest has trumped compassion and a genuine spirit of brotherhood.[24]

Notice that Roosevelt's approach to foreign policy parallels his domestic views. As he has both before and during his presidency, TR stresses the importance of marrying self-interest to duty and a concern for the rights of others. In both domestic and foreign matters, he writes, Americans must never act selfishly and without respect for the common good. Through their words and actions, he reminds readers, Washington and Lincoln taught their fellow countrymen that a government that recognizes the rights and liberties of individuals must be strong enough to preserve these rights and liberties from the aggression of thoughtless and selfish thugs, both foreign and domestic. According to TR, what made these two the greatest Presidents in American history was their refusal to believe that goodness meant weakness, as well as their hostility to the idea that strength justified wrongdoing. "No abundance of the milder virtues will save a nation that has lost the virile qualities, and, on the other hand, no admiration of strength must make us deviate from the laws of righteousness."[25] Good character is as essential in international affairs as it is in our business, family, and community relationships.

TR clearly regards preparedness as an extension of "the strenuous life," which encourages individuals to act with honesty, courage, discipline, physical vigor, patriotism, and a desire to serve the community-at-large. Indeed, in *America and the World War*, he advocates universal military training as a way to teach young Americans the importance of *both* personal responsibility and brotherhood. He does not believe in a large standing army, nor does he believe in militarism, but he does believe that men do not deserve freedom unless they are able and willing to defend it.[26] Far from distracting young men from their personal/civil pursuits, universal military training would give them the skills needed to succeed in life. Personal advantages would thereby accrue from service to others. Moreover, the system would be democratic. No man would be exempted from duty, and all would be expected to perform the same tasks.[27] Military training would have a leveling effect, bringing together "the son of the capitalist and the son of the day laborer, the son of the Railway President and the son of the brakeman, the sons of farmer, lawyer, doctor, carpenter and clerk would all go in together, would sleep in the same dog tents, eat the same food, go on the same hikes, profit by the same discipline, and learn to honor and take pride in the same flag." Promotion would depend on merit, not race, ethnicity, religion, or class. Thus, Roosevelt concludes, universal military training promises to foster individual fitness and discipline, while teaching the advantages of cooperation and permitting all young men to interact on a level playing field. In addition to military proficiency, it is certain to increase "social and industrial efficiency."[28]

For TR, having a nation prepared for war entails more than merely building up a military. It requires a nation built securely on a foundation of social and economic justice for all. As is so often the case, he recalls the lessons of

Lincoln to buttress his view. "There can be no sound relationship toward other nations," Roosevelt writes, "unless there is also sound relationship among our own citizens within our own ranks." In this, the nation must strike a balance. It must permit ample financial reward and incentive to those whose economic activities prove successful and responsible for the nation's prosperity, and simultaneously, it must assure that justice is done to the countless laborers who contribute to industrial success.[29] Roosevelt invokes Lincoln, recalling that, while the Great Emancipator correctly treated the preservation of the Union and the destruction of slavery as paramount over all other matters of public policy, he did not ignore various social and industrial questions. Lincoln thought that the rights of property were secondary to the personal rights of men, and he was "for both the man and the dollar, but in case of conflict, the man before the dollar."[30]

Lincoln's words about the superiority of the rights of labor to those of capital, TR asserts, point us in the direction we should follow in addressing the problems of industrialization, even if they do not say precisely what should be done. While Lincoln believed in guarding the rights of capital, he also thought it only right that the benefits of capitalism be diffused as widely as possible. It is for this reason, Roosevelt concludes, that the Great Emancipator called for eliminating all artificial obstacles to a fair start in the world. "What he upheld as a desirable principle was that the average man — who can never be the man of large means — should himself own a piece of the world and do his own work as regards that piece of the world. What he saw has changed. What he upheld as the desirable principle has not changed."[31]

In arguing for the concept of *economic preparedness*, Roosevelt emphasizes his rejection of both "ultraindividualism" and "ultracollectivism." He calls upon everyone to rebuke both those who embrace the teachings of Herbert Spencer (and see nothing wrong with the gross injustices committed by capitalists and corporations) and those who embrace Marxist doctrines (and make unreasonable demands on a society that rightfully embraces the concept of a free marketplace).[32] Laborers, Roosevelt asserts, should not be worked to the limit for the lowest wages offered; however, it is equally to the disadvantage of a nation that they should do as little work as possible. TR believes that society must strike a balance between labor and economic reward. Unlimited and unregulated competition will not secure this end, while attacks on hard work and private property will do far less.[33]

Roosevelt contends that the doctrines of Socialism are as immoral and as absurd as the doctrines of extreme individualism.[34] To him, Socialism requires an exercise of governmental power that borders on despotism and, in the end, is nothing but "a glorified state free-lunch counter" that makes self-indulgence the ideal.[35] In essence, Roosevelt concludes, Socialists are as selfish as laissez-faire capitalists, for both types seek to enthrone privilege. Socialists advocate allow-ing each man to contribute to a common stockpile what he can afford and to take what he needs. Roosevelt can think of no system more likely to encourage the thriftless and vicious to exploit the rest of society, especially the intelligent, fore-sighted, and industrious. "To choose to live by theft or by charity necessarily means the complete loss of self-respect."[36]

Roosevelt thus sees preparedness for war in a larger social and moral frame in which individualism must be balanced with social justice. What is true of the military and political institutions of the nation is no less true of business and community life. There must be social, economic, and military prepared-ness, and these must be grounded in a type of character that places at least as much emphasis on duty as on rights. There can be no enjoyment of individ-ual rights, he insists, unless all citizens are willing to sacrifice and endure hardship for the sake of preserving these rights. The fruits of individualism are quite simply dependant upon collective self-sacrifice.[37] Roosevelt again uses Washington and Lincoln to illustrate that liberty must be served by duty. He writes that no American should ever forget Washington's devotion to the Union, his desire that the American people cherish their nationality, his courage in standing up to the tyranny of both the individual and the mob, his tireless preaching about the need for military preparedness, and his demand that Americans find a way to reconcile both liberty and order. Likewise, Roo-sevelt recalls, Lincoln refused to surrender vital rights to the defenders of slavery and was willing to maintain these rights by force of arms. Both Wash-ington and Lincoln understood that the kind of peace for which they prayed could be obtained only by armed strength supporting moral right.[38] Their ex-amples should forever guide the nation.

ROOSEVELT'S DEFENSE OF FREE SPEECH

Once the United States declared war against Germany, many Progressives saw an opportunity to remake the nation in true Progressive fashion.[39] The need to mobilize troops and to stimulate the production of food and war ma-terials required an expanded role for the federal government. The War Indus-tries Board, for example, set priorities for the production of essential war ma-terials, promoted the conservation of scarce resources, and fixed the prices of certain goods. Similarly, Herbert Hoover's Food Administration directed pro-duction, urged conservation, and set prices. Other agencies were involved: the Fuel Administration maintained the availability of coal; the United States Shipping Board was responsible for building, commandeering, and operating ships; the U.S. Railroad Administration nationalized the nation's railways; the

War Labor Policies Board set employment standards for federal agencies; the National War Labor Board was responsible for mediating disputes over wages and hours; and the War Finance Corporation distributed funds through the Federal Reserve banks. The national government also passed a revenue act that imposed a top tax rate of 63 percent on the largest individual incomes and levied an excess profits tax on businesses.[40]

To Progressives, the Great War also offered a unique opportunity for reformers to create a loyal and patriotic populace that was ready and willing to subordinate their individual needs and interests to the common good. Many Progressives, continuing to embrace the belief that individuals could be transformed by tinkering with environmental factors, proposed and implemented legislation that posed a serious threat to civil liberties, particularly freedom of speech. The Espionage Act, for example, forbade the publication or transmission of information that might help the enemy. These restrictions were interpreted broadly, even to the point of abuse, as local postmasters were directed to confiscate publications containing any material that might cause "insubordination, disloyalty, mutiny, or refusal of duty . . . or otherwise embarrass or hamper the Government in conducting the war." In the first month of the law, fifteen publications were banned from the mails, most of them Socialist. In addition, the Sedition Act of 1918 outlawed any "disloyal, profane, scurrilous, or abusive language" about the federal government, the Constitution, the armed forces, the uniform, or the flag. The attorney general, who was responsible for the enforcement of this legislation, created a special Bureau of Investigation (later the Federal Bureau of Investigation) to investigate subversive activities. Private citizens were encouraged to spy on their neighbors and report any suspicious behavior. Not surprisingly, many citizens zealously embraced their new responsibility, forcing those suspected of disloyalty to kiss the flag and buy war bonds. Others were tarred and feathered, painted yellow, or simply beaten. One German-American, Robert Prager, was lynched in Collinsville, Illinois.[41]

Other efforts to transform Americans followed. The Trading with the Enemy Act of 1917 gave the federal government the power to confiscate enemy property; regulate the conduct of enemy aliens; censor any communication by mail, cable, or radio; and regulate the nation's foreign language press. The Alien Act of 1918 permitted the deportation of alien anarchists who believed in the violent overthrow of the government. It was this particular act that led to the imprisonment of Eugene V. Debs, the former Socialist candidate for President, and Victor Berger, the German-born mayor of Milwaukee. Finally, President Wilson issued an executive order that established the Committee on Public Information (CPI). The CPI was responsible for publicizing information about the war effort. Its chairman, George Creel, published 75 million pamphlets, used motion pictures, and employed some 75,000 volunteer speakers, the so-called "Four Minute Men," to defend the war, while denigrating anything and everything German. The Committee made a special effort to promote loyalty among German-Americans, establishing a Division of work with the Foreign-Born, which produced pamphlets and monitored foreign-language newspapers and magazines for any disloyal sentiment. But certain *nongovernmental* participants in this Americanization campaign were more coercive. The Daughters of the American Revolution, for instance, conducted campaigns to stop the teaching of German in schools; they burned German books; they protested the playing of German music; and they changed certain German words and names (e.g., hamburger became "liberty steak," and sauerkraut became "liberty cabbage").[42]

While supporting the general expansion of governmental authority during the war, Roosevelt had misgivings about some aspects of the government's effort to purge disloyalty. He agreed that all immigrants should drop their dual allegiances. Thus, German-Americans had to become either "outright Germans or outright Americans." They could not continue to be both, and those who referred to themselves as both were, according to him, hypocrites who pretended to be Americans in order to serve Germany and undermine the interests of America. "At this moment," TR declared, "the vital thing to remember about these half-hidden traitors is that to attack America's allies, while we are at death grips with a peculiarly ruthless and brutal foe, or to champion that foe as against our allies, or to apologize for that foe's infamous wrongdoing, or to clamor for an early and inconclusive peace, is to be false to the cause of liberty and to the United States. In this war, either a man is a good American, and therefore is against Germany, and in favor of the allies of America, or he is not an American at all, and should be sent back to Germany where he belongs."[43] At the same time, Roosevelt reminded his countrymen that single-minded Americanism meant more than the obligation of foreigners to become Americans. True Americanism also meant the duty of native-born Americans to respect those immigrants who decided to become Americans in both heart and mind. "If a man in good faith, in soul and in body, becomes an American, he stands on a full and entire equality with everybody else, and must be so treated, without any mental reservation, without any regard to his creed, or birthplace, or descent. . . . It is both weak and wicked to permit any of our citizens to hold a dual or divided allegiance; and it is just as mischievous, just as un-American, to discriminate against any good American, because of his birthplace, creed, or parentage."[44]

Roosevelt agreed that the government should not permit the publication of any newspaper or magazine published in the language of America's enemies, but he stressed that patriotism meant standing by the country and not necessarily the President or any other public official. Certainly, he declares in *The Great Adventure*, it is patriotic to support the President insofar as he serves the country efficiently and faithfully, but it is also patriotic to oppose the President if he fails to perform his duty.[45] Roosevelt acknowledges that sedition is not constitutionally protected; the government has a right to defend itself by punishing those who directly advise or counsel resistance to the laws of the land. But this should be differentiated from mere discussion of the wisdom or folly of governmental actions, or the honesty and competency of public officials. The latter, Roosevelt writes, falls clearly within the protection of the First Amendment, for the voters cannot be expected to perform their duty to remove incompetent public servants and to secure the repeal of unwise laws unless such questions can be discussed freely. During the Mexican War, he notes, Lincoln did not hesitate to denounce the conduct of President James K. Polk. Lincoln was able to distinguish between the President's cause and the country's cause.[46] Like Lincoln, Roosevelt maintains that his loyalty is to the United States. He charges that his opponents mistakenly believe that loyalty is automatically due to the President. "Stand by the President," they declare, forgetting to add the proviso: "so long as he serves the Republic."[47]

Roosevelt concludes by declaring that the Sedition Act is absolute treason. Under the terms of the act, Lincoln would have been imprisoned for what he repeatedly said of Presidents Polk, Pierce, and Buchanan. Under its terms, TR adds, President Wilson is free to speak against any citizen or governmental official, but the opposite is not allowed. From Roosevelt's standpoint, the Sedition Act is a proposal to make the American people subjects instead of citizens. In a self-governing country, it is imperative that the people be treated as citizens. Only a despotism or an autocracy regards and treats the people as subjects. This, he says, is the crucial difference between Germany and the United States, although the actions of the Wilson administration threaten to blur that difference. "Our loyalty," Roosevelt stresses, "is due entirely to the United States. It is due to the President only and exactly to the degree in which he efficiently serves the United States. It is our duty to support him when he serves the United States well. It is our duty to oppose him when he serves it badly. This is true about Mr. Wilson now and it has been true about all our Presidents in the past."[48] Roosevelt believes that the Sedition Act is unconstitutional, and he hopes to give the government the opportunity to test its constitutionality. Whenever the need arises, he declares, he will speak truthfully about the President, exactly as he has done in the past. When, in the past, Wilson spoke about being too proud to fight, Roosevelt criticized him. In doing so, he did not care whether the supporters of the President regarded the remarks as slurs. If the President wages the war efficiently and manages to secure an honorable peace, Roosevelt promises that he will support him happily. But, if he wages an inefficient war, TR will speak of him as he has done in the past. "I am an American and a free man," he asserts.[49]

Despite his support for the regulation of the foreign press and the deportation of subversive individuals, Roosevelt remained a prominent critic of an administration that posed a serious threat to free expression and therefore to the values that he held dear. It cannot be stressed enough that TR spent his entire public career resisting those who rejected individualism outright, believing that it was the responsibility of the national government to preserve and protect individual rights. He often stressed that Americans should never concern themselves more with rights than with duty, but as his reaction to the Sedition Act shows, Roosevelt saw political dissent as a combination of a right and a duty. His defense of those (including himself) who criticized governmental policy and decision-making during the war was part of his overall dedication to individual liberty and collective responsibility. As always, the Rough Rider was willing to support with real action a firm commitment to both individualism and collectivism—his American ideal.

LEADING BY EXAMPLE

Even before Wilson asked Congress for a declaration of war against Germany, the fifty-eight-year-old Roosevelt sought permission from the President to raise his own division of volunteers to fight for American values. "If they [Wilson and War Secretary Baker] will give me permission," he informed Hiram Johnson, "I can get into the trenches within six months with my division." Roosevelt even offered to stop criticizing the administration. "If President Wilson would give me a free hand, and send me to the front, I would support him as loyally as any man possibly could, behaving exactly as Thomas and Farragut behaved in the days of the Civil War," he vowed.[50] Of course, Wilson was not about to give his greatest political rival yet another opportunity to enhance his heroic reputation. Nevertheless, a little more than a week after Congress declared war, Roosevelt was sitting and talking with the President at the White House.

According to sources, the meeting began awkwardly. "The President doesn't like Theodore Roosevelt, and he was not one bit effusive in his greeting," wrote Thomas Brahany, an aide to Wilson. But Roosevelt was not deterred by the chilly reception. Despite his strong hatred of Wilson (not to mention his certainty that *he* should be the one leading the nation through such difficult and uncertain times, not Wilson), TR employed every ounce of his personal charm. "Mr. President," he stated, "what I have said and thought, and what others have said and thought, is all dust in a windy street, if we can now make your message good." The message to which Roosevelt referred was Wilson's call for a war that would make the world "safe for democracy." "Of course," Roosevelt continued, "it amounts to nothing, if we cannot make it good. But, if we can translate it into fact, then it will rank as a great state paper, with the great state papers of Washington and Lincoln." Before long, Wilson had "thawed out" and the two men were laughing. Roosevelt used this laughter as an opportunity to reiterate his proposal to raise a division. He explained that it was imperative for the United States to hit the enemy "hard" and "at once." Acknowledging the administration's belief that forces should be raised under the direction of the regular army's officer corps, Roosevelt explained that a division of motivated volunteers could be ready for combat long before a larger expeditionary force of regular recruits. Moreover, he continued, Wilson did not have to worry about the volunteers taking resources from the regular army. "I explained that all necessary expense could be provided out of private funds," TR later recounted. "I also explained to him that I would not take a man the draft might get." This argument seemed to appeal to Wilson. "The fact that I proposed to use material that otherwise would be unavailable seemed new to him. He seemed interested and he asked many questions." Indeed, Wilson was interested, but the interest was more in Roosevelt than in his proposal. "Well," asked Wilson's secretary, "and how did the Colonel impress you?" "I was, as formerly, charmed by his personality," Wilson replied. "There is a sweetness about him that is very compelling. You can't resist that man. I can easily understand why his followers are so fond of him." Sensing Wilson's favorable impression, Roosevelt was confident in his presentation. But Wilson again refused TR's request, a decision that impressed Roosevelt as additional proof of Wilson's ineptitude.[51]

Although he was denied one last opportunity to show, through his actions on the battlefield, the real meaning of courage, hardiness, camaraderie, and sacrifice, Roosevelt could hope that the American people were looking to his wilderness writings for guidance about the essentials of good character. Books like *Hunting Trips*, *Ranch Life*, and *The Wilderness Hunter*, as well as the more recently published *African Game Trails*, were intended to instruct readers in the qualities that will make them better citizens, capable of supporting themselves and the common good. Like the earlier stories of game hunting and wilderness life, *African Game Trails* also sold widely and captured the popular imagination. Over a million copies of this later adventure tale were sold, and it was even made into a movie, "Hunting Big Game in Africa," which many viewers accepted as real. An animated cartoon of terrified animals hiding from the Rough Rider was also based on his African safari. Roosevelt was not the least bothered by the publicity, although he never stopped thinking about how the success or failure of his wilderness adventures would be interpreted by the American people, especially young men, many of whom dressed in khaki, bought "Roosevelt tents" from Abercrombie and Fitch, and dreamed of adventure in distant lands.[52]

Success in the wild, as in civilization, requires the right kind of character, Roosevelt argues in *African Game Trails*. "No new country is a place for weaklings; but the right kind of man, the settler who makes a success in similar parts of our own West, can do well in East Africa. . . . It means hard work, of course; but success generally does imply hard work."[53] Roosevelt notes that a number of ranchers can be found working hard and doing well as a result. Equally important to TR, though, is the fact that these settlers exhibit the qualities of thoughtfulness and courtesy.[54] Because they have endured similar difficulties and hardships, they have grown into what Roosevelt refers to as "a companionship of mutual respect, regard, and consideration such as that which, for our inestimable good fortune, now knits closely together in our own land the men who wore the blue and the men who wore the gray and their descendants."[55]

When tracking the dangerous game of Africa, Roosevelt continues, a hunter always faces a certain risk to life and limb; however, a good hunter minimizes such risk by coolness, caution, sound judgment, and skill. He is resourceful and self-reliant, defined by his hard work, indifference to fatigue and hardship, willingness to take risks, and experience with every conceivable emergency.[56] Roosevelt also observes that the best hunters do not view hunting as a business. Nor does hunting in any way interfere with the serious occupations and responsibilities of their lives, whether public or private. At the same time, Roosevelt stresses that these men treat hunting as more than a mere pastime. Simply put, they understand that it is a craft, "a pursuit of value in exercising and developing hardihood of body and the virile courage and resolution which necessarily lie at the base of every strong and manly character."[57]

Through various vignettes, Roosevelt also stresses that successful hunters often depend on teamwork. One day, TR recalls, he and his various companions were engaged in an all-day lion hunt. Roosevelt and his friend Harold Hill were paired together, which proved fortunate, for Hill's eyes were much better than Roosevelt's. "He saw everything first," Roosevelt admits, "and it usually took some time before he could make me see it." At first, nothing came their way. Suddenly, Hill said, "Lion" and pointed it out to Roosevelt. Roosevelt could not see it right away; finally, he thought he spotted the creature and fired. The shot missed, although it made the lion "start up," which allowed Roosevelt's second shot to hit him squarely behind the shoulders.[58] On another occasion, while elephant hunting in Kenya, Roosevelt writes that he was grateful to have more than the keen observation of a trusted companion. After following the trail of an elephant herd, Roosevelt came in sight of an elephant resting his tusks on the branches of a small tree. The elephant was a male and as it turned its head toward the hunting party, TR fired at a spot that he thought would lead to the brain. "I struck exactly where I aimed," Roosevelt explains, "but the head of an elephant is enormous and the brain small, and the bullet missed it." The massive beast stumbled forward, half falling, but he quickly recovered, as Roosevelt fired a second shot, again aiming for the brain. This time the bullet hit its mark, and as he lowered the rifle from his shoulder, the Rough Rider watched the massive beast crash to the ground. Suddenly, at that very same instant, before there was a moment's time in which to reload, another massive elephant came charging through the thick brushes. "He was so close," Roosevelt recalls, "that he could have touched me with his trunk. I leaped to one side and dodged behind a tree trunk, opening the rifle, throwing out the empty shells, and slipping in two cartridges. Meanwhile, [R.J.] Cunningham fired right and left, at the same time throwing himself into the bushes on the other side. Both his bullets went home, and the bull stopped short in his charge, wheeled, and immediately disappeared in the thick cover. We ran forward, but the forest had closed over his wake. We heard him trumpet shrilly, and then all sounds ceased."[59]

Still, this teamwork was nothing compared to that of the Nandi warriors, whom Roosevelt and his friends accompanied on a lion hunt. According to TR, these were truly admirable men. Not only were they all lean, muscular, fearless, and "lithe as panthers," but "they had lived on nothing but animal food, milk, blood, and flesh." As a result, Roosevelt declares, "they were fit for any fatigue or danger." This much was proved as the party came upon a magnificent but ferocious lion. The life of this lion, Roosevelt observes, "had been one unbroken career of rapine and violence; and now the manned master of the wilderness, the terror that stalked the night, the grim lord of slaughter, was to meet his doom at the hands of the only foes who dared molest him." One by one, the African warriors formed a ring around the beast. "Each, when he came near enough, crouched behind his shield, his spear in his right hand, his fierce, eager face peering over the shield rim. As man followed man, the lion rose to his feet. His mane bristled, his tail lashed, he held his head low, the upper lip now drooping over the jaws, now drawn up so as to show the gleam of the long fangs. He faced first one-way and then another, and never ceased to utter his murderous grunting roars. It was a wild sight; the ring of spearmen, intent, silent, bent on blood, and in the center the great man-killing beast, his thunderous wrath growing ever more dangerous." Once the ring was complete, the Nandi warriors rose and closed in on their foe. The lion looked quickly from side to side, saw where the line of men was thinnest, and charged at top speed. "The crowded moment began," Roosevelt writes, borrowing a phrase that he uses in *The Rough Riders* to describe his charge up San Juan Hill. "With shields held steady, and quivering spears poised, the men in front braced themselves for the rush and the shock; and from either hand the warriors sprang forward to take their foe in flank." The leader of the group threw a long spear at the lion. Another warrior threw his spear. Rearing, the lion struck the second man. At that instant, a flurry of spears darted toward the lion. The entire battle took no more than ten seconds; "but what a ten seconds!"[60]

Roosevelt stresses that, for natives like the Nandi warriors, life is hard and cruel. According to Roosevelt, the uncivilized man of today shows us what life was like for our ancestors. Indeed, he says, the primitive tribes of the past faced the constant threat of harsh elements and wild beasts. "It is only in nightmares that the average dweller in civilized countries now undergoes the hideous horror which was the regular and frequent portion of his ages-vanished forefathers. . . . But the dread is short-lived, and its horror vanishes with instantaneous rapidity."[61] Roosevelt recalls that he experienced his share of dreadful conditions in Africa. The Rough Rider admits that he and his party of guides, taxidermists, porters, and gun bearers never wanted for food or shelter, yet they faced real and constant danger from the wildlife. In his account, Roosevelt mentions how many of those he met were maimed or disabled for life by vicious lions, charging rhinos, and stampeding buffalo. In addition, members of his group were constantly meeting accidents or falling ill.[62]

Some of Roosevelt's men complained of minor injuries and other "trifles," but most never complained at all. One man, Gosho, belonged to the latter category. One evening, Roosevelt noticed that Gosho was limping. Only after asking several questions was it learned that the previous night, while in his tent, Gosho had been bitten by a poisonous snake. His leg "looked angry and inflamed," but Gosho never even mentioned the incident until he was questioned by the others. Fortunately, after a few days, he was fine.[63] Roosevelt expresses pride in having known and traveled with Gosho. Indeed, Gosho is but one of the many fine men whom Roosevelt came to admire for their bravery, patience, hardihood, and loyalty. By telling stories about them, Roosevelt wants to inspire his fellow countrymen to practice such resolve, independence, and self-deprivation. Only thus does America have any hope of meeting the challenges of a new century.

NOTES

1. Theodore Roosevelt to Henry Cabot Lodge, September 9, 1913. Quoted in H. W. Brands, *T.R.: The Last Romantic* (New York: Basic Books, 1997), 735.

2. Theodore Roosevelt, "Speech at the National Conference of the Progressive Service," in *Social Justice and Popular Rule*, vol. 17 of *The Works of Theodore Roosevelt*, National Edition (New York: Charles Scribner's Sons, 1926), 380.

3. Roosevelt, "Speech at the National Conference," 385–86.

4. Roosevelt, "Speech at the National Conference," 380.

5. Roosevelt, "Speech at the National Conference," 386–87.

6. Theodore Roosevelt, "The Progressive Party," in *Social Justice and Popular Rule*, vol. 17 of *The Works of Theodore Roosevelt*, National Edition (New York: Charles Scribner's Sons, 1926), 392.

7. Roosevelt, "The Progressive Party," 393–94.

8. Roosevelt, "The Progressive Party," 399–400.

9. Roosevelt, "The Progressive Party," 400–401.

10. Roosevelt, "The Progressive Party," 403–4.

11. H. W. Brands, *Woodrow Wilson* (New York: Henry Holt and Company, 2003), 31–39; Kendrick A. Clements, *The Presidency of Woodrow Wilson* (Lawrence: University Press of Kansas, 1992), 49–51, 40–44, 81; Arthur S. Link, *Wilson: Confusions and Crises, 1915–1916* (Princeton: Princeton University Press, 1964), 321–27, 356–62.

12. Roosevelt, "The Progressive Party," 397.

13. Roosevelt, "The Progressive Party," 398.

14. Roosevelt, "The Progressive Party," 398–99.

15. For further discussion of Wilson's change of mind, see Clements, *The Presidency of Woodrow Wilson*, 81; Melvyn Urofsky, *Big Steel and the Wilson Administration: A Study in Business–Government Relations* (Columbus: Ohio State University Press, 1969) xii; Walter Dean Burnham, "The System of 1896: An Analysis," in *The Evolution of American Electoral Systems*, ed. Paul Kleppner (Westport, Conn.: Greenwood Publishing, 1981), 148.

16. Michael P. Riccards, *The Ferocious Engine of Democracy: From Teddy Roosevelt through George W. Bush* (New York: Cooper Square Press, 2003), 52–53; Clements, *The Presidency of Woodrow Wilson*, 115–17; Brands, *Woodrow Wilson*, 51–53; Arthur S. Link, *Wilson: The Struggle for Neutrality, 1914–1915* (Princeton: Princeton University Press, 1960), 5–6.

17. Theodore Roosevelt, *America and the World War*, vol. 18 of *The Works of Theodore Roosevelt*, National Edition (New York: Charles Scribner's Sons, 1926), 9.

18. Roosevelt, *America and the World War*, 8.

19. Roosevelt, *America and the World War*, 18.

20. Roosevelt, *America and the World War*, 19.

21. Roosevelt, *America and the World War*, 10.

22. Roosevelt, *America and the World War*, 12.

23. Roosevelt, *America and the World War*, 19. Roosevelt is referring not only to the Armenian massacres of the 1890s, in which some two hundred thousand Armenians were killed by order of Sultan Abdul Hamid II, but also to the Armenian Genocide of 1915 at the hands of the Ottoman Turks. For TR, the Armenian massacres of 1915 were "the greatest crime" of World War I. "All of the terrible iniquities of the past year and a half, including the crowning iniquity of the wholesale slaughter of

the Armenians," he writes in *Fear God and Take Your Own Part*, "can be traced directly to the initial wrong committed on Belgium by her invasion and subjugation; and the criminal responsibility of Germany must be shared by the neutral powers, headed by the United States, for their failure to protest when this initial wrong was committed." In other words, if the U.S. government had resisted Germany's invasion of Belgium, the Turk government, an ally of Germany, might have been discouraged from implementing genocide behind the cover of war. Later, after America declared war on Germany, Roosevelt frequently criticized Wilson's failure to ask Congress for a declaration of war against Turkey: "The perpetuation of Turkish rule is the perpetuation of infamy. . . . I feel that we are guilty of a peculiarly odious form of hypocrisy when we profess friendship for Armenia and the downtrodden races of Turkey, but don't go to war with Turkey. To allow the Turks to massacre the [Armenians] and then solicit permission to help the survivors, and then to allege the fact that we are helping the survivors as a reason why we should not follow the only policy that will permanently put a stop to such massacres is both foolish and odious. . . . The Armenian massacre was the greatest crime of the war, and failure to act against Turkey is to condone it; because the failure to deal radically with the Turkish horror means that all talk of guaranteeing the future peace of the world is mischievous nonsense; and because when we now refuse to war with Turkey we show that our announcement that we meant 'to make the world safe for democracy' was insincere claptrap." Note: The Armistice came, and the United States had remained neutral toward Turkey. See Theodore Roosevelt, *Fear God and Take Your Own Part*, vol. 18 of *The Works of Theodore Roosevelt*, National Edition (New York: Charles Scribner's Sons, 1926), 384; Theodore Roosevelt to Cleveland Dodge, May 11, 1918, *The Days of Armageddon: 1914–1919*, vol. 8 of *The Letters of Theodore Roosevelt*, ed. Elting Morison (Cambridge: Harvard University Press, 1954), 1316–18; Peter Balakian, *The Burning Tigris: The Armenian Genocide and America's Response* (New York: HarperCollins, 2003), 293–94, 307–8.

24. Roosevelt, *America and the World War*, 20.

25. Roosevelt, *America and the World War*, 25–26.

26. Roosevelt, *America and the World War*, 92.

27. Roosevelt, *America and the World War*, 94.

28. Roosevelt, *America and the World War*, 140.

29. Roosevelt, *Fear God*, 225.

30. Theodore Roosevelt, *The Foes of Our Own Household*, vol. 19 of *The Works of Theodore Roosevelt*, National Edition (New York: Charles Scribner's Sons, 1926), 54–55.

31. Roosevelt, *Foes of Our Own Household*, 58–59.

32. Roosevelt, *Foes of Our Own Household*, 74.

33. Roosevelt, *Foes of Our Own Household*, 75–76.

34. Roosevelt, *Foes of Our Own Household*, 97.

35. Roosevelt, *Foes of Our Own Household*, 100.

36. Roosevelt, *Foes of Our Own Household*, 104–5.

37. Roosevelt, *Fear God*, 395.

38. Roosevelt, *Foes of Our Own Household*, 49–50, 52–53.

39. Michael McGerr, *A Fierce Discontent: The Rise and Fall of the Progressive Movement in America (1870–1920)* (New York: Free Press, 2003), 281.

40. McGerr, *Fierce Discontent*, 285–87.

41. McGerr, *Fierce Discontent*, 288–90; Jerome M. Mileur and Ronald Story, "America's Wartime Presidents: Politics, National Security, and Civil Liberties," in *The Politics of Terror: The U.S. Response to 9/11*, ed. William Crotty (Boston: Northeastern University Press, 2004), 102–3.

42. McGerr, *Fierce Discontent*, 289–92; Mileur and Story, "America's Wartime Presidents," 103–4.

43. Roosevelt, *Foes of Our Own Household*, 31.

44. Roosevelt, *Foes of Our Own Household*, 34.

45. Theodore Roosevelt, *The Great Adventure*, vol. 19 of *The Works of Theodore Roosevelt*, National Edition (New York: Charles Scribner's Sons, 1926), 289.

46. Roosevelt, *The Great Adventure*, 290–92.

47. Roosevelt, *The Great Adventure*, 293.

48. Roosevelt, *The Great Adventure*, 296–97.

49. Roosevelt, *The Great Adventure*, 298–99.

50. Theodore Roosevelt to Hiram Johnson, February 17, 1917. Quoted in Brands, *The Last Romantic*, 777.

51. Brands, *The Last Romantic*, 781–82, 784. It should be noted that Roosevelt's correspondences with Secretary of War Baker are included as an appendix to *The Foes of Our Own Household*. Brands suggests that, by providing extensive documentation of his desire to return to the battlefield, Roosevelt was perhaps guarding his legacy against those who, in the absence of proof, would deny the story as an exaggeration. Regardless, it seems likely that these letters to Baker, which present Roosevelt's arguments about the need to serve the national interest, are intended to persuade and inspire readers to embrace the Rough Rider's outlook.

52. Kathleen Dalton, *Theodore Roosevelt: A Strenuous Life* (New York: Vintage Books, 2002), 353–54.

53. Theodore Roosevelt, *African Game Trails*, vol. 4 of *The Works of Theodore Roosevelt*, National Edition (New York: Charles Scribner's Sons, 1926), 28.

54. Roosevelt, *African Game Trails*, 32.

55. Roosevelt, *African Game Trails*, 34.

56. Roosevelt, *African Game Trails*, 50.

57. Roosevelt, *African Game Trails*, 273.

58. Roosevelt, *African Game Trails*, 65–67.

59. Roosevelt, *African Game Trails*, 210–11.

60. Roosevelt, *African Game Trails*, 295–97.

61. Roosevelt, *African Game Trails*, 168–69.

62. Roosevelt, *African Game Trails*, 50–51, 55–59, 205.

63. Roosevelt, *African Game Trails*, 275–76.

Conclusion

As a result of Charles Darwin's profound influence on their generation, TR and his Progressive brethren viewed society as a living organism, the product of growth and adaptation over time. In addition, like many conservative adherents to Darwinian theory, Roosevelt could not avoid seeing the world in the context of struggle, but his argument that competition was necessary for progress was tempered by a conviction that it should not be too severe. Specifically, he maintained that the rivalry associated with natural selection worked against progress. Intense competition did more than undermine population growth: where the struggle for survival was a constant concern, individuals had no opportunity to perform the great deeds that advanced society. This belief led TR to conclude that the state had the right and the responsibility to make competition more even, but not to abolish it completely. By relying on its police powers, the state could assure that everyone competed on a relatively equal level. This would better guarantee that the economic marketplace remained a true test of individual merit. It was possible, Roosevelt concluded, for the state to extend its sphere of activity without diminishing individual liberty and the happiness of the people.

Roosevelt thought that evolutionary biology and the experience of history taught the need for a national government that was much more expansive than the one envisioned by the framers of the Constitution, but he never completely rejected the constitutional structure of the founders. In several early essays. Roosevelt even praised *The Federalist Papers*, recommending the book for its excellent blend of theory and practice. Moreover, while he supported the energetic use of executive power to address the problems of an industrial society, Roosevelt (at least during his presidential years) appeared to accept James Madison's system of separated but overlapping powers (checks and balances). Even when TR made direct appeals to the people in order to pressure Congress, he did so in a way that demonstrated a clear appreciation for the role of Congress in passing legislation. As Jeffrey Tulis notes in his groundbreaking study of the rhetorical presidency, Roosevelt's campaigns for reform legislation, such as the Hepburn Act, managed to strike a middle path between nineteenth century statecraft, which tended to reject addresses to the people in favor of communications between the branches of government, and the rhetorical presidency of the twentieth century—the popular or mass appeals that Presidents make when "going over the heads" of Congress to obtain support for their policy initiatives. Roosevelt did not preempt Congress. In fact, his speaking tour began and ended before Congress began its reconsideration of the Hepburn Act. Then, as Congress deliberated, he did not make public remarks on the question of railroad regulation, though he maintained private contact with key congressmen, leaked news items, and quietly encouraged others to speak on behalf of reform. Roosevelt also did not speak directly to the people on the eve of crucial votes in Congress, nor did he attack any individual congressmen during the debate. Finally, he never bargained with Congress in his public addresses, although he was not averse to the idea of compromise and frequently explained, after the fact, that his willingness to negotiate did not mean the abandonment of principle.[1]

Admittedly, though, Roosevelt had much less respect for the independent power of the courts to strike down popular legislation that attempted to regulate the use of private property. Viewing the courts as beholden to special interests that cared nothing for the public good and the right of the people to improve their chances of economic success, TR defended various direct democracy reforms like the public's right to override judicial decisions. What is more, he mistakenly invoked Abraham Lincoln to support his position that the people should be "masters of the courts as regards constitutional questions." It was Lincoln, Roosevelt explained, "who advocated and secured what was practically the recall of the *Dred Scott* decision, and who trusted the Constitution as the living force of righteousness." The Progressives were simply "carrying out the principles set forth by Lincoln in this his first Inaugural Address."[2] But Roosevelt overlooked Lincoln's staunch belief that the majority did not have the right to decide any and all constitutional questions. In Lincoln's view, the problem with the *Dred Scott* decision was that it involved a right (the right to hold slaves in territories) that was merely inferred by a particular interpretation of the Constitution (and one that was not substantiated by the historical record on which it was based). Moreover, it was only because the Constitution did not expressly answer the territorial question that the people had the right to do so. But Lincoln held out hope that the *Dred Scott* decision would eventually be overturned by the justices themselves.[3] In reality, it took a long and bloody civil war, as well as the passage of the Thirteenth and Fourteenth Amendments, to overturn *Dred Scott*. This understanding is altogether absent from Roosevelt's speeches and writings pertaining to the right of the people to exercise judicial review.

Similarly, Roosevelt incorrectly relied on Lincoln's example to justify his "stewardship theory" of presidential power. According to this theory, the President was the "steward of the people," meaning that he was "bound actively and affirmatively to do all that he could for the people," unless this action was forbidden by "specific restrictions and prohibitions appearing in the Constitution or imposed by Congress in its Constitutional powers." Roosevelt famously observed that there were two kinds of Presidents—strong "Lincoln Presidents," which Roosevelt claimed to represent, and weak "Buchanan Presidents," which Roosevelt saw his successor, William Howard Taft, as representing.[4] But, as Taft retorted, Lincoln's broad and discretionary actions, unlike TR's, proceeded from the Constitution. When suspending *habeas corpus*, for example, "Lincoln always pointed out the source of authority which in his opinion justified his acts, and there was always a strong ground for maintaining the view which he took. His claim of a right to suspend the writ of *habeas corpus* . . . was well founded."[5] In short, Lincoln avoided making undefined claims of responsibility for "the welfare of all the people." Rather, he was always careful to link his actions to the specific provisions of the Constitution.

In addition to Lincoln, TR drew on the writings of another hero—Alexander Hamilton—to defend his broad understanding of presidential power; however, the Rough Rider's praise of Hamilton was qualified. While both the Square Deal and New Nationalism relied on a Hamiltonian understanding of energetic national power, especially a strong presidency, Roosevelt was the first to admit that Hamilton supported a strong executive because he believed it would check the will of the people, not give fuller expression to it. In addition, as Jean Yarbrough explains, Roosevelt neither accepted Hamilton's thoroughgoing promotion of a commercial republic nor echoed the Federalist's unabashed admiration of eastern entrepreneurs. "Purely commercial ideals" were, in Roosevelt's view, "mean and sordid," producing weak, self-indulgent, and cowardly individuals who were "incapable of the thrill of generous emotion." Material prosperity was necessary for national happiness, but it was not sufficient. Moreover, TR accused wealthy easterners of being much more decadent and effeminate than the self-reliant yet compassionate westerners with whom he proudly lived and worked on the frontier. Not only could the West teach the eastern elite how to be manlier, but also it represented the proper balance between individualism and collectivism. Finally, it is worth noting that Roosevelt rejected the rather sober view of human nature that is expressed in *The Federalist Papers*. Unlike Thomas

Jefferson, who exposed government as the main source of human oppression, the Federalist defenders of the Constitution—Hamilton and Madison—asserted that the forces of oppression are rooted in human nature, and that government is necessary because men are not "angels." In stark contrast, Roosevelt told the people that they were not the problem; rather, "the special interests"—corrupt businessmen and their willing puppets in government—were to blame for defiling the soul of the nation. Again and again, Roosevelt levied this charge and often employed religious language in doing so.[6]

To be sure, Roosevelt's conviction that the state could act as a positive force on behalf of individual interest and the public good had its roots in the Social Gospel movement. In the beginning, Social Gospel Christians did not place much emphasis on solving social problems through state action. Rather, they stressed the need for social regeneration through individual self-sacrifice and the voluntary adoption of Christian ethics. Over time, however, they came to realize that it was not enough to hope that individuals would voluntarily embrace the Golden Rule. In achieving desired social and economic reform, state action might be needed as a vital supplement to New Testament teaching. The Social Gospel fit with TR's particular brand of "muscular Christianity," which focused on Jesus as a vigorous and energetic crusader for righteousness. Jesus, Roosevelt reminded his countrymen, had been willing to disregard peace, order, and tradition for the sake of justice, and if America wanted to get right with Jesus, it had to demonstrate the same willingness to fight and sacrifice for the cause of righteousness. "Peace is not the end. Righteousness is the end. When the Savior saw the money-changers in the Temple he broke the peace by driving them out. At that moment peace could have been obtained readily enough by the simple process of keeping quiet in the presence of wrong. But instead of preserving peace at the expense of righteousness, the Savior armed himself with a scourge of cords and drove the money-changers from the Temple."[7] For many Progressives like Roosevelt, the achievement of economic and social justice was a sign of true Christian faith.

Because of his Social Gospel views, Roosevelt insisted that the complexities of life did not excuse wrongdoing, and he coupled this moral certainty with a Pragmatist's faith in experimentation. Indeed, William James' notion that ideas are tools that must be applied to real problems and judged by their results conformed to America's tradition of experimentation, and James' belief in the power of the autonomous and creative individual was reminiscent of the Declaration of Independence. Of course, the major difference between the Declaration and Pragmatic thought is that the former refers to universal laws—"the Laws of Nature and of Nature's God"—that the founders believed were discoverable through the use of human reason. As opposed to being an expedient justification for dissolving the political bands that had connected the American colonists with Great Britain, the Declaration is an expression of "self-evident" truths that are applicable to all people, in all places, at all times. The proposition that "all men are created equal" is the first self-evident truth proclaimed in the Declaration; it is the foundation upon which all subsequent truths are built. According to the Declaration, the equality of all humans means that all people have a right to liberty, because no person deserves to be the natural slave or the natural master of another. This is a political fact concerning human beings, and it stems from the natural fact that we are a certain kind of being with a certain kind of nature. While TR celebrated the Declaration of Independence as a great document, and while he understood that its philosophy was based on a belief that individual rights are grounded in an objective, natural order, he never insisted on this principle.

Yet Roosevelt's greatest hero believed that devotion to human equality and natural rights was the true measure of a government's goodness and legitimacy. Drawing on a verse from the Bible's Book of Proverbs—"A word fitly spoken is like apples of gold in pictures of silver"—Lincoln praised the Declaration's principles as the essence of the American regime: "The assertion [that all men are created equal] at the time was the word 'fitly spoken' which has proven an 'apple of gold' to us. The Union, and the Constitution, are the pictures of silver, subsequently framed around it. The picture was made, not to conceal, or destroy the apple, but to adorn and preserve it."[8] Lincoln took seriously the doctrines of the Declaration and believed that the document's most important function was to serve as "a stumbling block to those who in after times might seek to turn a free people back into the hateful paths of despotism."[9] For their part, scholars like Garry Wills charge that Lincoln romanticized the original purpose of the Declaration, but Lincoln's interpretation of the Declaration echoes Jefferson's own words.[10] In a letter to Roger C. Weightman, the last letter he is known to have written, Jefferson declared, "May it [the Declaration] be to the world, what I believe it will be, (to some parts sooner, to others later, finally to all) the signal of arousing men to burst the chains under which monkish ignorance and superstition had persuaded them to bind themselves, and to assume the blessings and security of self-government."[11]

Despite Roosevelt's rejection of Natural Law as the product of a universe of fixed things, both he and Lincoln sympathized with the less privileged and were willing to use the powers of government to assure that every individual had a chance. As James G. Randall writes, it is difficult to say "how far Lincoln 'would have' gone in extending the functions of government, and in using the government to promote the welfare of the country . . . but there is ample evidence that his philosophy of man and the state did not begin and end with laissez faire."[12] For one, Lincoln's Whig philosophy led him to support "internal improvements," or the use of federal funds for all kinds of public works. He also supported public education, the creation of an agriculture department, and the Homestead Act, which was intended to expand economic opportunities for the urban poor by enabling western settlers to claim up to 160 acres of federal land if they agreed to settle that land for five years.[13] Lincoln's rejection of a purely negative state was expressed in various public and private remarks as well. Consider the following fragment: "Government is a combination of the people of a country to effect certain objects by joint effort. . . . The legitimate object of government is 'to do for the people what needs to be done, but which they can not, by individual effort, do at all, or do so well, for themselves.'" In other writings, Lincoln declared that he wanted every man to have a fair chance in the race of life. "While we do not propose any war upon capital, we do wish to allow the humblest man an equal chance . . . with everybody else." It was to achieve this end that Lincoln defended the cause of the Union. Describing the Civil War as "a people's contest," he proclaimed, "On the side of the Union it is a struggle for maintaining in the world that form and substance of government whose leading object is to elevate the condition of men—to lift artificial weights from all shoulders—to clear the paths of laudable pursuit for all—to afford all, an unfettered start, and a fair chance, in the race of life."[14]

These basic ideas were shared by Roosevelt. Believing that Americans living in the early twentieth century faced the same challenge to eliminate artificial privilege and thereby equalize opportunity for all, the Rough Rider embraced the Great Emancipator's concept of positive liberty, as well as his willingness to use the national government to ensure that all Americans had a chance to realize their individual potential. In the same vein, Roosevelt celebrated George Washington's opposition to the tyranny of both the majority and minority, as well as his devotion to American unity. According to Roosevelt, what made Washington and Lincoln so worthy of praise was their defense of individual freedom *and* their nationalist spirit, which was intended to unite the American people in the service of the common good. Roosevelt urged all Americans to exhibit the same dedication to both rights and duty.

It is no hermeneutical stretch to say that Roosevelt's equal emphasis on independence and communal concern weaves through the lion's share of his speeches, essays, and books. TR's review of Benjamin Kidd (1895); his autobiography (1913); the many articles and addresses contained in books like *The Strenuous Life* (1900); the various presidential speeches that elucidate the principles of the Square Deal (1901–1909); the New Nationalism (1910–1912), which echoes the Square Deal; his criticisms of Woodrow Wilson's domestic policies (1913–1916); and his books about American preparedness and foreign policy—*America and the World War* (1915), *Fear God and Take*

Your Own Part (1916), *The Foes of Our Own Household* (1917), and *The Great Adventure* (1918)—all speak to individualism and collectivism as inseparable values, as two sides of the same coin. Even Roosevelt's seemingly nonpolitical writings on nature, hunting, ranching, military life, and history are part and parcel of this view, for they were intended to teach the American people about the importance of balancing self-reliance and discipline with such positive collectivistic values as an appreciation for mutual support and concern for the good of the community. In these writings, TR expresses his belief that, while government can level the economic playing field and help individuals realize their potential, regulation alone will not cure all of society's ills—a belief that also is apparent in Roosevelt's approach to such social/moral issues as divorce, temperance, and civil rights.

For Roosevelt, the concepts of personal autonomy and civic concern were not mutually exclusive. TR emphasized repeatedly that individualism and collectivism were two halves of the same whole. Unless it was backed by such individualistic values as hard work, personal responsibility, and self-restraint, the spirit of compassion could easily excuse idleness and irresponsibility. On the other hand, an excess of individualism, unrestricted by the lack of a feeling of brotherhood and a denial of obligation to the rest of the community, bred selfishness and permitted the exploitation of the weak. According to Roosevelt, it was not possible to devise legislation by which everyone would achieve success and have happiness. Individuals had a right to pursue happiness; they did not have a right to happiness itself. For Roosevelt, the only action a person could take was to secure, in part through government, an equal opportunity for each and every individual to show his "stuff." In Roosevelt's view, increased governmental action did not necessarily mean the weakening or the destruction of liberty. In an age of consolidated economic power and greater complexity, TR saw the marriage of collective action and individual ability as essential to success.

Roosevelt advocated and was responsible for a great expansion in the regulatory powers of the national government, but his devotion to American individualism prevented him from relying exclusively on governmental coercion to effect needed economic and social change. In contrast to many other Progressive reformers, TR understood that inspirational rhetoric and positive example could be a powerful means of compelling individuals to stay mindful of the public interest. This reliance on the power of noble words and moral leadership, coupled with certain institutional solutions like statutes and regulatory boards, was how TR sought to establish a middle path between a self-interested individualism and a moral zeal that abandoned individual freedom and rights for the sake of "the social good." TR thought this a timeless solution.

NOTES

1. See Jeffrey K. Tulis, *The Rhetorical Presidency* (Princeton: Princeton University Press, 1987), 95–116.

2. Theodore Roosevelt, "The Heirs of Abraham Lincoln," in *Social Justice and Popular Rule*, vol. 17 of *The Works of Theodore Roosevelt*, National Edition (New York: Charles Scribner's Sons, 1926), 369–70.

3. See Abraham Lincoln, "Speech at Peoria," in *The Collected Works of Abraham Lincoln*, vol. 2, ed. Roy P. Basler (New Brunswick: Rutgers University Press, 1953–55), 265–66; Abraham Lincoln, "Seventh Debate at Alton," in *The Collected Works of Abraham Lincoln*, vol. 3, ed. Roy P. Basler (New Brunswick: Rutgers University Press, 1953–55), 317–18; Abraham Lincoln, "First Inaugural Address," in *The Collected Works of Abraham Lincoln*, vol. 4, ed. Roy P. Basler (New Brunswick: Rutgers University Press, 1953–55), 268–69, 271.

4. Theodore Roosevelt, *Autobiography*, vol. 20 of *The Works of Theodore Roosevelt*, National Edition (New York: Charles Scribner's Sons, 1926), 352–55.

5. William Howard Taft, *Our Chief Magistrate and His Powers* (New York: Columbia University Press, 1925), 147, 144–45.

6. Jean M. Yarbrough, "Theodore Roosevelt and the Stewardship of the American Presidency," in *History of American Political Thought* (Lanham, MD: Lexington Books, 2003), 537–38, 548; Theodore Roosevelt, "American Ideals," in *American Ideals*, vol. 13 of *The Works of Theodore Roosevelt*, National Edition (New York: Charles Scribner's Sons, 1926), 3–12; Theodore Roosevelt, *Gouverneur Morris*, vol. 7 of *The Works of Theodore Roosevelt*, National Edition (New York: Charles Scribner's Sons, 1926); Theodore Roosevelt, *The Wilderness Hunter*, vol. 2 of *The Works of Theodore Roosevelt*, National Edition (New York: Charles Scribner's Sons, 1926); Theodore Roosevelt, *Hunting Trips of a Ranchman*, vol. 1 of *The Works of Theodore Roosevelt*, National Edition (New York: Charles Scribner's Sons, 1926); Theodore Roosevelt, *Ranch Life and the Hunting Trail*, vol. 1 of *The Works of Theodore Roosevelt*, National Edition (New York: Charles Scribner's Sons, 1926).

7. Theodore Roosevelt, *Fear God and Take Your Own Part*, vol. 18 of *The Works of Theodore Roosevelt*, National Edition (New York: Charles Scribner's Sons, 1926), 206.

8. Abraham Lincoln, "Fragment on the Constitution and the Union," in *The Collected Works of Abraham Lincoln*, vol. 4, ed. Roy P. Basler (New Brunswick: Rutgers University Press, 1953–55), 169.

9. Abraham Lincoln, "Speech at Springfield," in *The Collected Works of Abraham Lincoln*, vol. 2, ed. Roy P. Basler (New Brunswick: Rutgers University Press, 1953–55), 405–6.

10. See Garry Wills, *Lincoln at Gettysburg: The Words That Remade America* (New York: Simon and Schuster, 1993).

11. Thomas Jefferson to Roger Weightman, June 24, 1826, in *The Writings of Thomas Jefferson*, ed. Merrill Peterson (New York: The Library of America, 1984), 1517.

12. James G. Randall, "Lincoln the Liberal Statesman," in *Lincoln's American Dream: Clashing Political Perspectives*, eds. Kenneth L. Deutsch and Joseph R. Fornieri (Dulles: Potomac Books, 2005), 41.

13. Randall, "Lincoln the Liberal Statesman," 41–42.

14. Abraham Lincoln, "Fragment on Government," in *The Collected Works of Abraham Lincoln*, vol. 2, ed. Roy P. Basler (New Brunswick: Rutgers University Press, 1953–55), 182–83; Abraham Lincoln, "Special Message to Congress," in *The Collected Works of Abraham Lincoln*, vol. 4, ed. Roy P. Basler (New Brunswick: Rutgers University Press, 1953–55), 321.

Bibliography

PRIMARY SOURCES

Churchill, Winston S. *Thoughts and Adventures*. London: Thornton Butterworth, 1932.

Croly, Herbert. *Progressive Democracy*. New York: The Macmillan Company, 1914.

———. *The Promise of American Life*. New York: The Macmillan Company, 1909.

Dewey, John. "Evolution and Ethics." *Monist* 8 (1898).

———. *Human Nature and Conduct*. New York: Henry Holt and Company, 1922.

———. *Psychology*. New York: Henry Holt and Company, 1887.

———. *Reconstruction in Philosophy*. New York: Henry Holt and Company, 1920.

James, William. *Collected Essays and Reviews*. New York: Longmans, Greens and Company, 1920.

———. *Pragmatism and Other Writings*. New York: Penguin Books, 2000.

———. *The Principles of Psychology*. 2 vols. New York: Henry Holt and Company, 1890.

———. *The Will to Believe*. New York: Longmans, Green and Company, 1897.

———. *The Works of William James*. Edited by Frederick H. Burkhardt. 3 vols. Cambridge: Harvard University Press, 1975–88.

Jefferson, Thomas. *Notes on the State of Virginia*. Edited by William Peden. Chapel Hill: University of North Carolina Press for the Institute of Early American History and Culture, 1954.

Kidd, Benjamin. *Social Evolution*. New York: Macmillan and Company, 1894.

Lincoln, Abraham. *The Collected Works of Abraham Lincoln*. Edited by Roy P. Basler. 9 vols. New Brunswick: Rutgers University Press, 1953–55.

———. *The Language of Liberty: The Political Writings and Speeches of Abraham Lincoln*. Edited by Joseph R. Fornieri. Washington, D.C.: Regnery Publishing, 2003.

Madison, James, Alexander Hamilton, and John Jay. *The Federalist Papers*. New York: The New American Library, Inc., 1961.

Richardson, James D., ed. *A Compilation of the Messages and Papers of the Presidents.* 20 vols. Washington: Bureau of National Literature and Art, 1917.

Roosevelt, Theodore. *A Book-Lover's Holiday in the Open.* 1916. Vol. 3 of *The Works of Theodore Roosevelt*, National Edition. New York: Charles Scribner's Sons, 1926.

———. *African Game Trails.* 1910. Vol. 4 of *The Works of Theodore Roosevelt*, National Edition. New York: Charles Scribner's Sons, 1926.

———. *America and the World War.* 1915. Vol. 18 of *The Works of Theodore Roosevelt*, National Edition. New York: Charles Scribner's Sons, 1926.

———. *American Ideals.* 1897. Vol. 13 of *The Works of Theodore Roosevelt*, National Edition. New York: Charles Scribner's Sons, 1926.

———. *American Problems.* 1901–1909. Vol. 16 of *The Works of Theodore Roosevelt*, National Edition. New York: Charles Scribner's Sons, 1926.

———. *Autobiography.* 1913. Vol. 20 of *The Works of Theodore Roosevelt*, National Edition. New York: Charles Scribner's Sons, 1926.

———. *Campaigns and Controversies.* 1882–1900. Vol. 14 of *The Works of Theodore Roosevelt*, National Edition. New York: Charles Scribner's Sons, 1926.

———. *Fear God and Take Your Own Part.* 1916. Vol. 18 of *The Works of Theodore Roosevelt*, National Edition. New York: Charles Scribner's Sons, 1926.

———. *Gouverneur Morris.* 1888. Vol. 7 of *The Works of Theodore Roosevelt*, National Edition. New York: Charles Scribner's Sons, 1926.

———. *Hero Tales from American History.* 1895. Vol. 10 of *The Works of Theodore Roosevelt*, National Edition. New York: Charles Scribner's Sons, 1926.

———. *Hunting Trips of a Ranchman.* 1885. Vol. 1 of *The Works of Theodore Roosevelt*, National Edition. New York: Charles Scribner's Sons, 1926.

———. *Letters from Theodore Roosevelt to Anna Roosevelt Cowles, 1870–1918.* Edited by Anna Roosevelt Cowles. New York: Charles Scribner's Sons, 1924.

———. *Letters to Kermit from Theodore Roosevelt, 1902–1908.* Edited by Will Irwin. New York: Charles Scribner's Sons, 1946.

———. *Literary Essays.* 1890–1919. Vol. 12 of *The Works of Theodore Roosevelt*, National Edition. New York: Charles Scribner's Sons, 1926.

———. *Men of Action.* 1891–1917. Vol. 11 of *The Works of Theodore Roosevelt*, National Edition. New York: Charles Scribner's Sons, 1926.

———. *New York.* 1891. Vol. 10 of *The Works of Theodore Roosevelt*, National Edition. New York: Charles Scribner's Sons, 1926.

———. *Oliver Cromwell.* 1900. Vol. 10 of *The Works of Theodore Roosevelt*, National Edition. New York: Charles Scribner's Sons, 1926.

———. *Outdoor Pastimes of an American Hunter.* 1905. Vols. 2 & 3 of *The Works of Theodore Roosevelt*, National Edition. New York: Charles Scribner's Sons, 1926.

———. *Presidential Addresses and State Papers*, Homeward Bound Edition. 8 vols. New York: The Review of Reviews Company, 1910.

———. *Ranch Life and the Hunting Trail.* 1888. Vol. 1 of *The Works of Theodore Roosevelt*, National Edition. New York: Charles Scribner's Sons, 1926.

———. *Roosevelt in the Kansas City Star: War-Time Editorials by Theodore Roosevelt.* Edited by Ralph Stout. Boston: Houghton Mifflin Company, 1921.

——. *Selections of the Correspondence of Theodore Roosevelt and Henry Cabot Lodge, 1884–1918.* Edited by Henry Cabot Lodge. 2 vols. New York: Charles Scribner's Sons, 1925.

——. *Social Justice and Popular Rule.* 1910–1912. Vol. 17 of *The Works of Theodore Roosevelt*, National Edition. New York: Charles Scribner's Sons, 1926.

——. *State Papers as Governor and President.* 1899–1909. Vol. 15 of *The Works of Theodore Roosevelt*, National Edition. New York: Charles Scribner's Sons, 1926.

——. *The Foes of Our Own Household.* 1917. Vol. 19 of *The Works of Theodore Roosevelt*, National Edition. New York: Charles Scribner's Sons, 1926.

——. *The Great Adventure.* 1918. Vol. 19 of *The Works of Theodore Roosevelt*, National Edition. New York: Charles Scribner's Sons, 1926.

——. *The Letters of Theodore Roosevelt.* Edited by Elting Morison. 8 vols. Cambridge: Harvard University Press, 1951–54.

——. *The Naval War of 1812.* 1882. Vol. 6 of *The Works of Theodore Roosevelt*, National Edition. New York: Charles Scribner's Sons, 1926.

——. *The New Nationalism.* Gloucester: Peter Smith, 1971.

——. *The Rough Riders.* 1899. Vol. 11 of *The Works of Theodore Roosevelt*, National Edition. New York: Charles Scribner's Sons, 1926.

——. *The Strenuous Life.* 1900. Vol. 13 of *The Works of Theodore Roosevelt*, National Edition. New York: Charles Scribner's Sons, 1926.

——. *The Wilderness Hunter.* 1893. Vol. 2 of *The Works of Theodore Roosevelt*, National Edition. New York: Charles Scribner's Sons, 1926.

——. *The Winning of the West.* 1889–1896. Vols. 8 & 9 of *The Works of Theodore Roosevelt*, National Edition. New York: Charles Scribner's Sons, 1926.

——. *Theodore Roosevelt and His Time Shown in His Own Letters.* Edited by Joseph Bucklin Bishop. 2 vols. New York: Charles Scribner's Sons, 1920.

——. *Theodore Roosevelt's Diaries of Boyhood and Youth.* New York: Charles Scribner's Sons, 1928.

——. *Theodore Roosevelt's Letters to His Children.* Edited by Joseph Bucklin Bishop. New York: Charles Scribner's Sons, 1919.

——. *Thomas Hart Benton.* 1887. Vol. 7 of *The Works of Theodore Roosevelt*, National Edition. New York: Charles Scribner's Sons, 1926.

——. *Through the Brazilian Wilderness.* 1913. Vol. 5 of *The Works of Theodore Roosevelt*, National Edition. New York: Charles Scribner's Sons, 1926.

Sinclair, Upton. *The Jungle.* Edited by James R. Barrett. Urbana: University of Illinois Press, 1988.

Spencer, Herbert. *Principles of Ethics.* 2 vols. New York: D. Appleton and Company, 1895–98.

——. *Social Statics.* New York: D. Appleton and Company, 1864.

——. *The Man versus the State.* New York: D. Appleton and Company, 1885.

——. *The Principles of Sociology.* 3 vols. New York: D. Appleton and Company, 1876–97.

——. *The Study of Sociology.* New York: D. Appleton and Company, 1896.

Sumner, William Graham. *Essays of William Graham Sumner.* Edited by Albert G. Keller and Maurice R. Davie. 2 vols. New Haven: Yale University Press, 1934.

——. *What Social Classes Owe to Each Other*. New York: Harper and Brothers, 1883.

Taft, William Howard. *The Collected Works of William Howard Taft*. Edited by David H. Burton. 8 vols. Athens: Ohio University Press, 2001–03.

Turner, Frederick Jackson. *The Frontier in American History*. New York: Henry Holt and Company, 1953.

Ward, Lester. *Dynamic Sociology*. New York: D. Appleton and Company, 1883.

——. *Glimpses of the Cosmos*. 6 vols. New York: G. P. Putnam's Sons, 1913–18.

——. *Outlines of Sociology*. New York: The Macmillan Company, 1898.

——. *The Psychic Factors of Civilization*. Boston: Ginn and Company, 1893.

Washington, George. *Writings of George Washington*. Edited by John C. Fitzpatrick. 39 vols. Washington: Government Printing Office, 1931–44.

Wilson, Woodrow. *A Crossroads of Freedom: The 1912 Campaign Speeches of Woodrow Wilson*. Edited by John Wells Davidson. New Haven: Yale University Press, 1956.

——. *A History of the American People*. 5 vols. New York: Harper, 1902.

——. *Congressional Government: A Study in American Politics*. Boston: Houghton Mifflin, 1885.

——. *Constitutional Government in the United States*. New York: Columbia University Press, 1908.

——. *State Papers and Addresses*. New York: The Review of Reviews Company, 1918.

——. *The New Freedom*. Englewood Cliffs: Prentice-Hall, 1961.

——. *The State*. Boston: D. C. Heath and Company, 1918.

NEWSPAPERS AND OTHER PERIODICALS

Atlanta Constitution
Literary Digest
Memphis Scimitar
New York Times
New York Tribune
Richmond Dispatch
Richmond News
St. Louis Mirror
Washington Post

SECONDARY SOURCES

Balakian, Peter. *The Burning Tigris: The Armenian Genocide and America's Response*. New York: HarperCollins, 2003.

Berns, Walter. "Religion and the Founding Principle." In *The Moral Foundations of the American Republic*, edited by Robert H. Horwitz. Charlottesville: University Press of Virginia, 1998.

Blum, John Morton. *The Republican Roosevelt*. Cambridge: Harvard University Press, 1981.

Braeman, John et al., eds. *Change and Continuity in Twentieth Century America*. Columbus: Ohio State University Press, 1964.

———. *Albert Beveridge: American Nationalist*. Chicago: University of Chicago Press, 1971.

Brands, H. W. *T.R.: The Last Romantic*. New York: Basic Books, 1997.

———. *The Reckless Decade: America in the 1890s*. Chicago: University of Chicago Press, 2002.

———. *The Strange Death of American Liberalism*. New Haven: Yale University Press, 2001.

———. *Woodrow Wilson*. New York: Times Books, 2003.

Bringhurst, Bruce. *Antitrust and the Oil Monopoly: The Standard Oil Cases, 1890–1911*. Westport, CT: Greenwood Press, 1979.

Broderick, Francis L. *Progressivism at Risk: Electing a President in 1912*. Westport, Conn.: Greenwood, 1989.

Burnham, Walter Dean. "The System of 1896: An Analysis." In *The Evolution of American Electoral Systems*, edited by Paul Kleppner. Westport, Conn.: Greenwood, 1981.

Burns, James MacGregor and Susan Dunn. *The Three Roosevelts*. New York: Grove Press, 2001.

Butt, Archibald Willingham. *Taft and Roosevelt, 1900–1912*. 2 vols. New York: Harper and Brothers, 1958.

Cashman, Sean Davis. *America in the Age of the Titans: The Progressive Era and World War I*. New York: New York University Press, 1988.

Ceaser, James W. *Presidential Selection: Theory and Development*. Princeton: Princeton University Press, 1979.

Chace, James. *1912: Wilson, Roosevelt, Taft, and Debs—The Election That Changed the Country*. New York: Simon and Schuster, 2004.

Chamberlain, John. *Farewell to Reform: The Rise, Life and Decay of the Progressive Mind in America*. Chicago: Quadrangle Books, 1965.

Chernow, Ron. *Titan: The Life of John D. Rockefeller, Sr.* New York: Random House, 1998.

Chessman, G. Wallace. *Theodore Roosevelt and the Politics of Power*. Prospect Heights: Waveland Press, 1994.

Clemens, Will M. *Theodore Roosevelt: The American*. New York: F. Tennyson Neely, 1899.

Clements, Kendrick A. *The Presidency of Woodrow Wilson*. Lawrence: University Press of Kansas, 1992.

———. *Woodrow Wilson: World Statesman*. Chicago: Ivan R. Dee, 1999.

Coletta, Paolo. *The Presidency of William Howard Taft*. Lawrence: University Press of Kansas, 1973.

Commager, Henry Steele. *The American Mind: An Interpretation of American Thought and Character Since the 1880s*. New Haven: Yale University Press, 1950.

Connor, Valerie Jean. *The National War Labor Board: Stability, Social Justice, and the Voluntary State in World War I*. Chapel Hill: University of North Carolina Press, 1983.

Cooper, John Milton. "If TR Had Gone Down with the *Titanic*." In *Theodore Roosevelt: Many-Sided American*, edited by Natalie A. Naylor, Douglas Brinkley, and John Allen Gable. Interlaken, N.Y.: Heart of Lakes Publishing, 1992.

——. "Progressivism and American Foreign Policy: A Reconsideration." *Mid-America* 51 (Oct. 1969): 260–77.

——. *The Warrior and the Priest: Woodrow Wilson and Theodore Roosevelt*. Cambridge: Belknap Press, 1997.

Crossan, John Dominic and Richard G. Watts. *Who is Jesus?* Louisville: Westminster John Knox Press, 1996.

Crunden, Robert M. *Ministers of Reform: The Progressives' Achievement in American Civilization, 1889–1920*. New York: Basic Books, 1982.

Dalton, Kathleen. *Theodore Roosevelt: A Strenuous Life*. New York: Vintage Books, 2002.

Davis, Allen F. "Welfare, Reform and World War I." *American Quarterly* 19 (Autumn 1967): 520.

Donald, David Herbert. *Liberty and Union: The Crisis of Popular Government, 1830–1890*. Boston: Little, Brown and Company, 1978.

Duffy, Herbert S. *William Howard Taft*. New York: Minton, Balch and Company, 1930.

Eisenach, Eldon. *The Lost Promise of Progressivism*. Lawrence: University Press of Kansas, 1994.

Farb, Peter and George Armelagos. *Consuming Passions: The Anthropology of Eating*. Boston: Houghton Mifflin, 1980.

Fausold, Martin. *Gifford Pinchot, Bull Moose Progressive*. Westport: Greenwood Press, 1961.

Ferrell, Robert H. *Woodrow Wilson and World War I, 1917–1921*. New York: Harper and Row, 1995.

Filler, Louis. *The Muckrakers*. University Park: Pennsylvania State University Press, 1976.

Fine, Sidney. *Laissez Faire and the General-Welfare State: A Study of Conflict in American Thought, 1865–1901*. Ann Arbor: University of Michigan Press, 1964.

Fitzpatrick, Edward A. *McCarthy of Wisconsin*. New York: Columbia University Press, 1944.

Foner, Eric. *Reconstruction: America's Unfinished Revolution, 1863–1877*. New York: Harper and Row, 1988.

——. *The Story of American Freedom*. New York: W. W. Norton and Company, 1999.

Forcey, Charles. *The Crossroads of Liberalism: Croly, Weyl, Lippmann and the Progressive Era, 1900–1925*. London: Oxford University Press, 1961.

Gable, John Allen. *The Bull Moose Years: Theodore Roosevelt and the Progressive Party*. Port Washington, N.Y.: Kennikat Press, 1978.

Gabriel, Ralph Henry. *The Course of American Democratic Thought*. New York: The Ronald Press Company, 1956.

Gamble, Richard M. *The War for Righteousness: Progressive Christianity, the Great War, and the Rise of the Messianic Nation*. Wilmington: ISI Books, 2003.

Garraty, John. *Right-Hand Man, The Life of George W. Perkins*. New York: Harper-Collins, 1960.

Goodwin, Lorine Swainston. *The Pure Food, Drink, and Drug Crusaders, 1879–1914*. Jefferson, N.C.: McFarland, 1999.

Gould, Lewis. *Reform and Regulation: American Politics, 1900–1916*. New York: Wiley, 1978.

———. *The Presidency of William McKinley*. Lawrence: University Press of Kansas, 1982.

———. *Grand Old Party: A History of the Republicans*. New York: Random House, 2003.

———. *The Modern American Presidency*. Lawrence: University Press of Kansas, 2003.

———. *The Presidency of Theodore Roosevelt*. Lawrence: University Press of Kansas, 1991.

Grondahl, Paul. *I Rose Like a Rocket: The Political Education of Theodore Roosevelt*. New York: Free Press, 2004.

Guelzo, Allen C. *Abraham Lincoln: Redeemer President*. Grand Rapids: William B. Eerdmans Publishing, 1999.

Harlan, Louis J. *Booker T. Washington: The Wizard of Tuskegee, 1901–1915*. New York: Oxford University Press, 1983.

Harlow, Alvin F. *Theodore Roosevelt: Strenuous American*. New York: Julian Messner, 1943.

Hayes, Samuel P. *Conservation and the Gospel of Efficiency: The Progressive Conservation Movement, 1890–1920*. Cambridge: Harvard University Press, 1959.

Higgens-Evenson, R. Rudy. *The Price of Progress: Public Services, Taxation, and the American Corporate State, 1877–1929*. Baltimore: Johns Hopkins University Press, 2003.

Hirschfeld, Charles. "Nationalist Progressivism and World War I." *Mid-America* 45 (July 1963): 139–56.

Hofstadter, Richard. *Social Darwinism in American Thought*. Boston: Beacon Press, 1992.

———. *The American Political Tradition and the Men Who Made It*. New York: Vintage Books, 1989.

Jaffa, Harry V. *A New Birth of Freedom: Abraham Lincoln and the Coming of the Civil War*. Lanham: Rowman and Littlefield Publishers, 2000.

———. *Crisis of the House Divided: An Interpretation of the Issues in the Lincoln-Douglas Debates*. Chicago: University of Chicago Press, 1982.

Jeffers, H. Paul. *An Honest President: The Life and Presidencies of Grover Cleveland.* New York: HarperCollins Publishers, 2000.

Johnson, Donald. *The Challenge to American Freedom: World War I and the Rise of the American Civil Liberties Union.* Lexington: University of Kentucky Press, 1963.

Johnson, Walter. *William Allen White's America.* New York: Henry Holt and Company, 1947.

Kantrowitz, Stephen. *Ben Tillman and the Reconstruction of White Supremacy.* Chapel Hill: University of North Carolina Press, 2000.

Kaplan, Sidney. "Social Engineers as Saviors: Effects of World War I on Some American Liberals." *Journal of the History of Ideas* 17 (1956): 347–69.

Kazin, Michael. *The Populist Persuasion.* Ithaca: Cornell University Press, 1998.

Kennedy, David M. *Over Here: The First World War and American Society.* New York: Oxford University Press, 1980.

Kerr, K. Austin. *American Railroad Politics, 1914–1920.* Pittsburgh: University of Pittsburgh Press, 1968.

———. *Organized for Prohibition: A New History of the Anti-Saloon League.* New Haven: Yale University Press, 1985.

Kloppenberg, James T. *Uncertain Victory: Social Democracy and Progressivism in European and American Thought, 1870–1920.* New York: Oxford University Press, 1986.

Knott, Stephen F. *Alexander Hamilton and the Persistence of Myth.* Lawrence: University Press of Kansas, 2002.

Kolko, Gabriel. *Railroads and Regulation, 1877–1916.* Princeton: Princeton University Press, 1965.

———. *The Triumph of Conservatism.* Chicago: Quadrangle Books, 1963. Latham, Earl, ed. *The Philosophies and Policies of Woodrow Wilson.* Chicago: University of Chicago Press, 1958.

Lears, Thomas Jefferson Jackson. *No Place of Grace: Antimodernism and the Transformation of American Culture, 1880–1920.* New York: Pantheon, 1981.

Leech, Margaret. *In the Days of McKinley.* New York: Harper, 1959.

Letwin, William. *Law and Economic Policy in America: The Evolution of the Sherman Antitrust Act.* New York: Random House, 1965.

Leuchtenburg, William E. "Progressivism and Imperialism: The Progressive Movement and American Foreign Policy, 1898–1916." *Mississippi Valley Historical Review* 39 (Dec. 1952): 483–504.

Levy, David. *Herbert Croly of the New Republic: The Life and Thought of an American Progressive.* Princeton: Princeton University Press, 1985.

Link, Arthur S. *Wilson: Confusions and Crises, 1915–1916.* Princeton: Princeton University Press, 1964.

———. *Wilson: The Struggle for Neutrality, 1914–1915.* Princeton: Princeton University Press, 1960.

———. *Woodrow Wilson and the Progressive Era, 1910–1917.* New York: Harper and Brothers, 1954.

Lippmann, Walter. "The World Conflict in Relation to American Democracy." *Annals of the American Academy of Political and Social Science* 72 (1917): 1–10.

Livermore, Seward W. *Politics is Adjourned: Woodrow Wilson and the War Congress, 1916–1918*. Middletown: Wesleyan University Press, 1966.

Livingston, James. *Origins of the Federal Reserve System: Money, Class and Corporate Capitalism, 1890–1913*. Ithaca: Cornell University Press, 1986.

Lowi, Theodore J. *The Personal President*. Ithaca: Cornell University Press, 1985.

Manners, William. *T.R. and Will: A Friendship That Split the Republican Party*. New York: Harcourt, Brace, 1969.

McCarthy, G. Michael. *Hour of Trial: The Conservation Conflict in Colorado and the West, 1891–1907*. Norman: University of Oklahoma Press, 1977.

McCartin, Joseph Anthony. *Labor's Great War: The Struggle for Industrial Democracy and the Origins of Modern American Labor Relations, 1912–1921*. Chapel Hill: University of North Carolina Press, 1997.

McCullough, David. *Mornings on Horseback: The Story of an Extraordinary Family, A Vanished Way of Life, and the Unique Child Who Became Theodore Roosevelt*. New York: Simon and Schuster, 2003.

McDonald, Forrest. *The United States in the 20th Century, 1900–1920*. Reading: Addison-Wesley Publishing Company, 1970.

McGeary, Nelson. *Gifford Pinchot*. Princeton: Princeton University Press, 1960.

McGerr, Michael. *A Fierce Discontent: The Rise and Fall of the Progressive Movement in America (1870–1920)*. New York: Free Press, 2003.

———. "Theodore Roosevelt." In *The American Presidency*, edited by Alan Brinkley and Davis Dyer. Boston: Houghton Mifflin Company, 2004.

Meier, August. *Negro Thought in America, 1880–1915: Racial Ideology in the Age of Booker T. Washington*. Ann Arbor: University of Michigan Press, 1988.

Menand. Louis. *The Metaphysical Club: A Story of Ideas in America*. New York: Farrar, Straus, and Giroux, 2001.

Mileur, Jerome M. "The Legacy of Reform: Progressive Government, Regressive Politics." In *Progressivism and the New Democracy*, edited by Sidney M. Milkis and Jerome M. Mileur. Amherst: University of Massachusetts Press, 1999.

Mileur, Jerome M. and Ronald Story. "America's Wartime Presidents: Politics, National Security, and Civil Liberties." In *The Politics of Terror: The U.S. Response to 9/11*, edited by William Crotty. Boston: Northeastern University Press, 2004.

Milkis, Sidney M. *Political Parties and Constitutional Government: Remaking American Democracy*. Baltimore: Johns Hopkins University Press, 1999.

Miller, Nathan. *Theodore Roosevelt: A Life*. New York: William Morrow and Company, 1992.

Morris, Edmund. *The Rise of Theodore Roosevelt*. New York: The Modern Library, 2001.

———. *Theodore Rex*. New York: The Modern Library, 2001.

Mowry, George. *The Era of Theodore Roosevelt*. New York: Harper and Row, 1962.

———. *Theodore Roosevelt and the Progressive Movement*. New York: Hill and Wang, 1960.

Murphy, Paul L. *The Constitution in Crisis Times*. New York: Harper and Row, 1997.

Nash, George H. *The Life of Herbert Hoover: Master of Emergencies, 1917–1918*. New York: W. W. Norton, 1996.

Nevins, Allan. *John D. Rockefeller: The Heroic Age of American Enterprise*. 2 vols. New York: Charles Scribner's Sons, 1940.

Paludan, Philip Shaw. *The Presidency of Abraham Lincoln*. Lawrence: University Press of Kansas, 1994.

Pangle, Thomas L. *The Spirit of Modern Republicanism: The Moral Vision of The American Founders and the Philosophy of Locke*. Chicago: University of Chicago Press, 1990.

Parsons, Frank. "Municipal Ownership" and "Public Ownership." In *New Encyclopedia of Social Reform*, edited by W. D. P. Bliss. New York: Funk and Wagnalls Company, 1908.

Peterson, Merrill D. *Lincoln in American Memory*. New York: Oxford University Press, 1994.

Phillips, Kevin. *Wealth and Democracy: A Political History of the American Rich*. New York: Broadway Books, 2002.

———. *William McKinley*. New York: Henry Holt and Company, 2003.

Porter, Kirk H. and Donald B. Johnson, eds. *National Party Platforms, 1840–1964*. Urbana, Ill.: University of Illinois Press, 1966.

Pringle, Henry F. *Theodore Roosevelt*. New York: Barnes and Noble Books, 1956.

Putnam, Carleton. *Theodore Roosevelt: The Formative Years, 1858–1886*. New York: Charles Scribner's Sons, 1958.

Renehan, Edward J. *The Lion's Pride: Theodore Roosevelt and His Family in Peace and War*. New York: Oxford University Press, 1998.

Riccards, Michael P. *The Ferocious Engine of Democracy: From Teddy Roosevelt through George W. Bush*. New York: Cooper Square Press, 2003.

Roosevelt, Nicholas. *Theodore Roosevelt: The Man as I Knew Him*. New York: Dodd, Mead, 1967.

Sanders, Elizabeth. *Roots of Reform: Farmers, Workers, and the American State, 1877–1917*. Chicago: University of Chicago Press, 1999.

Sedgwick, Jeffery Leigh. "Abraham Lincoln and the Character of Liberal Statesmanship." In *Legacy of Disunion: The Enduring Significance of the American Civil War*, edited by Susan-Mary Grant and Peter J. Parish. Baton Rouge: Louisiana State University Press, 2003.

Sklar, Martin. *The Corporate Reconstruction of American Capitalism, 1880–1916*. New York: Cambridge University Press, 1988.

Skowronek, Stephen. *Building a New American State: The Expansion of National Administrative Capacities, 1877–1920*. Cambridge: Cambridge University Press, 1990.

Stephenson, Nathaniel W. *Nelson W. Aldrich: A Leader in American Politics*. New York: Charles Scribner's Sons, 1930.

Stettner, Edward. *Shaping Modern Liberalism: Herbert Croly and Progressive Thought*. Lawrence: University Press of Kansas, 1993.

Stid, Daniel. *The President as Statesman: Woodrow Wilson and the Constitution.* Lawrence: University Press of Kansas, 1998.

Thelen, David P. *Robert M. LaFollette and the Insurgent Spirit.* Boston: Little, Brown, 1976.

Thompson, Charles W. *Presidents I've Known and Two Near-Presidents.* Indianapolis: Bobbs-Merrill Company, 1929.

Thorelli, Hans B. *The Federal Antitrust Policy: Origination of an American Tradition.* Baltimore: Johns Hopkins University Press, 1954.

Timberlake, James H. *Prohibition and the Progressive Movement, 1900–1920.* New York: Antheneum, 1970.

Trattner, Walter I. "Progressivism and World War I: A Reappraisal." *Mid-America* 44 (July 1962): 131–45.

———. *Crusade for the Children: A History of the National Child Labor Committee and Child Labor Reform in America.* Chicago: Quadrangle Books, 1970.

Tulis, Jeffrey K. *The Rhetorical Presidency.* Princeton: Princeton University Press, 1987.

Urofsky, Melvyn. *Big Steel and the Wilson Administration: A Study in Business-Government Relations.* Columbus: Ohio State University Press, 1969.

Watts, Sarah. *Rough Rider in the White House: Theodore Roosevelt and the Politics of Desire.* Chicago: University of Chicago Press, 2003.

Webking, Robert H. *The American Revolution and the Politics of Liberty.* Baton Rouge: Louisiana State University Press, 1988.

Weisman, Steven R. *The Great Tax Wars: Lincoln, Teddy Roosevelt, Wilson —How the Income Tax Transformed America.* New York: Simon & Schuster, 2002.

West, Thomas G. *Vindicating the Founders: Race, Sex, Class, and Justice in the Origins of America.* Lanham: Rowman & Littlefield, 1997.

Westbrook, Robert B. *John Dewey and American Democracy.* Ithaca: Cornell University Press, 1991.

White, Charles T. *Lincoln and Prohibition.* New York: The Abingdon Press, 1921.

White, John Kenneth and Jerome Mileur. "In the Spirit of Their Times: 'Toward a More Responsible Two-Party System' and Party Politics." In *Responsible Partisanship?*, edited by John C. Green and Paul S. Herrnson. Lawrence: University Press of Kansas, 2002.

Wiebe, Robert H. *The Search for Order, 1877–1920.* New York: Hill and Wang, 1967.

Wilensky, Norman M. *Conservatives in the Progressive Era: The Taft Republicans of 1912.* Gainesville: University of Florida Press, 1965.

Willis, H. Parker. *The Federal Reserve System.* New York: Arno Press, 1975.

Wills, Garry. *Lincoln at Gettysburg: The Words That Remade America.* New York: Simon and Schuster, 1992.

Wister, Owen. *Roosevelt: The Story of a Friendship.* New York: Macmillan and Company, 1930.

Witcover, Jules. *Party of the People: A History of the Democrats.* New York: Random House, 2003.

Wolin, Sheldon S. *The Presence of the Past: Essays on the State and the Constitution.* Baltimore: Johns Hopkins University Press, 1990.

Yarbrough, Jean M. "Theodore Roosevelt and the Stewardship of the American Presidency." In *History of American Political Thought*, edited by Bryan-Paul Frost and Jeffrey Sikkenga. Lanham, MD: Lexington Books, 2003.

Young, James Harvey. *Pure Food: Securing the Federal Food and Drugs Act of 1906*. Princeton: Princeton University Press, 1989.

Index

About the Author

Paul M. Rego is assistant professor of politics at Messiah College. He holds a B.A. from Millersville University (2001), an M.A. from the University of Massachusetts at Amherst (2005), and a Ph.D. in political science also from the University of Massachusetts at Amherst (2006). His teaching and research interests include American national government and politics, the American presidency, American political thought, and constitutional law.